Creative Recording 2

Microphones, Acoustics, Soundproofing And Monitoring

Also by Paul White and available from Sanctuary Publishing:

Creative Recording 1: Effects And Processors (second edition)
Desktop Digital Studio
EMERGENCY! First Aid For Home Recording
Home Recording Made Easy (second edition)
Live Sound For The Performing Musician
MIDI For The Technophobe (second edition)
Recording And Production Techniques (second edition)

The Basic series:

Basic Digital Recording
Basic Effects And Processors
Basic Home Studio Design
Basic Live Sound
Basic Mastering
Basic Microphones
Basic MIDI
Basic Mixers
Basic Mixing Techniques
Basic Multitracking
Basic Sampling
Basic VST Effects
Basic VST Instruments

Printed in the United Kingdom by MPG Books, Bodmin

Published by SMT, an imprint of Sanctuary Publishing Limited, Sanctuary House, 45-53 Sinclair Road, London W14 0NS, United Kingdom

www.sanctuarypublishing.com

ISBN: 1-84492-002-X

Creative Recording 2

Microphones, Acoustics, Soundproofing And Monitoring

Paul White

smt

contents

CHAPTER 25

introduction

Though much of today's music is created by synthesis or sampling, the ability to record 'real' instruments and real voices is just as important as it ever was. All modern amplification and recording systems are, by their nature, electrical – so before a sound can be processed in any way, it must first be converted into an electrical signal that the system can handle. For this, we need a microphone. The problem is that, unlike the exquisitely designed human ear, there is no single microphone that is ideal for all jobs – microphones come in many types and sizes, all designed to handle a specific range of tasks. The first problem is deciding what microphone to choose for a particular application.

Having selected an appropriate microphone, there is still the question of how best to position it relative to the sound source in order to capture the desired sound. And in many cases, the sound you're after isn't necessarily the most natural sound, the close-miking of acoustic drums for rock or pop music being a prime example. In this case we tend to go for a sound that is somewhat larger than life.

The purpose of the first section of this book is to explain how the different types of microphone work, which types are best suited to which jobs, and how to use them in a recording situation. This includes the positioning of single microphones for solo instrument and vocal recording, classical stereo mic techniques and multi-mic setups such as are used for recording drum kits.

Unlike electronically produced sound, 'real' voices and instruments are affected by the acoustic environment in which they are recorded, so no book on microphones and mic techniques can be truly complete without taking these factors into consideration. Furthermore, most private studios don't have the same degree of acoustic isolation as professional facilities, so the subject of unwanted noise leaking in and out also merits attention. For this reason, the latter half of this book is given over to explaining the basics of soundproofing and acoustic treatment along with practical solutions to common problems.

chapter 1

sound & microphones

Sound is created when a vibrating object (such as the body of an acoustic guitar or the head of a drum) causes the air about it to vibrate within the frequency range of human hearing. When this vibration reaches our ears, it causes our eardrums to vibrate accordingly and our brains perceive this as sound.

But even our ears have limitations and the human hearing system can, at best, only detect air vibrations in the range of 20Hz to 20kHz (twenty vibrations a second to twenty thousand), though there is variation from individual to individual. The upper limit of hearing deteriorates with age, and as a rule of thumb, we lose around 1kHz for each decade of our age.

It is important to note that although sound travels at around 1100ft per second, the air itself doesn't move. The way in which sound travels is often explained in textbooks by comparison with the ripples formed in a pond after a stone has been thrown into the water. A cork placed on the water merely bobs up and down as the ripples pass by, it doesn't travel with them because the water itself isn't moving away from the point where the stone entered the water.

Sound behaves in much the same way except that the ripples travel out from the source in all directions in a spherical manner – and as the sphere expands, the sound energy gets weaker as the energy in the wavefront is spread over an increasingly large area. Even relatively loud sounds involve quite low amounts of acoustic energy, unless you're very close to them, which all conspires to make the microphone's job surprisingly difficult. It has to convert this tiny amount of acoustic energy into a meaningful electrical signal that can later be amplified to a useful level.

transducers

Any device designed to convert some form of physical energy to electrical energy (or vice versa) is known as a transducer. For example, there are pressure transducers used in electronic weighing machines, photo transducers such as the photocells used in automatic cameras, temperature transducers used in electronic thermometers and thermostats – and there are transducers that convert motion into electricity.

Microphones fall into the latter category. But there is, as yet, no practical way of converting the vibration of air directly into electricity so all commercially available microphones make use of some form of lightweight diaphragm. As the air vibrates, the air pressure in the vicinity of the microphone diaphragm fluctuates causing the diaphragm to move backwards and forwards over a small distance, closely following the vibrations of the original sound. To turn this tiny movement into an electrical signal, there needs to be some system for measuring the movement of this diaphragm. Exactly what this system is varies depending on the type of microphone. The result is an electrical signal that rises and falls in voltage to mirror the rise and fall in air pressure caused by the original sound.

It could be argued that as we only need one set of ears to hear any type of sound at any level, it should be possible to make a single microphone that is suitable for all recording jobs. Some of the more expensive models come pretty close to this ideal, but the truth of the matter is that microphone technology isn't perfect, and in order to make a microphone perform particularly well in one area, it's generally necessary to compromise its performance to some extent in another area. For example: a microphone designed for very low background noise may not have as good a frequency response as another or maybe it doesn't respond as accurately to off-axis sounds (sounds that don't occur directly in front of it). And remember that not everyone can afford the most exotic microphones so it is important to know what compromises have been made in the name of economy and how they will affect the performance of the microphone in specific recording (or sound reinforcement) situations.

directionality

Not all microphones pick up sound in the same way and which type we choose depends on the task in hand. Some pick up sound equally efficiently regardless of what direction the sound is coming from. In other words, you don't have to point the microphone directly at the sound source because it can 'hear' equally well in all directions.

Other microphones may be designed to respond mainly to sounds approaching them from a single direction while others still may pick up sound from both front and rear but not from the sides. These basic directional characteristics are known as omnidirectional (all directions), cardioid, meaning heart-shaped (unidirectional) and figure-of-eight, (which picks up from both front and rear but not from the sides).

It is possible to design a microphone incorporating two or more capsules, the outputs of which can be combined in different ways to give a selection of pickup patterns, and these will be discussed more fully later. First, a closer look at the individual pickup patterns.

omnidirectional

If the diaphragm of a microphone is fixed across the end of a sealed, airtight cavity, then the air pressure at the rear of the diaphragm will be essentially constant, while on the side open to the air, it will vary depending on the sound reaching the microphone. Figure 1.1 shows how this works in practice, and because this type of microphone responds directly to changes in air pressure, it is known as a pressure microphone. Pressure changes will occur regardless of the direction the sound is coming from so the microphone will be omnidirectional.

In practice there must be a small hole to allow air to flow into the cavity in order to compensate for any changes in outside air pressure. Failure to do this would produce a microphone that doubled as a barometer!

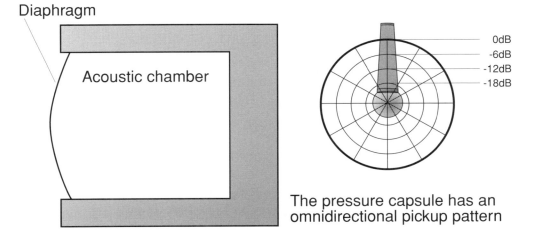

Diaphragm

Acoustic chamber

0dB
-6dB
-12dB
-18dB

The pressure capsule has an omnidirectional pickup pattern

Figure 1.1: Basic pressure capsule

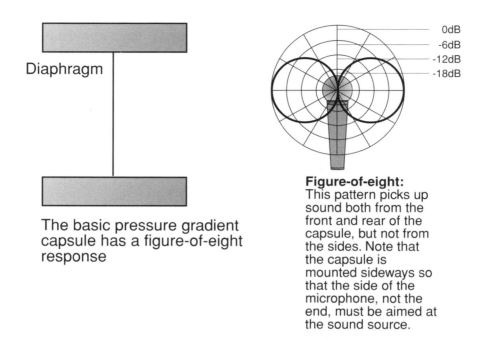

Diaphragm

The basic pressure gradient capsule has a figure-of-eight response

Figure-of-eight:
This pattern picks up sound both from the front and rear of the capsule, but not from the sides. Note that the capsule is mounted sideways so that the side of the microphone, not the end, must be aimed at the sound source.

Figure 1.2: Pressure gradient capsule

Because any microphone physically obstructs the soundfield it is trying to measure to some extent, the omnidirectional response is often less than perfect. This usually results in the mic's sensitivity to high frequencies being less at the sides and rear of the microphone than at the front. In theory, a perfect omnidirectional mic would be infinitely small so as not to interfere with the soundfield, but as this simply isn't possible in practice, some compromises have to be accepted. Fortunately, these need not be serious.

Omnidirectional microphones do not exhibit the proximity effect inherent in cardioid and figure-of-eight designs. The proximity effect is explained in the section on cardioid microphones.

figure-of-eight

The figure-of-eight pattern microphone uses a diaphragm that is open to the air on both sides. It is easy to see how this picks up sound from two directions but why doesn't it pick up sound coming from the sides too? The answer is quite simple when you think about it. A sound arriving from the side will reach both sides of the diaphragm at the same time so the air pressure on each side of the diaphragm will always be equal. If there is no difference in pressure, the diaphragm won't move and no electrical output will be produced. Figure 1.2 shows the general principle. Because this type of microphone works on the difference in pressure between the front and the rear, it is known as a pressure gradient microphone and consequently exhibits a proximity effect which tends to result in an increase in the mic's responsiveness to low frequency sounds when the microphone is used very close to the source.

cardioid

Another type of pressure gradient mic is the directional or cardioid mic which is similar to the figure-of-eight mic except that a specially designed sound path is used to delay the sounds reaching the rear of the diaphragm. The design of this sound path is critical and the top manufacturers keep their precise design details secret, but the outcome is that sounds arriving from the front of the microphone cause a pressure difference between the front and rear of the diaphragm while sounds arriving from the rear and sides cause the pressure to be the same on both sides. The practical outcome is that the microphone is most sensitive to sounds arriving from directly in front and least sensitive to sounds arriving from the rear. In reality, sounds arriving from the sides are still picked up to some extent, but less efficiently, than the ones from the front giving rise to the characteristic heart-shaped or cardioid pickup pattern from which this type of microphone derives its name. A simplified diagram of a unidirectional microphone is shown in Figure 1.3.

A microphone that is even more strongly directional is called a supercardioid or hypercardioid. An extreme hypercardioid with a very narrow pickup pattern can be produced by fixing the microphone capsule to the rear of a complex interference tube structure and these are known as shotgun mics because of their appearance. They are often used for spot miking during stage shows where it isn't possible to get the microphone close to the performer without spoiling the visuals, and they are also useful for wildlife recording and some forms of surveillance work. Their design makes them inefficient at low frequencies so they are seldom used in music studios. All cardioid microphones exhibit the proximity effect as explained below.

proximity effect

Pressure gradient microphones (cardioids and figure-of-eight) both exhibit the proximity effect which causes a boosting of low frequencies when the sound source is very close to the microphone. This comes about because the path lengths for sounds arriving at the front and rear of the diaphragm are not quite the same. If the distance between the mic and source is very small, then the difference between these two acoustic paths is proportionally more significant and the phase differences in the signals give rise to the characteristic low frequency boost. Typically, this happens at mic/source

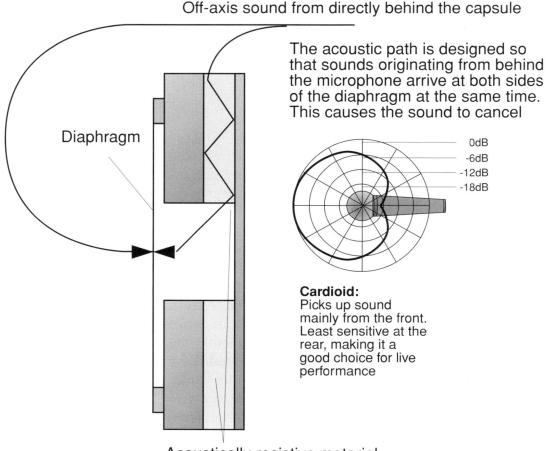

Off-axis sound from directly behind the capsule

Diaphragm

The acoustic path is designed so that sounds originating from behind the microphone arrive at both sides of the diaphragm at the same time. This causes the sound to cancel

0dB
-6dB
-12dB
-18dB

Cardioid:
Picks up sound mainly from the front. Least sensitive at the rear, making it a good choice for live performance

Acoustically resistive material

The pressure gradient capsule may be modied to produce a cardioid or unidirectional response

Figure 1.3: Directional microphone capsule

distances of a couple of inches or less and is used to advantage by some live vocalists to modify their performance.

attributes

These different directional patterns allow the microphones to be used in a variety of different situations. The unidirectional or cardioid, for example, is used where unwanted off-axis sound, such as room reverberation or spill from other instruments, needs to be kept to a minimum. This is often the case in recording studios where several musicians may be playing close together and also when miking the drum kit where the close proximity of the individual drums poses an even greater problem. But it should be borne in mind that such spill as does exist will be coloured by the off-axis frequency response of such microphones. In other words, if the microphone loses some top end when picking up sounds from the side or rear, any 'spill' from off-axis sources will tend to sound less bright than it really is.

Separation is particularly important in live situations so cardioid mics are extensively used with touring PA systems as well as for recording drum kits or other instruments that are physically close to each other.

The figure-of-eight pattern microphone is usually used only for specialist applications such as stereophonic miking which will be discussed in detail later in the book. They were also popular at one time for live backing vocal use as two singers could share one mic – one at the front and the other at the rear.

Omnidirectional microphones have an inherently more natural sound than cardioids because there is no need for any mechanical porting to modify their directional characteristics. This means that even off-axis sounds are reproduced reasonably faithfully. Other advantages include a higher immunity to handling noise than cardioid mics, lack of proximity effect, and a greater capacity for handling high sound pressure levels.

They are often used at conferences or in the production of radio programmes to pick up a group of speakers seated round a table but are also widely used in serious music recording, both for solo instrument or vocal miking, and for specialist stereo work. Figure 1.4 shows response plots for each of the common pickup patterns produced by studio microphones.

Even in situations where separation is a prime requirement, it can be argued that omnis give a more natural result, as any off-axis spill will be recorded faithfully rather than being distorted by an imperfect off-axis response as would be the case with most cardioid mics. Although the hypercardioid mic is designed to exclude as much off-axis sound as possible, it is interesting to note that if you position an omni mic at between half and two thirds the distance of a cardioid mic, the amount of spill will be comparable.

construction

The transducer that converts sound into electricity is built into a part of the microphone known as the capsule. This is usually mounted behind a protective grille and it is also commonplace for microphones to have some form of handle or main body which houses any electronics, transformers or connectors that might be needed.

Whatever principle the mic works on, the actual size of the diaphragm is important as will be explained in the section covering capsule dimensions.

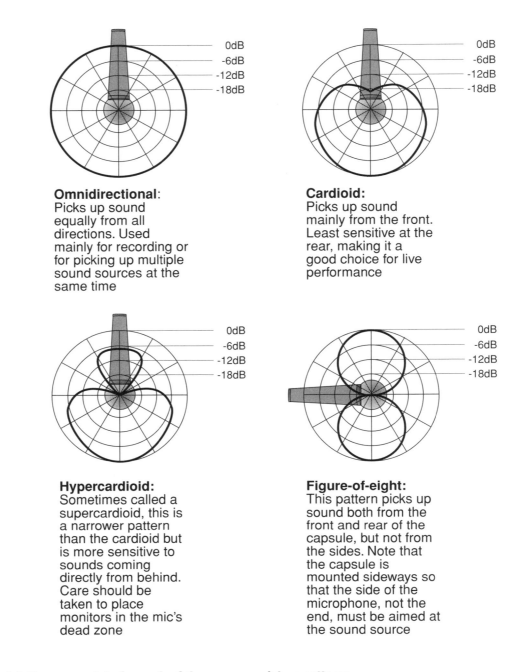

Omnidirectional:
Picks up sound
equally from all
directions. Used
mainly for recording or
for picking up multiple
sound sources at the
same time

Cardioid:
Picks up sound
mainly from the front.
Least sensitive at the
rear, making it a
good choice for live
performance

Hypercardioid:
Sometimes called a
supercardioid, this is
a narrower pattern
than the cardioid but
is more sensitive to
sounds coming
directly from behind.
Care should be
taken to place
monitors in the mic's
dead zone

Figure-of-eight:
This pattern picks up
sound both from the
front and rear of the
capsule, but not from
the sides. Note that
the capsule is
mounted sideways so
that the side of the
microphone, not the
end, must be aimed at
the sound source

Figure 1.4: Response plots for each of the common pickup patterns

Studio and live sound mics tend to use a flexible shock mounting to minimise
the level of handling noise reaching the capsule and the protective grille very
often incorporates a fine mesh wind shield to reduce the level of popping on
vocals. This metal mesh also provides essential electrical screening for the
capsule. As we shall see later, these shields are of very limited use, so some
form of external pop shield is necessary for discerning work. Fortunately,
these can be improvised for negligible cost.

chapter 2

dynamic microphones

The dynamic or moving coil microphone works on much the same principle as the generators that provide our mains electricity – but on a much smaller scale. A light, circular diaphragm, usually made from a thin plastic film, is attached to a very fine coil of wire which in turn fits into a gap in a permanent magnet such that it can move freely between the north and south poles of the magnet. In this respect, the dynamic microphone assembly looks very much like that of a moving coil loudspeaker except that the speaker works the other way round – it turns electrical signals back into sound.

When the diaphragm moves back and forth in response to a sound, the attached coil moves within the magnetic field which generates an electric current in the wire of the coil. This current is very small but can easily be amplified to a useful level by a preamplifier such as the input circuitry of a mixing console. Figure 2.1 shows the construction of a typical moving coil microphone.

pros and cons

Dynamic microphones have several advantages over other types of microphone: they are relatively inexpensive to manufacture and they are very rugged which means that they can be used live as well as in the studio. They can also tolerate extremely high sound pressure levels and require no power supply as there is no electronic circuitry in the microphone itself.

But they also have their disadvantages. Firstly, the movement of the diaphragm is restricted to some extent by the mass of the coil attached to it. The faster the diaphragm tries to move, the more the inertia of the coil impedes it, the result being that high frequency efficiency suffers. In practice, a conventional dynamic microphone can be made to work effectively up to around 16kHz but above that, the efficiency tends to fall significantly.

Some recent improvements have been achieved using Neodymium for

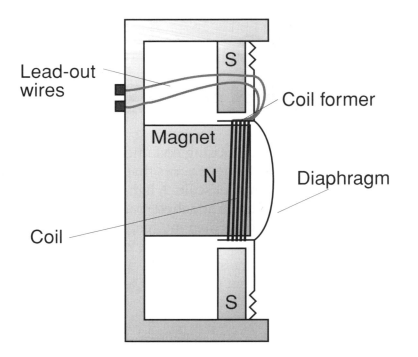

Figure 2.1: Construction of a typical moving coil microphone

the magnetic structure. Neodymium produces a more intense magnetic field which allows a shorter coil to be used and the reduced mass of the shorter coil allows the diaphragm to move more freely at higher frequencies. There is disagreement between manufacturers as to how great the advantages of Neodymium mics really are but there are several models on the market boasting a frequency response extending to above 20kHz.

The other great disadvantage of dynamic mics is that they produce a relatively small output signal which needs a lot of amplification to make it usable. This is no problem if the sounds being picked up are moderately loud and close to the microphone, but soft or distant sounds often require so much amplification that the results are unacceptably noisy. For this reason the dynamic mic is rarely used to record instruments like the acoustic guitar because it's difficult to get the mic close enough to pick up a reasonable amount of sound without compromising the tone of the instrument.

capsule dimensions

There is a common misconception that dynamic microphones themselves can't actually generate noise because they have no active circuitry. The truth is that any circuit having an electrical resistance produces electrical noise – the higher the resistance, the higher the noise. Furthermore, the impact of individual air molecules on the diaphragm of any type of microphone generates noise rather in the same way as individual oxide particles on recording tape contribute to the overall tape hiss, though this only tends to be significant in the case of very small capsules.

A larger diaphragm is better from the noise point of view as the sound picture is built up from the impact of more air molecules. This gives a statistically better result – much in the same way as a wider format of recording tape or faster tape speed gives lower tape hiss on a tape machine – but large diaphragms cause compromises in other areas.

Sounds approaching the microphone head on will reach all parts of the diaphragm at more or less the same time, but sounds coming at an angle will reach one side of the diaphragm before the other, so some of the higher frequencies will combine out-of-phase causing a deterioration in high frequency response for sounds arriving off-axis. Furthermore, the larger the diaphragm, the greater the handling noise of the microphone – if the microphone is knocked or moved suddenly, the higher inertia of the diaphragm makes it try to stay where it is, which means that it is in effect moving relative to the rest of the capsule. And movement between the diaphragm and the magnetic assembly is precisely the mechanism that creates an output signal, which is why suddenly moving a microphone can result in a thump!

The other drawback of a large diameter diaphragm is that the microphone's physical size will be large and so may interfere with the very soundfield that it is trying to capture, particularly at high frequencies where the wavelength of sound is shortest. As in most areas of design, the diaphragm diameter is a calculated compromise and differs from one model to the next depending on its applications. On the positive side, the lower resonant frequency of a large diameter capsule makes it more suitable for use with bass instruments.

Dynamic mics are generally available in omnidirectional, and cardioid versions; cardioid mics break down further into wide pattern cardioids, normal cardioids and hypercardioids where the hypercardioid is the most directional of the three.

Because of the physical construction of dynamic microphone capsules, it is generally considered impractical to utilise more than one diaphragm which means that each model is normally designed to offer only one fixed pickup pattern.

chapter 3

ribbon microphones

The ribbon microphone works on the same electrical principle as the dynamic microphone except that a thin conductive ribbon fills the role of both the diaphragm and the coil. This is electrically equivalent to a dynamic microphone with a single turn of coil so only a tiny voltage is developed across the ribbon in response to sound. Figure 3.1 shows how such a microphone is constructed. Because the electrical output from the ribbon is so low, a transformer is incorporated into the design to bring the voltage up to a usable level.

A well designed ribbon microphone can have a frequency response rising to 20kHz and the frequency response can be made very flat. The double-sided nature of the ribbon construction produces a pressure gradient microphone with a figure-of-eight pickup pattern though some modified

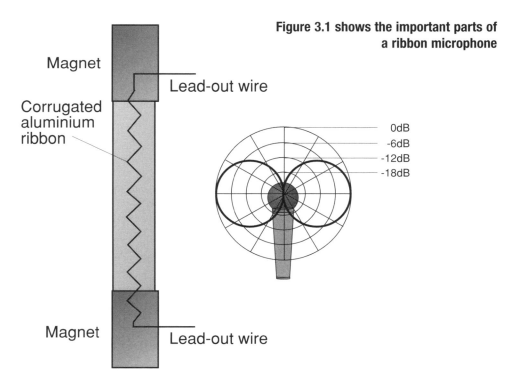

Figure 3.1 shows the important parts of a ribbon microphone

Magnet

Lead-out wire

Corrugated aluminium ribbon

0dB
-6dB
-12dB
-18dB

Magnet

Lead-out wire

The ribbon mic has a figure-of-eight response

designs are available with more directional characteristics.

It can be argued that because ribbon microphones are no more sensitive than moving coil microphones, and because their frequency response is comparable, they offer no real advantage over more conventional dynamic designs, and until recently, ribbon microphones had the severe disadvantage of being physically very fragile. But as in all things, technology has progressed and modern ribbon mics are relatively tough and innovations such as the printed ribbon where a metallic film is deposited on a light, plastic membrane give the ribbon higher reliability and a more extended frequency response. Ribbon mics are still popular for use in classical recording because they have a subjectively smoother sound than many dynamic or capacitor microphones and are often used for recording string sections.

chapter 4

capacitor microphones

A capacitor (or condenser as it is sometimes called) comprises a pair of parallel metal plates separated by an insulator. Its claim to fame is that it can store an electrical charge, and for those interested in technicalities, the relevant formula is: $Q=CV$ – where Q is the electrical charge in coulombs, C is the capacity in farads and V is the voltage across the two plates. Capacitors are used in all kinds of electronic circuitry, but the principles of capacitance also make it possible to build extremely good microphones.

If the capacitance is varied by altering the distance between the two plates of a charged capacitor, the voltage across the plates will change causing a current to flow into or out of the capacitor, through the resistor connecting it to the power supply. By monitoring the voltage across this resistor via a high impedance preamp, a signal can be derived.

A capacitor microphone comprises two such plates, one being a solid, fixed metal plate and the other a very thin, flexible plastic diaphragm onto which has been deposited an extremely thin metal coating to make it electrically conductive. If the plates are then electrically charged, any movement of the diaphragm caused by vibrations in the air will cause the capacitance to change accordingly, and when this change is translated into a voltage and amplified, you have an audio output.

charge

In addition to the capacitor capsule, some means of providing an electrical charge to the diaphragm and back-plate is needed. The charge is usually provided via the 48v phantom power source in the mixing console or mic preamp, or from a separate phantom power supply. Phantom powering will be discussed more fully later in the book.

In order to amplify the voltage changes on the capsule without allowing the electrical charge to leak away, a preamp with a very high input impedance is used. In early designs, these employed valves, but now FETs (field effect transistors) are more common. Valve designs are still popular however and well preserved older models change hands for considerable sums of money. There are also numerous new and reissued valve designs and it's thought that they sound so distinctive because valve circuitry tends to subtly colour the sound in a way that many engineers and producers consider to be appealing.

Aside from being cheaper, FETs don't require the heavy heater currents that valves do so the preamp too can be run from the phantom powering system – the microphone is completely self-contained. On the other hand, valve microphones require a complex and often costly power supply capable of supplying the capsule polarising voltage as well as the high tension and heater supplies for the valve itself. Figure 4.1 shows the internal construction of a typical solid-state capacitor microphone. Note that the fixed back-plate is perforated so that air can pass freely through it.

When compared with the moving coil or dynamic microphone, the capacitor mic seems rather complicated, and because many of the manufacturing stages still need to be done by hand, this complication is

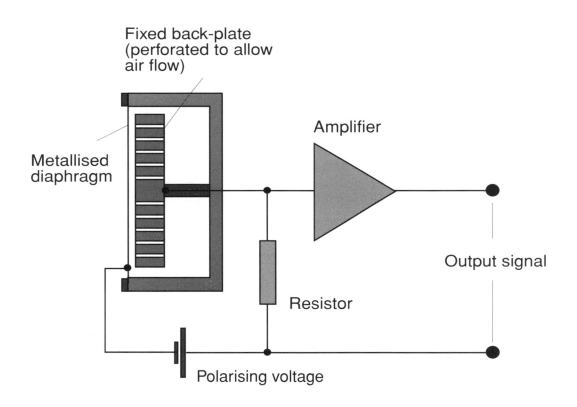

Figure 4.1: Internal construction of a typical capacitor microphone

advantages over other microphone types and the majority of serious recording work is carried out using capacitor microphones of one type or another. Fortunately, as private recording studios have become more popular, cost effective capacitor microphones have become available, many of which perform exceptionally well.

advantages

Probably the biggest advantage of the capacitor microphone capsule design is that the metal-coated plastic diaphragm can be made just a few microns thick, and that means that it is very light in weight. Less weight means less inertia, so the diaphragm can respond to higher frequencies more effectively than the dynamic microphone. In conjunction with a high quality on-board preamp, capacitor mics offer the best noise performance and the highest sensitivity of any studio microphone. Furthermore, their frequency response can easily exceed the range of human hearing at both the high and low ends of the spectrum.

Capacitor microphones can be made with virtually any response pattern and systems using two or more diaphragms are often found in studios because these enable the microphone to be switched over a range of different response characteristics.

refinements

Current capacitor microphone designs are rugged enough to be used in live situations as well as in the studio but many still suffer from sensitivity loss if used in a very humid environment. Even in an air-conditioned studio, the moisture from a singer's breath can cause problems. The reason for this is fairly simple – the moisture forms a conductive path that allows the electrical charge on the capsule to leak away.

rf capacitor

European microphone manufacturers Sennheiser have resurrected a system first used in the very early days of capacitor mics and refined it to a point where its advantages are clearly significant. What they do is to bias the capsule, not with a fixed electrical charge, but with a rapidly alternating voltage. This is provided by an oscillator running at around 8MHz and gives the technique its name: RF or radio frequency. What happens is that the audio signal is superimposed on this high frequency oscillation, just like the music on an FM radio signal, and circuitry within the microphone body extracts the audio frequency before feeding it out as normal.

A high frequency capsule working on this principle has an inherently high impedance so normal levels of moisture in the air have no significant effect on its performance. Early RF designs were unstable, noisy and susceptible to some forms of RF interference, but technology has moved a long way since then and the modern version is very reliable. Figure 4.2 shows a typical RF microphone system.

symmetry

One limitation of the basic capacitor microphone is that the capsule is not symmetrical, either electrically or acoustically. When the diaphragm

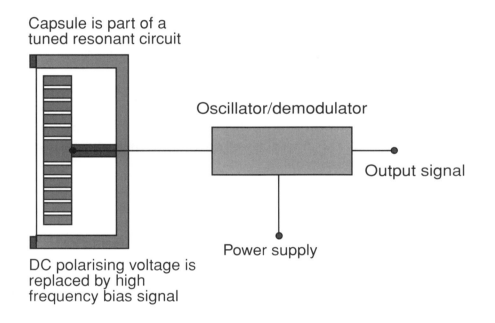

Capsule is part of a
tuned resonant circuit

Oscillator/demodulator

Output signal

DC polarising voltage is
replaced by high
frequency bias signal

Power supply

Figure 4.2: RF Microphone principle

moves towards the back-plate, the acoustic impedance is different to when it is moving away because the spacing is slightly different depending on whether the diaphragm is bending inwards or outwards. The electrostatic attraction exerted on the diaphragm by virtue of the electric field between it and the back-plate is also non-symmetrical for the same reason.

One solution to this problem involves building a microphone with two perforated plates – one in front of the diaphragm and one behind. These are both part of the electrical circuit and so the capsule is both electrically and acoustically symmetrical within the limits imposed by manufacturing accuracy. The symmetrical construction also reduces intermodulation distortion by a significant degree, though different manufacturers have different methods of optimising their capsule performance.

intermodulation distortion

Briefly, intermodulation distortion manifests itself in a system that is in some way non-linear, for example, an asymmetrical capsule design. The outcome is that when two different frequencies are fed into the mic at the same time, the output also contains small levels of the sum and differences of these two frequencies. For example, a tone of 2kHz and a tone of 3kHz would have intermodulation products at 1kHz and 5kHz. Even though the amount of intermodulation may be very small, it still affects the overall perceived sound quality and can make an otherwise good microphone sound harsh and confused. Improved capsule linearity reduces this undesirable effect.

electrets

Electret mics work on a very similar principle to the capacitor and have been around in one form or another for several years. The main difference is that the electrical charge on the diaphragm is not provided by a power supply but is built in at manufacture by a process involving heat and strong magnetic fields. Exactly how this is achieved is an industrial secret, but early models had the charge carrying elements built into the insulating material that formed the diaphragm. This was made of a highly insulating plastic so the charge would remain intact for many years. An FET preamp was still needed to process the signal from the capsule but this could run from batteries contained in the mic handle.

The real problem was, however, that the very process of making a charged diaphragm meant that the diaphragm had to be thicker and consequently heavier than a conventional capacitor mic's diaphragm. And as we saw in the section on dynamic mics, this results in a loss of sensitivity and high end frequency response. Even so, the microphones could be built very cheaply and needed no external power supply or phantom powering (most would run from a 1.5v battery) and were used extensively in domestic audio equipment such as cassette recorders and so on.

back-electret

Improvements in diaphragm technology enabled better mics to be built

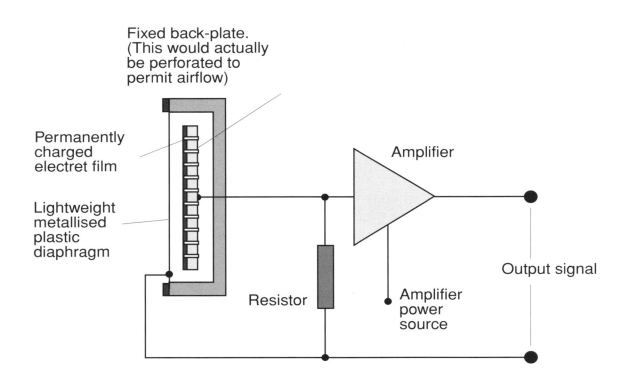

Fixed back-plate.
(This would actually
be perforated to
permit airflow)

Permanently
charged
electret film

Lightweight
metallised
plastic
diaphragm

Amplifier

Output signal

Resistor

Amplifier
power
source

Figure 4.3: Construction of a back-electret microphone

using the electret principle but the most significant improvement turned out to be the invention of the back-electret capsule. This works on much the same principle, but with one very important difference – the material carrying the permanent electrical charge is fixed to the stationary back-plate allowing the moving diaphragm to be made of exactly the same material as that used in a true capacitor microphone.

This back-electret technology has enabled a new range of cost-effective mics to be produced which offer virtually all the benefits of true capacitor mics at around the cost of a dynamic mic. The idea may seem obvious, but the manufacturing process took a lot of development as it transpired to be very difficult to find a reliable way to bond the charged material to the back-plate. Figure 4.3 shows the construction of a back-electret microphone. Back-electret microphones are available that can run on batteries as well as on phantom power, but as a rule, the higher phantom power voltage results in more headroom and a better dynamic range than can be achieved from batteries.

multipattern microphones

Though it is feasible (and indeed has been accomplished) to build a variable pattern microphone capsule using dynamic or ribbon transducers, the capacitor system lends itself far more readily to this application. This is partly because the capacitor capsule is both compact and mechanically simple in concept, and importantly, because the output of a capacitor capsule can be governed by varying the polarising voltage between the back-plate and the diaphragm. Unfortunately, the cheaper electret principle doesn't rely on an external polarising voltage and so can't be controlled in the same way, though some multipattern back-electret mics have been produced.

Many popular studio capacitor mics offer switchable response patterns, the Neumann U87 and AKG 414 being popular examples. The logic behind the variable pattern design is obvious; for the price of one microphone you get a model that can be used in a wide variety of recording situations.

dual cardioid

By combining two cardioid elements back to back, all the common response patterns can be produced by mixing the outputs from the two capsules in different amounts and phases. In physical terms, this might comprise a dual diaphragm capsule where the polarising voltage on one of the elements can be switched to vary the gain and phase of its output. Once the outputs from the two parts of the capsule are combined, the desired pattern is produced. By adding two cardioid patterns equally and in phase, an omnidirectional response is produced, while switching off one of the cardioids will obviously leave a straightforward cardioid response from the other. On the other hand, adding the two cardioids equally and out of phase will result in the classic figure-of-eight pattern. In addition to these three important basic patterns, varying the output level from one of the capsules can create all the patterns in between such as the wide cardioid and hypercardioid responses. Figure 4.4 shows the five most useful patterns that can be created in this way.

Another approach is to add the outputs from a figure-of-eight mic and an omni to produce a cardioid response and this has the advantage that no rear porting is required. In theory, this means that a better sounding cardioid can be produced, and by simply switching off one or other of the elements, the omni and figure-of-eight responses are also available.

All the gain and phase control needed to produce these pattern changes is produced by simply varying the polarising voltage to one side of the

Direction of sound

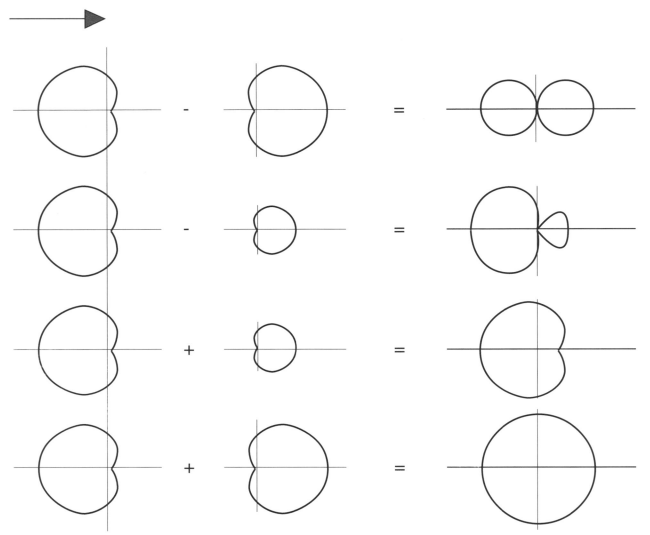

Figure 4.4: Patterns generated by two back-to-back cardioid capsules

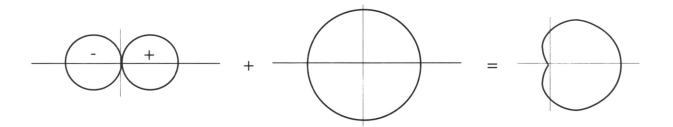

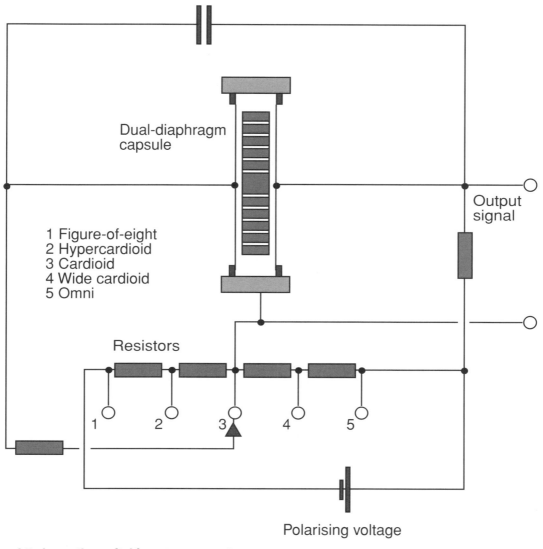

Dual-diaphragm capsule

1 Figure-of-eight
2 Hypercardioid
3 Cardioid
4 Wide cardioid
5 Omni

Output signal

Resistors

1 2 3 ▲ 4 5

Polarising voltage

Figure 4.5 shows the switching arrangement for a multipattern microphone

capsule – if a phase reversal is necessary, the polarising voltage is simply reversed. Because the voltage being switched is DC at a relatively high level (60 volts or so), the switching can be made remote, if need be, with no detrimental effect on the output signal of the microphone. Figure 4.5 shows the switching arrangement for a multipattern microphone.

sensitivity

The sensitivity of a microphone is calculated by measuring the electrical output for a given sound pressure level and a high sensitivity is an obvious advantage as it helps to provide a good signal-to-noise performance – if the microphone produces a large signal, then less amplification is necessary at the mixer end of the system and it is well known that the noise produced by an amplifier increases as its gain increases.

The usual method of measurement is to present the microphone with a constant SPL (Sound Pressure Level) of 1 Pascal or 10 microbars and then measure the output voltage of the microphone with a high impedance measuring system so as not to load the microphone in any way. This is known as open circuit measurement and a typical studio microphone might have an output of 8 to 10 mV/Pa.

Research has indicated that the threshold of hearing (for a 1kHz tone) is around 20×10^{-4} Pascals, so if this threshold is used as a 0dB reference, we can express the SPL on a dB scale for convenience. On this scale, 1 Pascal is equivalent to an SPL of 94dB.

Manufacturers often state the electrical noise generated by a particular microphone as an equivalent SPL or 'sound pressure level' – in other words, the level of an external sound that would produce the same signal level at the output of a perfectly noise-free microphone. This may be measured from 20Hz to 20kHz using a flat response meter (unweighted) or it may be measured using the so-called A weighting system which has a frequency characteristic designed to compensate for the sensitivity of the human ear to different frequencies. 'A weighted' figures generally look a dB or two more favourable than unweighted figures.

If we then subtract the equivalent noise SPL from the maximum SPL the microphone can tolerate before distortion becomes unacceptably high, we are left with the useful dynamic range. An example might be a microphone with a noise SPL equivalent of 15dB and an upper overload threshold of 135dB. Subtracting these gives a dynamic range of 120dB. When you consider that the dynamic range of 16-bit digital recording is only 96dB or so, this figure is very good. Of course for quieter sounds that don't approach the mic's upper threshold, the noise performance will be correspondingly worse. This is almost an exact analogy of what happens with analogue recording tape where the quieter the input signal, the louder the background hiss by comparison. For this reason, quiet sound sources should always be recorded using the most sensitive microphones available if the best signal-to-noise performance is to be preserved.

When the sensitivity of a microphone is measured, it is generally done so over a range of frequencies and at a range of angles around the microphone so that it can be established how the microphone behaves towards off-axis sounds. This may achieved by mounting the microphone under test on a turntable in closely controlled acoustic conditions such as

Cardioid mic pattern at
different frequencies

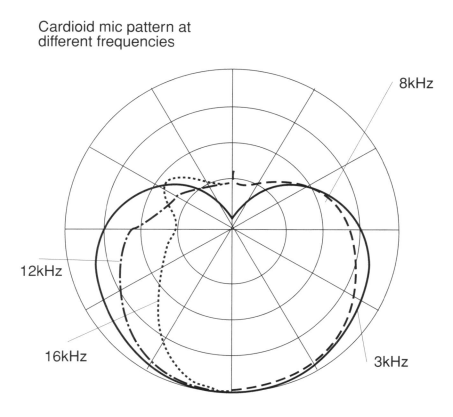

8kHz

12kHz

16kHz

3kHz

Note how the polar pattern
narrows at higher frequencies

**Figure 4.6: Polar plot of a typical studio
microphone**

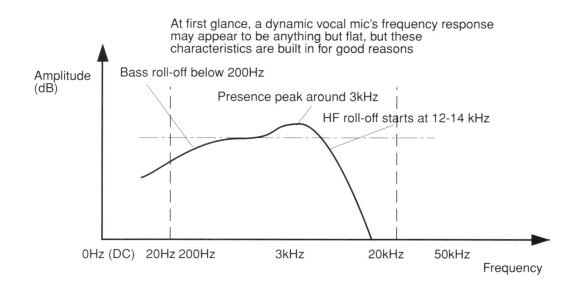

At first glance, a dynamic vocal mic's frequency response
may appear to be anything but flat, but these
characteristics are built in for good reasons

Amplitude
(dB)

Bass roll-off below 200Hz

Presence peak around 3kHz

HF roll-off starts at 12-14 kHz

0Hz (DC)   20Hz 200Hz   3kHz   20kHz   50kHz

Frequency

an anechoic chamber. A calibrated level of tone is provided by a loudspeaker system at a fixed distance from the turntable and the output of the microphone connected to a plotting device incorporating a microphone preamplifier and level measuring circuit. The recording paper is made to rotate to follow the microphone position while the position of a moving pen follows the output level from the microphone. In this way, the sensitivity may be plotted out over a full 360°. The test is repeated using various frequencies throughout the audio range and the results plotted out on a single circular diagram to form the familiar polar diagram response found in microphone documentation. Figure 4.6 shows a typical polar plot over a range of frequencies.

chapter 5

electrical considerations

balancing

Microphones used in domestic equipment or for low budget musical applications are connected to the amplification system by a standard, screened cable. This cable comprises a single, insulated centre core surrounded by a screen woven from fine wire. Outside the screen is a rubber or synthetic protective coating. The reason that this type of cable is used rather than, say, ordinary twin flex is because the output signal from a microphone is a very low voltage and is liable to corruption by electrical interference. Such interference is generated by equipment with unshielded mains transformers, mains power wiring and any electrical circuit that switches or interrupts the current such as thermostats, light dimmers, computer monitors and so on. Radio signals can also cause problems known as radio frequency or RF interference.

Screened cable offers some protection against interference but it is by no means totally effective. The idea is that any radiated interference is intercepted by the outer screen, which is connected to electrical earth, so that all the interference drains away to earth. In practice, a significant proportion of the interfering signal still ends up superimposed on the wanted signal from the microphone. Part of the problem is that the screen forms the return path for the electrical circuit as well as providing the screening.

A far more satisfactory approach is to use a so-called balanced system. Figure 5.1 shows that a balanced system uses not one but two central cores to the cable and these are again surrounded by a protective screen, though the screen does not form part of the signal path. Both the microphone and the preamplifier to which it is connected must be designed for balanced operation in order for this system to work.

split phase

Inside the microphone, the output signal is split into two opposite

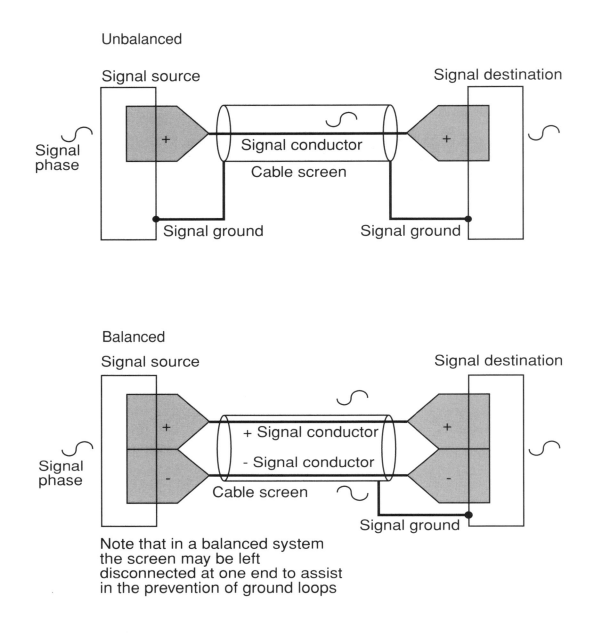

Figure 5.1: Balanced wiring system

phases, usually by means of a transformer or an electronic output balancing stage. These two phases are known as positive and negative or hot and cold and are fed down the two centre cores of the mic cable. The screen is connected to ground at the mixer end and to the body of the microphone at the mic end but doesn't carry any of the microphone output signal.

At the mixer or preamp end of the system, another transformer or electronically balanced input stage inverts one of the phases before adding its voltage to the other one. Because the signals are once again in phase when they are combined, they add rather than subtract leaving us with a usable signal.

Interference is treated rather differently because it affects both inner cores of the cable in the same way – an interference signal on the hot or positive lead will also be present in the cold or negative lead as both occupy virtually the same physical space. When this noise signal encounters the balanced amplifier input, one of the phases is inverted, so that when the signals are combined, the two equal noise signals are out of phase with each other and cancel out. The result is that the wanted signal is preserved but that virtually all the interference disappears. I say 'virtually' because for perfect operation, the system relies on the balanced amplifier or input transformer to be perfectly symmetrical and effective at all frequencies. In reality, component tolerances mean that the circuit doesn't behave symmetrically and most circuits are also less effective in cancelling interference at higher frequencies. In spec sheets, this ability to cancel noise is described as common mode rejection and is expressed in dBs, usually specified at a single frequency such as 1kHz.

Because balancing isn't 100% effective in rejecting unwanted interference, it is still wise to take precautions against interference by keeping cable runs as short as is practical and not routing cables close to mains cables or equipment containing transformers.

impedance

Microphones come in two impedance types: high and low. High impedance mics, typically 5-10kohms, are often used in domestic equipment and budget musical equipment because they have a relatively high output voltage compared to low impedance types. This means that the preamplifiers needn't be so electrically complex as they don't need to provide so much gain.

This sounds an ideal system but there are two major limitations. Firstly, the higher impedance makes the signal more susceptible to electromagnetic interference and secondly, the higher the impedance, the more the signal is affected by cable capacitance.

Because the centre core of a screened cable is in close proximity with the outer screen, a length of cable acts as capacitor and the longer the cable, the higher the capacitance. Different cables have different capacitance values and these are usually specified in picofarads per metre. The effect of this capacitance is to attenuate the higher frequencies (the impedance of a capacitor falls as the frequency increases) and because a typical microphone cable may have a capacitance in the order of 100pf per metre, the effect is significant. For this reason, high impedance microphones can only be used with relatively short cable runs. Ten or 20 feet is okay but the longer the length, the more treble loss will be experienced and the higher the susceptibility to interference. Cable capacitance can also result in handling noise – any distortion of the cable that results in the distance between the screen and cable core to be varied can cause the cable to act like a capacitor microphone, inducing noise onto the wanted signal.

For professional applications, low impedance microphones are always used and these have impedances of 250 ohms or less. Usually the microphone preamplifier will have an impedance of five to ten times that amount because we are concerned with transferring the maximum signal voltage to the preamp, not the maximum power. Also, by making the input impedance higher than that of the microphone, the effect of cable impedance is less significant than it would be if the input and output impedances were identical. With this system, it is possible to use cable lengths of around 50 metres with only a dB or so of high frequency loss at 20kHz. With both low and high impedance microphones, the effect of cable resistance is negligible for any practical cable length.

cable types

It is important to select a microphone cable with a low capacitance, especially if long runs are to be used. A woven, braided screen generally offers better protection against interference than the type where the screen conductor is merely wrapped around the centre cable, and indeed, this latter type should be avoided in any application except possibly for very short runs of line-level signal. The main reason for this is that the helically wound screen of a wrapped cable can open up where the cable is bent, thus compromising its effectiveness against interference.

There's another type of cable that uses a conductive plastic screen that may be used to make up microphone leads and, though it doesn't offer quite the same level of screening as the woven screen type, it is still good enough for short to medium length cables and has the distinct advantages of being resistant to kinking and having a low handling noise. It is also easy to use, as an uninsulated wire runs alongside the conductive plastic screen to form the screen connection. This saves time in stripping back and preparing the screen, and the only special

**Figure 5.2: Wiring details
for jacks and XLRs**

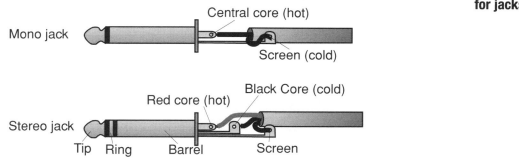

Mono jack

Central core (hot)

Screen (cold)

Stereo jack

Red core (hot)

Black Core (cold)

Tip   Ring   Barrel   Screen

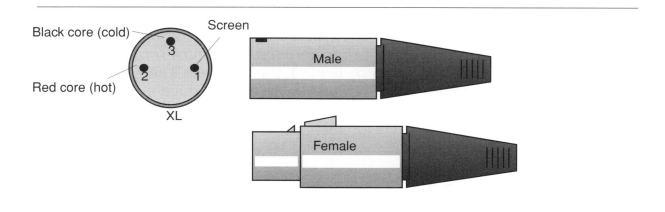

Black core (cold)

Screen

Red core (hot)

XL

Male

Female

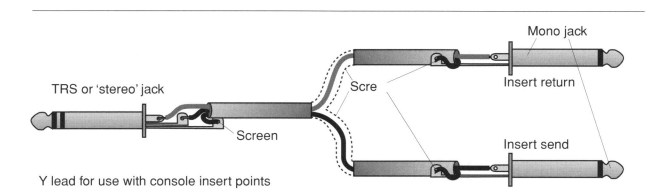

TRS or 'stereo' jack

Screen

Y lead for use with console insert points

Mono jack

Scre

Insert return

Insert send

precaution is to ensure that the conductive plastic screen is stripped back far enough to prevent it shorting out on any part of the connectors to which it is soldered.

connectors

Unbalanced microphones are often supplied with a fixed lead or a lead that fixes to the microphone using a non-standard, proprietary connector. The other end may be soldered to a standard quarter-inch jack or an XLR connector wired for unbalanced use by linking the earth and cold pins.

Balanced microphones tend to rely on a separate XLR cable which plugs into the microphone handle, though some budget systems use stereo, quarter-inch jacks wired tip hot, ring cold. A standard mic cable uses a female XLR 3-pin connector at the mic end and a male 3-pin XLR at the other. The three pins of the XLR plugs and sockets are numbered (usually by numerals moulded into the plastic holding the pins) and the easy way to remember what connects to what is to think: 1,2,3 = XLR where X is earth, L is live (or hot) and R is return (or cold). In other words, the screen connects to pin 1, the hot to pin 2 and the cold to pin 3. This applies to all balanced systems though some American companies still build equipment where pin 3 is hot and pin 2 is cold. Figure 5.2 shows the wiring details for both balanced and unbalanced jacks and XLRs.

phase problems

If a microphone cable is wired with pins 2 and 3 swapped over, it will still work as normal – until it is used in a multi-mic setup. A properly wired mic translates a positive increase in air pressure at the diaphragm into a positive voltage at the hot terminal but crossed wiring anywhere along the chain will cause a positive pressure to produce a negative voltage.

If two correctly wired mics are placed in close proximity and their outputs added in a mixing console, the combined signal level will be around 6dB higher than the output from a single mic. But if one of these microphones is wired out of phase, the output signals will largely cancel each other out.

This effect can be used as the basis of a simple test which can be used to check whether all your mics are in fact wired in phase – even if all your cables are correct, you could have a mic which is wrongly wired internally.

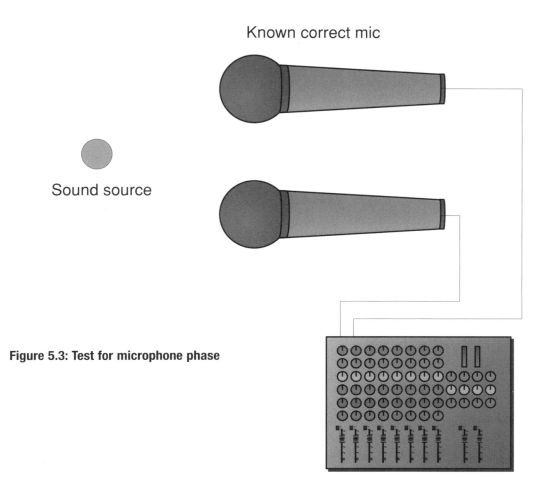

Known correct mic

Sound source

Figure 5.3: Test for microphone phase

Add the mics together at equal levels and monitor the levels on the meters. If switching off one mic causes an increased reading, the microphones are out of phase. If wired correctly, the level should be slightly higher when both mics are switched on

Set up the two mics side by side, one of which you know is correct, and place a loudspeaker a little way in front of them. Feed the speaker from a test oscillator (around 200Hz) or synth pitched at around one octave below middle A and set up the gain controls on the mixer (one mic at a time) so that both mics give the same VU meter reading. When both mic faders are up, the combined signal should give an increased meter reading. If it drops, there's a phasing problem.

The actual test frequency isn't critical but it should be kept fairly low to ensure that the small spacing between the mics isn't causing any problems. If sound is arriving at one mic slightly before the other one, some phase cancellation will occur but only at high frequencies where the wavelength is short – at lower frequencies these effects are negligible. Figure 5.3 shows how this test might be arranged.

phantom powering

All capacitor mics and electret microphones require power to operate, and though some electret mics will work from a low enough voltage and require little enough current to make battery powering practical, true capacitors normally utilise an external source of power because of the higher voltages needed. The standard power supply voltage for microphones is 48v though some models are designed to operate over a range of voltages from 9v to 48v allowing them to be operated from different power supplies.

The most popular way of powering a capacitor microphone is to use a so-called phantom power supply. This ingenious system supplies the necessary DC power along the signal leads in the microphone cable which means that no extra wiring is necessary. However, the microphone wiring must be balanced to accommodate this system.

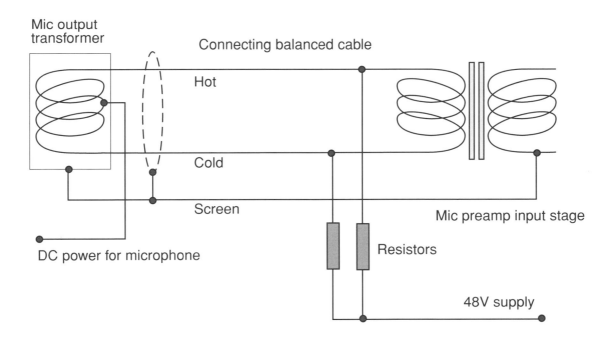

Figure 6.1: Phantom powering schematic

A phantom power supply may be a stand-alone unit that is connected in series with the microphone cable at some convenient point or, more often, it is generated within the mixing console or microphone preamplifier and fed via the microphone input sockets. Less expensive consoles allow the phantom powering to be switched on or off globally, while more serious designs allow individual switching for each mic input.

Connecting a dynamic mic to a phantom powered input will cause no problems so long as the mic is wired for balanced operation. In this situation, the same voltage appears at both ends of the voice coil and so no current flows. But, if the mic is wired for unbalanced use, the phantom powering voltage will be present across the coil and a potentially damaging current will flow. Even if the microphone is wired for balanced use, it is good practice not to plug it in with the phantom power turned on just in case one pin makes contact before the other causing current to flow through the coil momentarily. This is unlikely to cause any damage but better safe than sorry! Figure 6.1 shows the schematic of a typical phantom powering system.

special microphone types

boundary microphones

So far we have looked at fairly conventional microphone types which are typically stand mounted or hand-held and are located fairly close to the sound being recorded. If these microphones are mounted at a greater distance, problems can occur as sound reflecting from walls or other solid objects arrives at the microphone slightly later than the direct sound causing partial cancellation of some frequencies. This gives rise to peaks and troughs in the output frequency and an often used term for this effect is comb filtering, a more severe version of which is deliberately created in phaser and flanger effects units. This comb filtering can result in a distant and highly unnatural sound.

One microphone which neatly avoids this problem is the 'pressure zone microphone' or PZM, initially developed by Crown. Other companies produce similar designs but these are generically termed 'boundary effect microphones' to avoid copyright problems:

The boundary effect microphone, as its name implies, is designed to be used at a boundary such as a wall or floor, but models with integral boundary plates are available allowing them to be positioned more freely. It should be noted, however, that the size of the boundary plate affects the low frequency response of the microphone so the mic should still be mounted on a plate at least one metre square if the whole audio bandwidth is to be faithfully reproduced. At frequencies below which the boundary plate is effective, the boundary effect ceases to work and a drop in low frequency response is evident. As a rule of thumb, the frequency response shelves off by 6dB when the wavelength of sound is longer than six times the length of the side of the boundary plate (assuming a square plate).

boundary effect

The boundary effect principle relies on the fact that at a solid boundary, there can be no air movement because the mass (and consequentially the inertia) of the boundary prevents it. At such boundaries, reflected sound

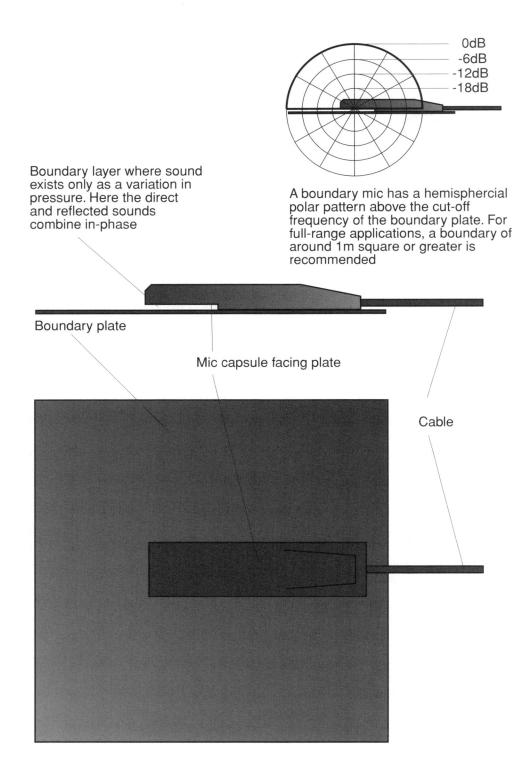

Boundary layer where sound exists only as a variation in pressure. Here the direct and reflected sounds combine in-phase

A boundary mic has a hemisphercial polar pattern above the cut-off frequency of the boundary plate. For full-range applications, a boundary of around 1m square or greater is recommended

Boundary plate

Mic capsule facing plate

Cable

Figure 7.1: Boundary effect microphone

manifests itself instead as a change in air pressure and a pressure type microphone capsule located at the boundary can accurately respond to these pressure changes.

Some designs use a pressure capsule recessed so as to be flush with the plate while others rely on a capsule suspended at a small distance above the plate and facing towards it. It is this latter approach that is used in the popular (but now sadly discontinued) Tandy/Radio Shack PZM where the capsule senses pressure changes in the gap between the capsule and the boundary. So long as the capsule is within a tenth of an inch of the boundary plate, the direct and reflected sound will remain in phase up to 20kHz.

The advantage of this design is that direct and reflected sounds arrive at the capsule simultaneously which gives an inherently consistent frequency response over the whole hemisphere of the microphone's pickup pattern. Furthermore, the direct and reflected sounds arrive in-phase and so add to double the output of the microphone.

polar pattern

You can think of the boundary mic as being like an omni mic with half of its pattern cut off by the boundary. Figure 7.1 shows how a typical boundary effect microphone might be constructed and how direct and reflected sound arrive at the capsule.

Directional boundary mics are also available incorporating a cardioid capsule, usually pointing along the plate where the advantages of in-phase direct and reflected sound are maintained.

contact microphones

In situations where acoustic feedback or spill from nearby sound sources is a serious problem, it may be possible to use a contact microphone. These react to the surface vibration of part of the instrument directly so they are less prone to picking up unwanted airborne sound. Most such microphones work on either the moving coil principle or the piezo electric principle, the latter being popular for acoustic guitar pickups, especially where the transducer is permanently built into the instrument.

piezo electric

The piezo electrical principle is also used in cheap microphones supplied with domestic equipment, but for technical reasons, these tend to sound rather tinny, and their very high output impedance makes them susceptible

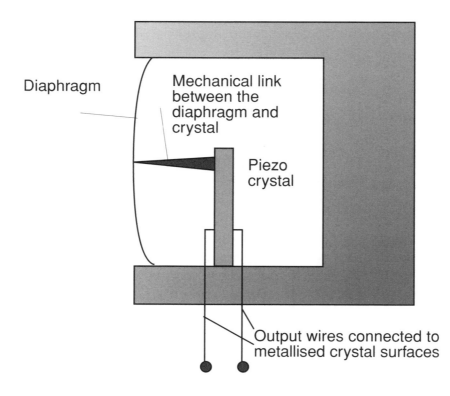

Figure 7.2: Simple piezo-electric microphone

to noise and interference. However, the principle can be adapted to contact miking giving a relatively high sound quality, providing a suitable high input impedance preamplifier is fitted close to the pickup itself.

The principle on which the microphone works is simple: some crystalline substances, when bent or twisted in certain ways, will develop an electrical voltage between their faces. If these faces are plated with metal, then the voltage can be fed to an amplifier. The crystal microphone is designed to apply a bending motion to a crystal, one end of which is fixed and the other of which is joined to a moving diaphragm. Their natural frequency response is far from flat but a little EQ can improve matters considerably. Figure 7.2 shows the basic operating principle of a piezo-electric microphone.

contact principle

In the contact mic application, the diaphragm is not moved by the air but by direct contact with a vibrating surface such as the soundboard of a guitar or piano to which the microphone is attached. In reality, there may be no diaphragm as such, the important consideration being that the vibration of the instrument is in some mechanical way translated into a bending of the crystal. Referring back to the acoustic guitar example, the pickup is often mounted within the bridge assembly as this gives a usable tone and a relatively high output signal.

Contact mics are available in many forms, from self-adhesive tapes to tiny blocks of wood or plastic that can be fixed to an instrument using double-sided adhesive pads – but they all have one serious limitation: the sound of an instrument cannot be represented by the vibration of a single part of that instrument – the sound is made up of all the vibrations emanating from every part of it.

contact mic limitations

A violin produces some sound from the strings themselves, some from the resonance of the air within the body of the instrument and some from the vibration of the wood from which the instrument is built. Using the vibrations from only one part of the surface can never do a good instrument full justice. In the case where a contact mic must be used, the skill is in finding a mounting position that gives the best representation of

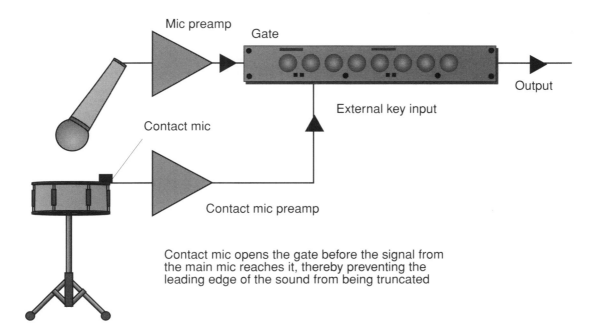

Figure 7.3: Keying a gate from a contact mic

the actual sound of the instrument and some EQ will almost certainly be needed to achieve this. For this reason, contact mics (whether attached or inbuilt) are often used in conjunction with conventional mic techniques when recording.

triggering

Contact mics may also be used to trigger gates or samplers: because they are mounted directly on the instrument, they receive their signal before the sound reaches nearby conventional microphones. By controlling the key input of a gate using a contact mic, the gate can be made to open before the sound from the conventional mic reaches its input and this ensures that none of the leading edge of the sound is removed by the gate. Figure 7.3 shows how this works.

chapter 8

stereo mic techniques

Most of what we hear on pop records is not true stereo but a collection of separately recorded mono sounds panned to different positions in the left/right soundfield. What's more, it is frequently enhanced by digital reverberation using synthesised stereo outputs. But there's a world of difference between true stereo and what I tend to think of as panned mono.

The underlying theory of stereo is all to do with the fact that we have two ears, one on each side of our head. The reason we have two ears rather than just one is so that we can tell from which direction sounds are coming. How we differentiate between sounds arriving from the front or from behind is a complex subject where the shape of the outer ear is just one factor, but the important parameters covering left/right positioning are fairly well understood.

direction

If we hear a sound that is directly in front of us, then providing there are no strong reflections from nearby objects, it is reasonable to assume that each ear will receive the same sound at the same time, because the human head is symmetrical. However, if we now hear a sound that is to our right, the sound will reach the right ear a fraction of a second before it reaches the left. Furthermore, when the sound does reach the left ear, it will be slightly quieter due to the masking effect of the head and its frequency content will be altered – low frequencies tend to pass around the head, whereas high frequencies will be absorbed or shadowed.

precedence

Our brains are equipped to analyse this level, phase and spectral information, which is what enables us to estimate the direction from which a sound is coming without any conscious effort on our behalf. Of course the introduction of reflecting surfaces can confuse the listener, but there is yet another effect of nature on our side – the precedence effect.

If two equal intensity sounds are separated by more than around 15ms, but are still close enough to sound like a single event rather than a sound followed by an echo, the brain locks onto the sound that arrives first and works out the direction from that. In a large, reverberant room, the original sound is often far enough ahead of the first reflections to allow the precedence effect to work, but in a small, highly reflective room, the result may be more confusing.

dummy head

It might seem from the above description of human hearing that the only way to record a concert in true stereo would be to sit in the audience with a small microphone jammed in each ear. Surely this would capture exactly the sound the listener would hear normally? Bizarre though it may sound, work has actually been done utlilising tiny microphone capsules fitted within the ear, and when the sound is replayed over headphones, it appears to retain many of the stereo cues of the original performance. A far less uncomfortable approach is to build a dummy head and build the microphones into that.

Promising though this line of research appears at first glance, there is one serious limitation – if the sound is picked up from within the ear, then to accurately play back a recording, the sound must be generated in the ear by tiny speakers positioned exactly where the microphones were. Though this isn't practical, the use of headphones is close enough to the theoretical ideal to yield excellent results, though front and rear sounds still appear to be confused. Several records have been released using dummy head recording and it is worth listening to some of these through really good headphones just to see what can be achieved.

loudspeaker reproduction

Unfortunately the technique doesn't work nearly so well when the sound is replayed via loudspeakers. This is because when we hear stereo loudspeakers, some of the sound from the left speaker reaches the right ear and vice versa. To create a convincing stereo image with loudspeakers, different microphone techniques are necessary.

To this day, we still don't have an entirely satisfactory system for capturing and reproducing a soundfield via a pair of stereo loudspeakers. After all, when we attend a concert, sound arrives from a wide variety of directions – left/right, up/down, front/back and every conceivable angle in between. When we listen to speakers, all the sound comes from two small boxes with a little room reverberation thrown in.

spacial recording

One can speculate on how a true spacial recording might be made in the future, perhaps by covering the surface of a sphere with microphones and then replaying the recording via a similar sphere, the inside of which was entirely covered with loudspeakers. The listener would occupy the centre of the sphere. The real problem is to intercept all the sound arriving at the listener and then recreate that same soundfield at the same points in space when we come to replay the recording. This is rather like the audio equivalent of a hologram, but to date, the technology doesn't exist to pursue this avenue, at least, not in any practical way.

Fortunately, our ears are fairly forgiving organs and there are a variety of stereo recording techniques that produce a reasonably convincing illusion of space without going to all this trouble.

coincident or xy pair

Probably the oldest, and still one of the most popular, methods of stereo miking is the coincident or XY pair. This comprises two high quality cardioid or figure-of-eight mics of similar characteristics mounted at around 90° to each other and with their capsules as close to each other as is practically possible. Because the microphones are directional, one will tend to pick up sound mainly from one side of the soundstage and the other from the opposite side. If we use figure-of-eight mics, then we'll also capture the left and right sound from the rear of the room including audience noise and room reverberation.

This arrangement provides the necessary change in level from left to right but makes no serious attempt to simulate the masking effect of the human head or the phase effects caused by the distance between one ear and the other. However, because cardioids often have a poor high frequency response off-axis, the high frequency attenuation caused by the presence of the human head may be simulated to some extent, purely by accident! Figure 8.1 shows a basic coincident pair set up relative to a sound source.

phase integrity

One of the great advantages of the coincident or XY system is that the lack of spacing avoids any phase problems that might compromise mono compatibility, but there are also drawbacks. Firstly, the lack of the phase information 'dilutes' the stereo effect and secondly, because cardioids and figure-of-eight mics tend to have their most accurate frequency response on or near their axes, the important central area of the soundstage may end up

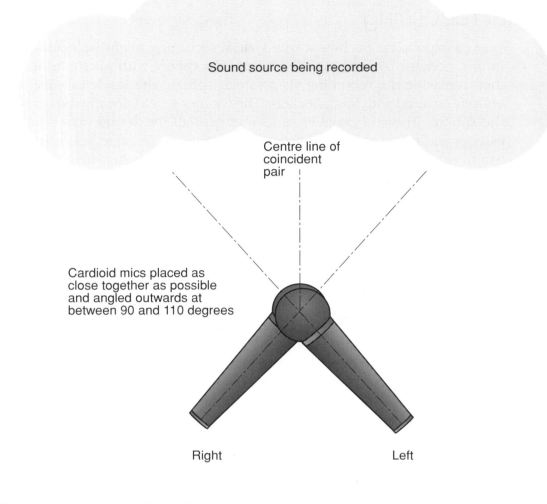

Figure 8.1: Coincident cardioid mic array

sounding less clear than the edges. The degree to which this occurs depends on the off-axis characteristics of the particular microphones used. Despite these shortcomings, the coincident pair is widely used and is capable of excellent and predictable results. What's more, the negligible spacing between the two mics means that mono compatibility is good.

When using figure-of-eight microphones rather than cardioids, It must be borne in mind, that there is no way of discriminating between front and rear sounds so the replayed recording will always present all the information in front of the listener.

The angle subtended by a coincident pair is about 90° and sounds occurring outside this angle will be inaccurately represented in the stereo

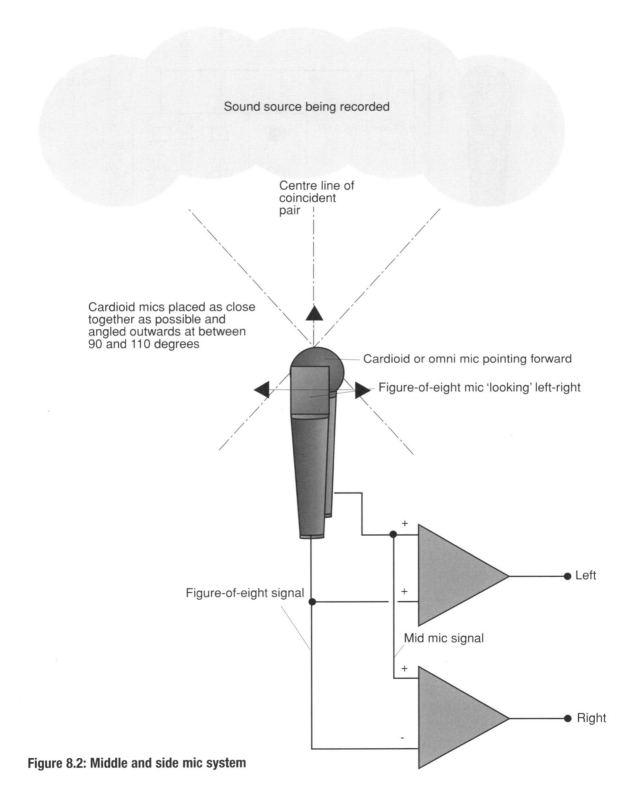

Sound source being recorded

Centre line of
coincident
pair

Cardioid mics placed as close
together as possible and
angled outwards at between
90 and 110 degrees

Cardioid or omni mic pointing forward

Figure-of-eight mic 'looking' left-right

Left

Figure-of-eight signal

Mid mic signal

Right

Figure 8.2: Middle and side mic system

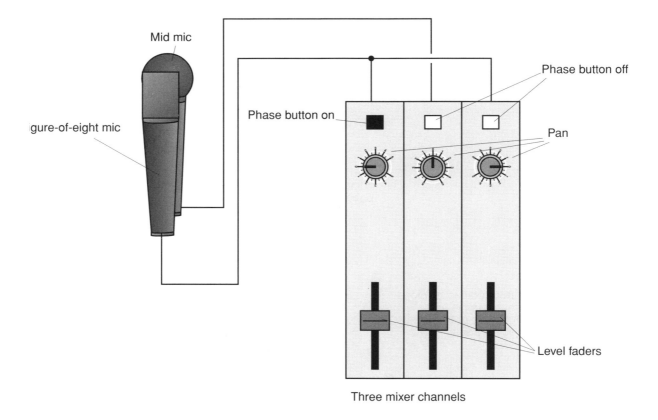

**Figure 8.3: Decoding M&S
outputs using a mixing console**

recording. The stereo width can be widened slightly by increasing the mic angle to 110° but more than this is likely to be at the expense of the centre stage sound quality.

middle and side (ms)

Another coincident microphone technique is available which produces a more stable centre image than the XY pair and which is completely mono compatible. Figure 8.2 shows the arrangement which again uses two coincident microphones – this time one figure-of-eight and one omni. In situations where sound from behind the mic array should be excluded, the omni may be exchanged for a cardioid.

This system uses one microphone – the 'middle' – to capture the centre stage sound in mono. The figure-of-eight microphone is positioned so that it 'listens' left and right, which is why this is called the 'side' mic. Essentially, the centre mic provides an accurate mono image while the side mic provides the information that, when properly decoded, describes how the left and right signals are different from the mono centre signal. To extract discrete left and right signals, it is necessary to sum the outputs of the two mics to give one side of the stereo image, and subtract the side signal from the middle to give the other side. This may be done using a specially constructed sum and difference box, or it may be done using a mixing console that has phase reversal buttons as shown in Figure 8.3.

Note that three mixer channels are needed to do the decoding: the middle mic is panned dead centre while the side mic is split to feed two channels, one panned left and the other panned right. On one of these channels, the phase button is pressed and this pair of channels, one in-phase and the other out-of-phase, gives us the necessary sum and difference signal.

variable width

By varying the level of the 'side' signal channels, the stereo width can be modified. With the side signals turned right down, we are left with mono, and if the side signals are turned up higher than the centre signal, then we end up with an artificially widened stereo image. Care must be taken when using a mixer to set the two 'side' channels to the same level and this may be done by panning both to the centre (with the mid signal switched off) and adjusting the levels so that the two signals cancel each other out. Once this has been done, the channels may be panned back to their original left and right positions.

For location recording, it is quite in order to record the outputs from the two mics directly to two tracks of a stereo tape recorder and these may be decoded later when mixing or transferring to another stereo machine.

The MS pair has the advantage that it is always mono compatible – the in- and out-of-phase side signals cancel completely when summed to mono, and the centre stage signal is captured with greatest accuracy because it is directly on the axis of the mid mic. Despite the minor inconvenience involved in decoding the output signals to give the left and right stereo signals, the technique can be very rewarding and is highly recommended.

However, because this is still a coincident technique, there is no spacing to yield phase information. Furthermore, the figure-of-eight mic picks up a lot of its information off-axis, so we have the reverse situation to the XY pair – the centre stage sound is accurate but the edges of the soundstage may be less well defined.

spaced xy

So far I have looked at systems that create a level difference between left and right sounds but no account has been paid to the time delay caused by the distance between the ears. We can space the microphones of our coincident pair by a few inches to create an additional sense of space, but the phase cancellations that occur should the signal be summed to mono cause comb filtering effects which may significantly colour the sound. If there is no need to reproduce the recording to a high standard in mono, then the technique is perfectly acceptable. In fact this system is favoured by some European broadcast institutions where it is known as the ORTFE (Office de Radiodiffusion Television Francais) system. To be ORTFE compatible, the microphones must subtend an angle of 100° and be precisely seven inches or 17cm apart. A variation on this setup is used by the Dutch Broadcast Organisation – their NOS pair subtends 90° with a 12 inch or 30cm spacing.

spaced omnis (ab)

If, on the other hand, we use omni mics and space them by several feet rather than inches, the comb filtering effects become less pronounced, except at low frequencies where they still persist. This is a popular stereo technique known as the AB pair and is used for recordings destined to be replayed over loudspeakers, but positioning is important if the soundstage isn't to suffer from a 'hole in the middle' caused by too great a mic spacing. If such a hole is evident, then a third omni mic can be added centre stage, but then additional care has got to be taken to avoid phasing problems. If such problems are manifest, then all you can do is change the mic position and spacing so that the effect is minimised, trying to keep the inter-mic spacing as large as possible relative to the distance between microphone and sound source. Figure 8.4 shows a spaced omni setup which might be used for a small musical ensemble.

The distance of the microphones from the performers must be carefully adjusted so that the desired balance of direct and reverberant sound is being picked up. If the sound is too ambient, then the mics need to be brought closer to the performers. Conversely, if the sound is too dry, the microphones may be moved further away. Don't move the microphones too far in one go because a relatively small change in distance can significantly change the sound. If you can arrange to monitor a rehearsal using good headphones while you 'fine tune' the mic positions, this will save a lot of trial and error.

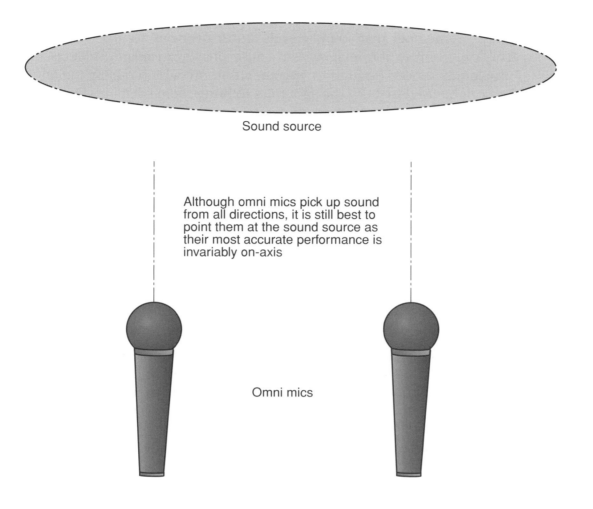

Sound source

Although omni mics pick up sound
from all directions, it is still best to
point them at the sound source as
their most accurate performance is
invariably on-axis

Omni mics

Figure 8.4: Spaced omnis set up to record a small ensemble

spot microphones

With very large ensembles, it is sometimes impossible to achieve the desired
balance by using just a stereo pair of mics, so additional spot mics are often
brought into use. These are positioned close to those performers needing
reinforcement and then added to the main stereo mix after being panned to
the appropriate position. The technique for positioning these spot mics is
exactly the same as if you were miking an individual or small group of players
and either cardioid or omnis are applicable.

One potential problem when employing spot mics is that the sound arrives
at the spot mics several milliseconds before reaching the main stereo mic

array – remember that sound travels at just over one foot per millisecond. This can confuse the imaging and cause phase cancellation effects. If the problem is serious enough to warrant attention, a high quality digital delay line can be used to delay the spot mics to bring them back into line with the stereo mics. A stereo delay patched into a pair of mixer subgroups would be one practical way to achieve this and around a millisecond of delay should be added for each foot between the spot mics and the main stereo array.

Whenever spot mics are used, they should be added to the stereo mix in as small a proportion as possible so that the main stereo mics still provide the majority of the signal. This will prevent the stereo image from becoming too confused as it could if several high level spot mics were competing with the stereo pair.

stereo with boundary mics

Boundary mics are capable of excellent stereo recordings and like conventional mics, there are a number of different ways of achieving essentially the same result. The simplest method is the equivalent of spaced omnis, and two boundary mics placed four feet or so apart on a low table top make an effective and easy way of recording a solo player. Alternatively, the two boundary mics may be fixed to a wall and spaced apart by the necessary distance to form an equilateral triangle with the performer at the apex. Both arrangements are shown in Figures 8.5a and 8.5b. It is also possible to mount the microphones directly on the floor but this leaves them open to the danger of picking up low frequency vibrations and thumps from the floor itself.

The equivalent of a coincident pair is the arrangement whereby two boundary mics are fixed to either side of a wooden or perspex sheet around four feet square. Ideally the mics should be positioned a few inches away from the exact centre of the board to randomise edge diffraction effects, and the board should be suspended edgeways to the performers in a similar position to that which would be used for coincident cardioids. Again the exact distance has to be determined empirically so that the desired balance of direct and reverberant sound is picked up.

rear pickup

This set-up will pick up sounds from the front and rear of the room with equal efficiency, so if it is desired to reject some of the rear sound, for example, audience noise at a live concert, then two sheets of material may be employed, hinged at the front edge. By increasing the angle between the two sheets, the mic array can be made less sensitive to sound coming from

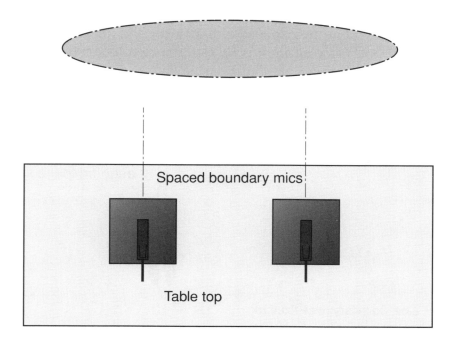

Spaced boundary mics

Table top

Figure 8.5a: Spaced boundary mics on a table top

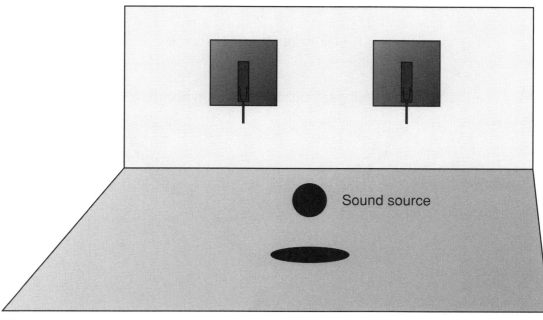

Boundary mics fixed to wall

Sound source

Floor

Figure 8.5b: Spaced boundary mics fixed to a wall

behind at the expense of narrowing the image of sounds arriving from the front. Once again, it is up to the user to choose a suitable compromise and both methods are illustrated in Figures 8.6a and 8.6b.

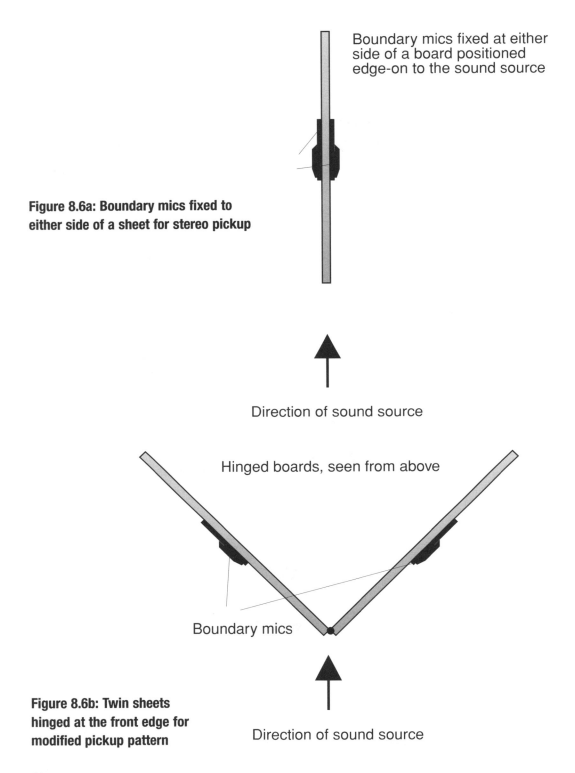

Boundary mics fixed at either side of a board positioned edge-on to the sound source

Figure 8.6a: Boundary mics fixed to either side of a sheet for stereo pickup

Direction of sound source

Hinged boards, seen from above

Boundary mics

Figure 8.6b: Twin sheets hinged at the front edge for modified pickup pattern

Direction of sound source

recording vocals

Recording a vocal performance in the studio isn't difficult but there are, as you might expect, a few key points to keep in mind. Firstly, the choice of microphone is important. For live performance, vocal microphones are nearly always unidirectional in order to minimise feedback and are usually dynamics, preferred for their rugged construction and their non-reliance on phantom powering. Furthermore, many live vocal mics incorporate a deliberate treble boost of a few dBs at around 3 to 5kHz in order to help the vocal sound compete with the rest of the band. This so-called presence peak, while undoubtedly useful in preserving clarity of diction, is not necessarily a good thing in the studio where the general aim is to capture as natural a performance as possible.

Most studio professionals will use capacitor mics for vocal use because of their high sensitivity and wide frequency response. Dynamic microphones tend to perform poorly above 16kHz or thereabouts and are less sensitive than capacitors. On the other hand, some rock vocalists prefer to use their live dynamic mic in the studio because it gives them a hard-hitting, powerful sound and their voices are usually loud enough not to require a highly sensitive mic. Here the choice is made for artistic reasons rather than to capture the most accurate rendition of the performer's voice.

frequency response

One seldom aired point is that the wide frequency response of capacitor microphones can emphasise sibilance in a performer's voice (a whistling sound accompanying 's' and 't' sounds) and modern bright sounding digital reverb units tend to further exacerbate the situation. The traditional cure for this problem is to use an electronic de-esser to attenuate the sibilant sounds. But a more pragmatic approach might be to use a suitable dynamic microphone on performers known to suffer from excessive sibilance as the limited frequency response will tend to hide the problem. Moving the mic position so that the performer sings over rather than directly into the microphone can also help avoid sibilance.

polar pattern

Referring again to live performance, I've indicated that cardioid pattern mics are the preferred choice because of their ability to reject off-axis sounds, thus minimising the spill from other instruments or performers. They are also less prone to acoustic feedback. In the studio, vocals tend to be recorded as separate overdubs where the singer monitors the existing instrumental backing via headphones. Because of this, the need to use a cardioid pattern mic is not so great, but unless the studio is acoustically fairly dead, then it may be a good idea to use a directional mic anyway to minimise the effect of the room acoustic on the recorded sound. If the acoustic is compatible with the use of an omni pattern mic, then the result will probably sound more natural because, as a general rule, omni pattern mics produce a more accurate result than an equivalent cardioid. And, because omni mics have the same nominal response in all directions, such room ambience as is captured will sound more accurate than it would if a cardioid were used. The off-axis response of a cardioid mic can exaggerate the boxy sound of a room.

Whichever type of microphone you opt to use, it is as well to keep in mind the fact that no single microphone is ideal for all vocalists. If a singer has a bright voice, then a mic with a presence peak may tend to make the overall sound harsh, whereas the same mic used on a person who has an indistinct or soft voice could yield a significant improvement. Attempting to achieve the same effect by means of EQ seldom succeeds and current thinking indicates that subtle phase effects occurring in audio equipment are more important to the tonality than simple equalisation involving the cutting or boosting of certain frequencies. For this reason, I would recommend recording vocals with little or no EQ and if the sound isn't right, then try a different mic or change its position slightly before resorting to EQ.

handling noise

In order to minimise handling noise, microphones should be mounted on a solid boom stand and a shock-mount cradle employed if possible. If your mixing console has a low frequency, hi-pass filter, this can be used to reduce the effect of any low frequency vibrations transmitted from the floor via the stand, but it's far better to avoid them in the first place.

Some singers can't perform properly without a hand-held mic, in which case let them try it and see what result you get. If their mic technique is poor, set up another mic on a stand a couple of feet in front of them telling them that you need a mix of the sound from both mics. This is of course a white lie and the recording is made entirely using the output from the stand-mounted mic!

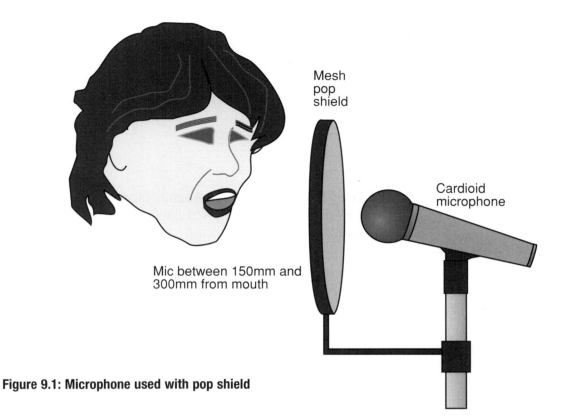

Mesh
pop
shield

Cardioid
microphone

Mic between 150mm and
300mm from mouth

Figure 9.1: Microphone used with pop shield

pop shields

Many people experience problems with popping on the plosive 'p' and 'b' sounds, and experience has shown that simple foam wind shields are generally ineffective in preventing this. The popping is caused by blasts of air from the performer's mouth slamming into the microphone diaphragm giving rise to a high level, low frequency output signal which manifests itself as a loud, breathy pop or thump. Fortunately, the solution is simple.

Commercial pop filters simply comprise a fine plastic or metal gauze stretched over a circular frame somewhere between four and six inches in diameter and positioned between the performer and the microphone. Normal sound, which consists of vibrations within the air, is not affected, but blasts of moving air are intercepted and their energy dissipated as turbulence as the air forces itself through the small holes in the mesh. A commercial pop shield may seem expensive, but it is possible to improvise your own at a fraction of the cost and it will work just as well.

The important part of the pop filter is the grille or mesh and a piece of nylon stocking works perfectly. This may be stretched over a wire frame (many engineers use wire coat-hangers) and is then fixed around six inches in front of the microphone. Figure 9.1 shows a typical setup.

An alternative ready-made pop filter can be bought in the form of a frying pan splash guard – these simply consist of a fine metal mesh fixed to a wire hoop with a handle. The provision of a handle makes fixing the filter to a mic stand easy and the overall result is a little tidier than the stocking approach.

positioning

There is generally no need for a singer to work really close to a microphone as is common in live performance, though those performers who have mastered the art of using the proximity effect of the microphone in a creative way may wish to do so. Working too close to a microphone will cause significant changes in both level and timbre as the singer moves his head so only very experienced vocalists should be recorded this way as a general rule.

Normally, a working distance of between six and 18 inches is ideal with the microphone pointing either just above or just below the singer's mouth. This usually gives a little more immunity to popping and sibilance than pointing the mic straight at the mouth, though you should take care not to move too far from the main axis of the microphone's response. The reason for this is that most cardioid mics only have an accurate frequency response over an angle of plus or minus thirty degrees or so, and outside this range, the top end response usually falls off with the consequence that off-axis sounds are reproduced sounding duller than they should.

The best position for a stand-mounted mic is in front of and just above the performer's mouth. If the stand will permit the mic to hang rather than supporting it from underneath, the vocalist will find it easier to arrange lyric sheets so that they can be consulted during the performance without changing the head position.

acoustics

Most studio vocal recordings are done in a relatively dead environment so that the desired reverb can be added artificially during the mix. If the acoustic you are working in is adversely affecting the recorded sound, then you can achieve excellent results by applying sound-deadening material to one corner of a room and then getting the performer to stand in the corner singing towards the centre of the room. Any sounds reflected from the rest of the room and bounced back into the corner will be absorbed by the acoustic treatment before they can be bounced back into the microphone (so long as you use a cardioid microphone). Acoustic foam tiles are very efficient at the frequencies normally found in speech and can either be fixed

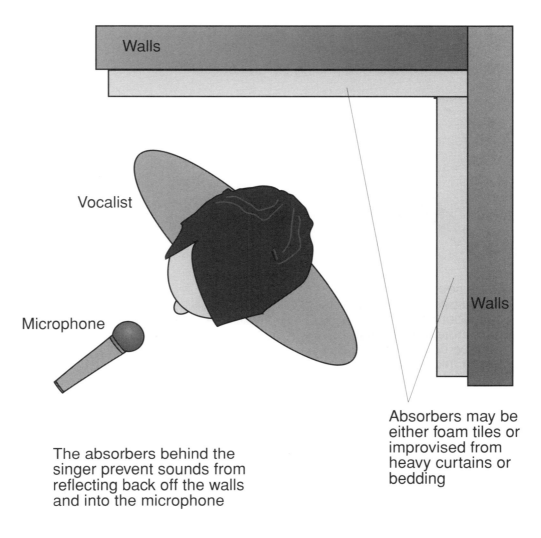

Walls

Vocalist

Microphone

The absorbers behind the singer prevent sounds from reflecting back off the walls and into the microphone

Walls

Absorbers may be either foam tiles or improvised from heavy curtains or bedding

Figure 9.2: Use of acoustic treatment in a corner for recording vocals

directly to the wall or onto the surface of a hinged screen. If such a screen is made with the other side reflective (hardboard or varnished wood), then it may be used one way round to deaden an environment or the other way to increase its liveness. Figure 9.2 shows how such an acoustically treated corner might be used in practice. Note that it is inadvisable to move too far into the corner as the boundary effect of the walls can introduce an unwanted low frequency boost.

Musical ensemble comprising several sections

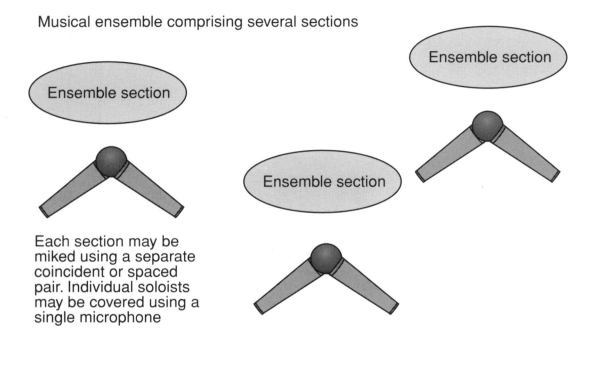

Each section may be miked using a separate coincident or spaced pair. Individual soloists may be covered using a single microphone

Additional stereo pair may be used to capture the overall sound. Some engineers prefer to delay the close mics so as to get the signal in phase with the more distant mics

Figure 9.3: Multiple stereo pairs used to record large choral group

multiple vocalists

If several vocalists are to be recorded at one time, it is advisable to position the mics so that spill between them is at a minimum (unless you are using a single stereo pair). The distance between mics should be at least three times the distance between the microphone and the vocalist to avoid phase cancellation effects and some form of acoustic screening is advisable. This three-to-one rule applies whenever multiple microphones are being used in close proximity.

If just two performers must be recorded at the same time, it is quite acceptable for a figure-of-eight mic to be used with a performer on each side. This avoids any phase cancellation problems but precludes the rebalancing of levels at the mixing stage.

For larger groups of singers such as choirs or ensembles, it may be desirable to record them in stereo and suitable techniques are discussed in the section on stereo miking. As a rule, one stereo pair should be used for each section of the chorus with the microphone pairs mounted above the performers' head heights and several feet in front of the front row of the section. Figure 9.3 shows how several stereo pairs might be used to mic up a large choral group.

processing

Because most vocalists find it difficult to control their dynamics with any accuracy, some compression may be needed during the recording to ensure a healthy signal level onto tape at all times (or digital recording system) while arresting any peaks that might cause overload distortion. Soft-knee compressors are ideal for use with analogue recorders, though digital recorders may also benefit from being used with a separate limiter to avoid brief peaks that the compressor might allow through. Try setting the compressor to give a gain reduction of eight or so during the louder sections as a starting point – a performer with a very wide dynamic range may need a ratio type controller set to a ratio of 4:1 or even higher. The same degree of gain reduction should be aimed for, and as with all signal processing, if you can get away with using less, then by all means do so as you'll almost certainly end up with a more natural sound. Always under-compress rather than over-compress when recording as you can always add more compression while mixing, but reversing the effects of excessive compression is far more difficult.

headphones

It is also worth a few lines on the subject of monitoring. Fully enclosed

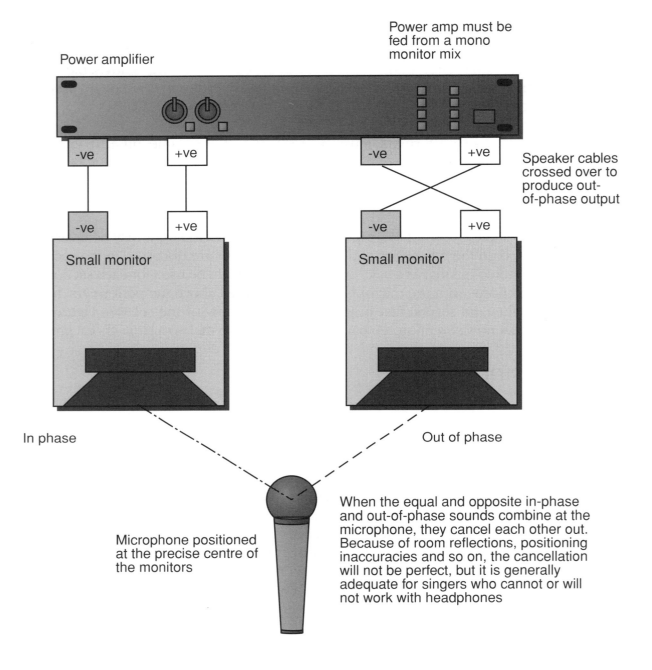

Power amp must be
fed from a mono
monitor mix

Power amplifier

-ve   +ve   -ve   +ve

Speaker cables
crossed over to
produce out-
of-phase output

-ve   +ve   -ve   +ve

Small monitor   Small monitor

In phase   Out of phase

Microphone positioned
at the precise centre of
the monitors

When the equal and opposite in-phase
and out-of-phase sounds combine at the
microphone, they cancel each other out.
Because of room reflections, positioning
inaccuracies and so on, the cancellation
will not be perfect, but it is generally
adequate for singers who cannot or will
not work with headphones

Figure 9.4: Using out-of-phase monitors to avoid spill

headphones are the preferred choice as they are less prone to spillage problems, but some vocalists find that they have trouble singing in tune using this method. This is why you often see videos of recording sessions where the singer has one phone on and the other off.

Semi-enclosed phones that you can actually hear through feel more comfortable to work with but they leak more sound so you could end up with a small but audible level of the backing track on the vocal track. This is acceptable so long as you don't suddenly decide to use part of the take unaccompanied because the spill will become obvious when there is no music to hide it.

The same is true if any sort of click track is being used and the mid-range beeps provided by some sequencers tend to spill quite badly, even with enclosed headphones.

alternative monitoring

For those vocalists who simply cannot work with phones at all, there is one method of working with speakers that gives surprisingly little spill. If the backing track is switched to mono and the phase of one of the monitor speakers reversed by swapping the red and black terminal connections on the rear of the speaker cabinet, then a microphone positioned equidistantly from both speakers will pick up an equal amount of in-phase and out-of-phase sound. According to theory, this should cancel out leaving no signal picked up by the mic. Nothing is perfect and so some signal is always audible, but by carefully positioning the mic and by balancing the levels fed to the speakers, spill can be reduced to a bare minimum. Because the vocalist is listening to the speakers with two ears, the out-of-phase effect doesn't cause cancellation and the monitored sound is perceived as being quite normal. Figure 9.4 shows how this arrangement could be set up in practice.

spoken word

Spoken word recording is more critical of room acoustics than singing because in the latter case, clarity of diction is not quite so important and there are likely to be other instruments playing which will hide the more subtle room effects or cover extraneous noises. Ideally, a very dead acoustic is necessary and again, this can be arranged locally by means of acoustic tiles, a portable sound booth, hanging blankets or rugs around the recording area.

A high quality capacitor microphone is the ideal choice and a cardioid model will exclude more room ambience than an omni. If some degree of reverberation is necessary, this may be added artificially after the recording has been made. Reverb should be used very sparingly unless a special effect is sought and dedicated ambience programs often work better than more obvious reverb treatments.

early reflections

It is particularly important to minimise early reflections from nearby objects such as tables or walls and it is common for specially absorbent or acoustically transparent table tops to be employed. An absorbent table top could be made by placing a layer of two inch foam rubber on its surface while a transparent table could be made from perforated metal sheet or wire mesh. Some form of table is generally necessary to support scripts or notes and care should be exercised to ensure that these don't rustle during the recording.

If a solid table must be used, an improvement in early reflections can be achieved by using a boundary mic flush with the table top. This arrangement ensures that reflections from the table will either miss the microphone altogether or arrive in phase with the direct sound which avoids comb filtering effects and their inevitable coloration.

multiple voices

Where several speakers must be recorded at once, there's a choice of approaches that can be used. In the case of a conference where the main objective is to provide a record of what has been said, a single omni hanging above a table around which the speakers are seated will often suffice. A location about two feet above head height is normally adequate. This method has the advantage of simplicity but allows no balancing between the voices and the result is only monophonic.

For the recording of two voices, you can either use a figure-of-eight mic with a speaker at either end of it or employ two cardioids, ensuring that there is adequate space between them to maintain separation and prevent phase cancellation from colouring the sound.

The figure-of-eight option is the easiest and has no phase problems, but the result is again mono and the only way to balance the levels is to experiment with the position of the speakers during a test run. If their voices are significantly different in level, then separate microphones will yield a better result.

Floor divided in areas to mark actors' positions

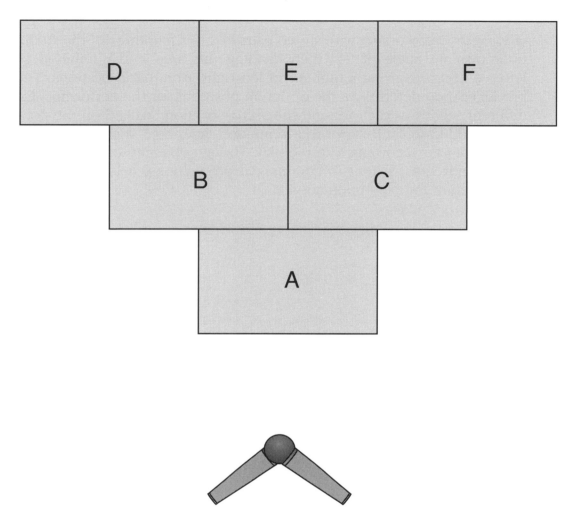

Figure 9.5: Floor layout for stereo play recording

Separate microphones have the advantage that they can be recorded onto different tape tracks to create a stereo spread and the levels can easily be adjusted individually. Either technique is suitable for commentary and basic radio play/jingle work.

plays

For more sophisticated radio plays, the two main approaches are separate cardioids or a single stereo pair. Arguably, the single stereo pair gives the most lifelike stereo imaging and also conveys some sense of distance when the performers are further from the mic. The disadvantage is that no rebalancing can be done later and the stereo positioning can't be changed.

One method of working with stereo pairs involves marking out the studio floor over an angle of 90° then dividing this area into numbered or lettered sections giving a number of left/right, front/back locations. The producer then determines the optimum positions for the performers for different scenes or sections and the sector location chalked on the floor can be added to their script as a reminder. Figure 9.5 shows a practical floor layout for recording a stereo play. Though this method is no longer used to any great extent in commercial productions, it is still a useful starting point for experimentation.

chapter 10

acoustic guitars

Acoustic guitars and similar fretted instruments often have a limited sound output, so a sensitive microphone is desirable if noise problems are to be avoided. Their sound also contains a lot of high frequency detail so a capacitor or good back-electret microphone is the obvious first choice, preferably one with a reasonably flat frequency response over the entire audio spectrum.

When miking an acoustic guitar live, it is tempting to put the microphone very close to the sound-hole as this produces the largest signal, but unfortunately, the tone is likely to be boomy and unpleasant. This is because the volume of air inside the guitar body resonates at a more or less fixed frequency which gives the guitar sound its depth of tone. Other important components of the sound come from elsewhere on the instrument (such as the body top and the strings), and it's only when they all combine that the true guitar tone is created.

If the guitar is miked too close to the sound-hole, some improvement can be achieved by cutting the lower mid EQ, but while this may be adequate for live work, it is not the right way to go about making a quality recording. Far better to find a microphone position that produces a more representative sound, even at the expense of signal level.

Most dynamic microphones are not sufficiently sensitive to do justice to the acoustic guitar and their lack of top end response can lead to a somewhat lifeless sound. If you must use a dynamic mic, use a good quality model and resist the temptation to position it too close purely to get a healthy signal as this will seriously compromise the tone.

vibrations

Like most acoustic instruments, the various parts of the guitar vibrate in different ways which means that different parts of the instrument generate different sounds: the volume of air inside the body produces one sound, the vibration of the table produces another and yet further sounds are produced directly from the strings and from the vibration of the neck and headstock. What the listener in the audience hears is a blend of all these sounds, plus reflections from the floor and walls of the room itself, so it is apparent that placing a microphone close to a single spot on the instrument's surface won't give a representative sound. It is for this reason that contact mics or bridge transducers seldom produce a sound that matches up to the natural tone of the instrument, though careful positioning combined with careful EQ circuitry can produce a close approximation. Though serious recordings are rarely made using transducers alone, it is fairly common practice to combine the output from a transducer with a microphone.

audience perception

To capture the sound that a member of the audience would expect hear, it is, in theory at any rate, necessary to place a mic or a stereo pair of mics at a comparable distance in a concert hall. In a studio, this approach may not be practical due to the constraints of spill, microphone sensitivity or the acoustic character of the environment, and in any event, the sound that we want to record isn't necessarily the exact sound the instrument would produce in a large venue. For example, a steel strung acoustic rhythm guitar may need to be made slightly brighter than real life and at the same time have some of the low end removed to prevent conflict with other instruments. A solo acoustic guitar on the other hand is normally miked to sound more natural but the top end is still often enhanced either by the choice and positioning of microphones or by the use of equalisation or electronic enhancement.

mic pattern

Either omni or cardioid mics may be used, omnis being preferable only when the room acoustics are particularly good. Strictly speaking, a flat frequency response is desirable but a mic with a subtle presence peak might enhance the top end allowing it to cut through a mix. Getting the desired tone by choosing a suitable mic and mic position always sounds better than using EQ. If two guitars are being recorded together, then it may be worth trying omnis rather than cardioids – the degree of spill will be higher, but due to the superior off-axis response of omnis, the spill will at least be of a high quality. In such a situation, use the 'three-to-one' rule for mic positioning – if the mics are placed two feet from the guitars, then make sure they are at least six feet apart. Any closer than this and the degree of spill may be enough to cause phase cancelling effects that will colour the sound making it appear distant and unnatural.

environment

In order to produce the best tone from the instrument, it should be played in a sympathetic room – one in which the acoustics are fairly live. If no such room is available, a localised live environment can be created by covering the floor with hardboard, shiny side up, and by placing reflective screens around the playing area. I've even heard of corrugated aluminium sheets being used to create a reflective environment, the main criteria being that the instrument actually sounds good in the room in which it is played. Don't worry if the acoustic isn't as live as you'd like as some artificial reverb can be added without compromising the sound quality.

mic placement

The sound that you actually capture can vary enormously depending on the microphone position. Experimentation has shown that there are quite a number of possible miking methods that produce excellent results, but a mic positioned around two feet from the instrument and pointing somewhere in between where the neck joins the body and the sound-hole is a good starting point. If the sound is too boomy, the mic can be positioned further away from the sound-hole or moved upwards so that it is 'looking down' on the instrument, and conversely, if the sound lacks body, it can be moved closer in.

Having said this, you might find a situation where the mic pointing at the floor to pick up mainly reflected sound gives a well balanced result. Try moving your head around the playing position as the performer warms up and listen out for any 'sweet spots'. When you've identified the sweet spots, try putting the mic there and see what kind of sound you get. If it's not quite right, you can always move it.

A quick way to find these sweet spots is to monitor the output from the mic using good quality closed headphones and then move the mic manually as the guitarist runs through the number. This way you can hear immediately the effect of changing the mic position.

stereo

If the guitar is the main instrument in a track, then try recording it in stereo as this will give a much more detailed sound. To do this, place a stereo pair of microphones two or three feet in front of the instrument and move the mic positions slightly if the sound is excessively thin or boomy. Remember that pointing a mic towards the sound-hole will give a more boomy sound whereas moving the mic along the neck, away from the body will give a thinner sound. Figure 10.1 shows some possible stereo mic positions. In practice, you can use any of the stereo miking methods discussed in Chapter 8.

It is also quite acceptable (and indeed, probably more common) to use two mics which can be panned to produce a stereo image, even though they may not be positioned to capture a true stereo picture. For example, you could

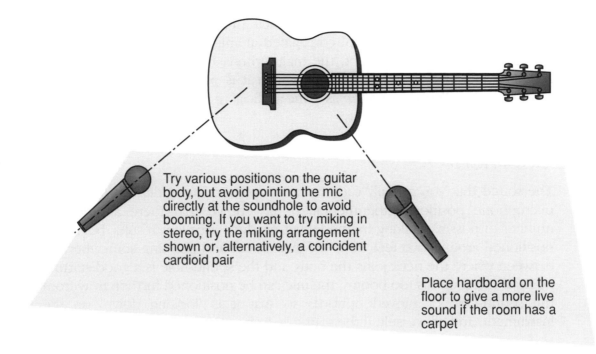

Try various positions on the guitar body, but avoid pointing the mic directly at the soundhole to avoid booming. If you want to try miking in stereo, try the miking arrangement shown or, alternatively, a coincident cardioid pair

Place hardboard on the floor to give a more live sound if the room has a carpet

Figure 10.1: Stereo-miked acoustic guitar

have one close mic panned to one side and an ambience mic at a greater distance panned to the other. Unless you are after an accurate stereo picture, any setup that sounds good is artistically valid. Similarly, panning the miked signal to one side and the output from a transducer to the other often produces worthwhile results.

practical arrangement

One arrangement that works particularly well is to position one mic in the usual end-of-neck or 'looking down' position to capture the main part of the sound and then position another a foot or so away from the neck pointing towards the headstock. This gives a very articulate, detailed sound that works equally well with picked, rhythm or classical style playing. The microphones may be cardioids, omnis or even one of each and they may be balanced during the mix to create the desired tone. Figure 10.2 shows how this miking arrangement can be set up in practice.

If you have a pair of boundary mics, you can obtain a very natural sound by placing these on a table top a couple of feet in front of the performer with the mics three feet or so apart. This arrangement is also quite good for making quick demos of guitarist/vocalists. Alternatively, the boundary mics could be set up as a conventional stereo pair as outlined in the section on stereo mic techniques in Chapter 8.

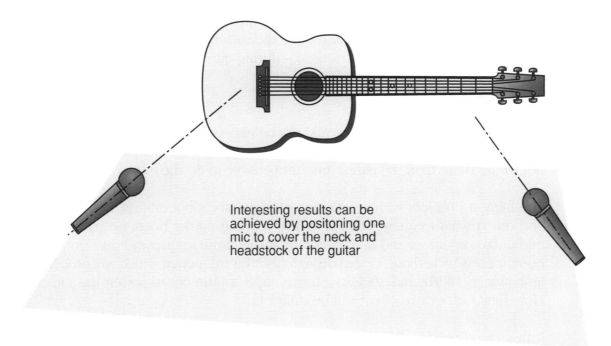

Interesting results can be achieved by positoning one mic to cover the neck and headstock of the guitar

Figure 10.2: Asymmetrical microphones to create a stereo effect

preparation

As with any instrument, the resulting sound quality depends on how good the instrument sounds in the first place. Any intonation problems or buzzes should be attended to before the session starts and with steel-strung instruments, a relatively new set of strings is a good idea, particularly if a bright, lively sound is sought.

The performer should play seated if possible to prevent undue movement of the guitar relative to the microphones and it should be ensured that the seat doesn't squeak or creak before recording begins. Also take care to exclude other sources of noise such as spill from headphones, particularly if click tracks are being used. Some finger squeak is normal, but if excessive, a little talcum powder on the player's hands may help.

external noise

Other sources of noise include the ticking from clockwork or even quartz watches, rustling clothing and excessive breathing noises. Some breath noise is obviously a natural part of the performance but some players tend to go a bit over the top, accompanying their music by grunting and snorting. If a click track has to be used, pick a sound that isn't too piercing, and if possible, rig it via a compressor set up in 'duck' mode so that the click track gets louder when the guitar is played louder and quietens down when the playing is quiet. This way the performer will always be able to hear the click but it will be turned down at the times it's most likely to be noticed – during quiet sections or pauses.

equalisation

In an ideal world, equalisation would not be necessary, but in the studio where reality is not always the main objective, some EQ may be needed. Even so, try not to use more than the barest amount possible to do the job.

The biggest problem with certain acoustics guitars is boominess, and you can find out at what frequency this occurs by turning up the boost on your lower mid or bass equaliser and then sweeping through the frequency range until the boominess is picked out. Once you've found this frequency, which will probably lie between 100Hz and 200Hz, you can apply a little cut to lessen the effect. Hopefully a dB or two of cut will be sufficient.

If the sound needs a little more top end sparkle, you could use your shelving 10kHz equaliser to add a dB or so of top boost. If this doesn't seem to be enough, then you may be better off creating the brightness you want by using an enhancer such as an Aphex Exciter or SPL Vitalizer. Those fortunate enough to have access to a parametric equaliser may prefer to use a broadband boost. Bite can be added to the sound by boosting between 5kHz and 7kHz while harshness in the upper mid-range may be minimised by cutting between 1kHz and 3kHz. As usual, the exact frequency you need to work on is identified by setting the relevant equaliser section to full boost and then sweeping through the frequency range. When you hit it, the offending frequency should stand out like a sore thumb!

Only apply as much cut as you need to do the job or the result is likely to be quite unnatural. The only area where excessive EQ might be justified is if you want to take out all the bottom end to give a bright rhythm sound with as little body as possible in order not to compete with other instruments in the mix. By the same token, switching in your sub-bass high-pass filter won't significantly alter the sound but it will keep unwanted low frequency information to a bare minimum. Interestingly, the digital EQ implemented in some computer audio workstations and digital mixers may work better with acoustic guitar than traditional analogue equalisers as they seem better able to adjust the tonal balance of a sound without the result sounding as though it's been EQ'd. Curiously though, some digital EQs seem to require a lot more cut or boost to achieve the necessary subjective result than analogue equalisers do. Of course every equaliser has its own character so some experimentation will be necessary.

chapter 11

electric guitar

T he electric guitar sound is unusual in that it depends not only on the instrument itself, but also on the amplification system and the loudspeaker system used. Add to this the effect of the room acoustics, the position of the speaker cabinet within that room and, most importantly, the way the instrument is played, and you can see why there are as many unique guitar sounds as there are guitarists.

amplification

Guitar speaker systems tend to comprise 10 or 12 inch drivers, either singly or in multiples, mounted in cabinets which may be fully sealed or open-backed. Tweeters or mid-range speakers are, as a rule, not employed. The distinctive overdrive sound is caused by harmonic distortion added in the amplifier, but fed through a full range speaker system such as a hi-fi, the result would be raspy and most unmusical. Guitar speakers have a poor high frequency response and tend to become inefficient above 2 or 3kHz, which has the effect of filtering out the undesirable harmonics resulting in a sound which still has plenty of edge or bite but doesn't sound buzzy or thin.

Many of the best loved guitar speakers are designed so that the cones themselves add distortion at high power levels. If you hear someone talking about loudspeaker break-up modes, they are referring to the way the sound is distorted at high power levels and not about driving a speaker to destruction!

Open-backed cabinets tend to have a fatter sound than closed ones but the approach to miking them is similar. There is also a vast difference in sound between one make of amplifier and another and most players still uphold that valve amplifiers sound better than solid state models.

microphone type

Because of the limited frequency response of guitar speaker systems, dynamic microphones are very often used to mic them up and a general purpose cardioid or omni will usually give quite adequate results. In situations where spill is a problem, a cardioid mic would be the obvious choice, but an omni used at half the distance will result in roughly the same amount of spill so the practical differences between the two mic types are not all that great.

Because guitar amplification systems aren't short on volume, you don't need to worry about microphone sensitivity and at the other end of the scale, most good dynamics can handle the extreme sound pressure levels (SPLs) produced by guitar amps.

Many American engineers still prefer to use a capacitor microphone on the electric guitar and this helps to produce the American rock sound which is not so fat as the British sound and has a more incisive edge. The bottom line is that if you get the sound you want, then you've used the right mic.

On some occasions a mic with a presence peak will help a sound cut through a mix more effectively whereas an already aggressive sound might benefit if a fairly flat mic is used. At the bass end, the lowest string on a guitar sounds at a little under 100Hz so an extended bass response is not really necessary. However, some amplifiers produce a definite low frequency clunk when the strings are picked hard and this may produce a significant amount of low frequency which a mic with a good low end response should interpret rather better. This so-called cabinet clunk is mainly featured in heavy rock guitar styles.

environment

Guitar cabinets can either be close-miked, miked from a distance or a combination of the two methods using two or more mics. In some ways you have to treat a guitar cabinet like an instrument in its own right because different sounds come from different parts of it. The majority of the sound may come from the speakers but even with a sealed cabinet, a significant amount of sound comes from the back and sides of the box. And with an open-backed cabinet, as much sound escapes from the back as from the front.

The traditional way to get the sound of a cranked-up stack played live is to set up the full stack and then mike it from ten feet or more in a large room. This way you capture the direct sound from the speakers, including any phase cancellation effects caused by multiple drivers, and you also get the sound reflected from the floor which creates further comb filtering. In other words, the mic hears the performance much as an audience would.

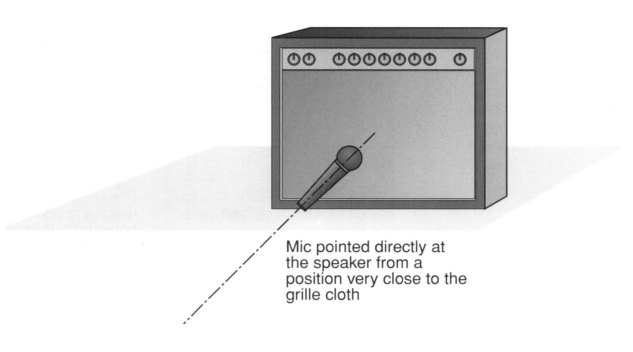

Mic pointed directly at
the speaker from a
position very close to the
grille cloth

Figure 11.1: Close-miked guitar amplifier

The problem is that few studios have the space to work this way, especially when several members of the band are playing together and some degree of acoustical separation is needed. Furthermore, although this gives a warm and loud sound quality, it doesn't sound as bright or intimate as a close-miked amp and so may not cut through in a complex mix.

A more basic approach is to position a single mic some 12 inches (or less) in front of one of the speakers in the cabinet. Many engineers actually prefer to work with the mic right up against the speaker cloth. If the mic is pointed directly along the axis of the speaker, then the sound will be relatively bright, but it can be mellowed by moving the mic towards the edge of the speaker. Figure 11.1 shows a typical close-miking situation.

open-backed speakers

In the case of open-backed cabinets, a fatter sound may be obtained by miking the rear of the cabinet and some engineers even like to mic the side of the cabinet and then add this sound to the direct miked sound. There is no reason not to mic both the front and rear of the cabinet

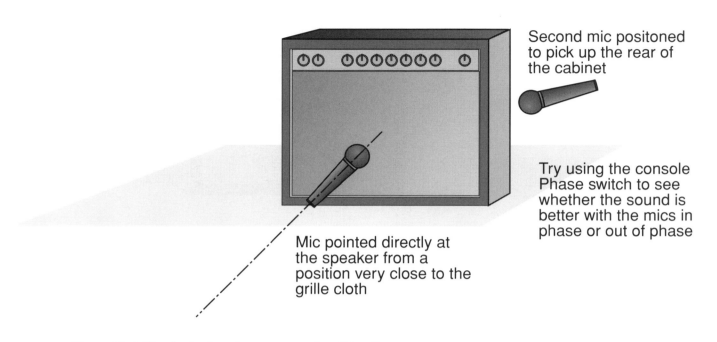

Second mic positoned to pick up the rear of the cabinet

Try using the console Phase switch to see whether the sound is better with the mics in phase or out of phase

Mic pointed directly at the speaker from a position very close to the grille cloth

Figure 11.2: The dual microphone approach, miking the front and rear of the cabinet

simultaneously but the phase of the rear mic should be inverted so that its output is in phase with that of the front mic.

The reason for this is pretty clear if you think about it – while the front of the speaker cone is travelling towards the front mic, the rear of the cone must be travelling away from the rear mic which will create an opposite polarity of signal. Without the use of phase inversion, these two signals would tend to cancel to some extent giving a quite different and less weighty one.

Having said that, if you prefer the sound without using phase reversal, then use the sound you like!

ambience

Another popular variation on the close-miked approach is to use an additional ambience mic, usually a capacitor model, several feet from the cabinet and then add this to the close-miked sound. A direct comparison of the two sounds in isolation will reveal that the close-miked sound is more clinical, brighter and indeed sounds closer. The ambience mic will have a softer tone and include a degree of room reverb giving the sound more spread and making the tone smoother.

If the guitar is played in a room other than the one in which the amplifier is located, then a capacitor microphone can be used to capture the direct sound from the guitar strings which can be added to the miked amplifier sound. On its own, the miked strings will seem thin and tinny, but when mixed in with the main sound, they will add definition to the notes rather like an exciter. This is definitely a technique worth experimenting with, especially for country or clean Strat-type guitar sounds.

equalisation

When it comes to the mix, some additional EQ may be needed to achieve the desired tone because the sound you hear in the studio is rarely exactly the same as the sound you get on tape. Much of the compensation can be done at the recording stage by adding EQ on the desk or the amplifier itself so that the sound you hear over the monitors is more or less correct. Even so, once the other instruments are added, the tone may need modifying to make it stand out against the rest of the mix.

If the sound is muddy, cut applied at between 100Hz and 250Hz can help reduce the problem and the usual method of determining the frequency to work at applies: crank up the low mid boost and then sweep through the frequency range until the offending frequencies are most prominent. At that point you can change from boost to cut and set the amount of cut by ear.

effects

It is often considered inadvisable to record effects along with a sound because you lose the option to change them at the mixing stage unless the effects can be recorded on separate tape tracks. However, in the case of the guitar, the effects are modified by the amplification system itself and so it may be impossible to duplicate these later. Furthermore, the player responds to the sound he is producing and often the effects are an integral part of the sound, particularly overdrive or delay. There are no hard and fast rules on which effects have to be recorded to tape and which you can add later but don't compromise the performance for the sake of some slight technical advantage. Discuss the options and their implications with the player and then agree on a method of working that you can both live with.

direct inject

It is possible to record the guitar without miking it up at all, and though DI'ing used to be the second best option, some of todays' digital recording guitar preamps based on physical modelling can sound superb. With DI'ing you have the advantage that the guitarist can play in the control room and hear the actual sound going to tape over the monitors as he plays. For clean guitar sounds, you don't even need a special recording preamp, but unfortunately, unless the electric guitar has active electronics, it can't be plugged directly into the mixing console.

There are several problems that stand in the way of a good DI'd electric guitar sound but most can be circumvented to some extent. Firstly, the output impedance of a non-active guitar pickup is too high for a mixer's mic or line input and the resulting mismatch causes loading on the pickups, which in turn gives a poor treble performance and may even reduce the sustain of the instrument.

A simple DI box (a model with a high impedance instrument input) will solve the impedance matching problem but the tone still won't quite be what you are used to. A guitar amplifier is usually voiced, or to put it another way, the frequency response isn't flat but is modified to sound good, usually by adding mid or high frequency boost. The other major factor is the way in which the speaker changes the tonal character of the sound. A basic rhythm sound can be achieved by using a DI box and then applying some corrective or creative EQ, but a dedicated guitar processor will give better results.

guitar processors

The first successful guitar processor was the Rockman which combined compression, delay, chorus, equalisation and overdrive to give a convincing clean or dirty guitar sound straight into the mixing desk. The designers realised the profound effect that the speaker has on the overdrive sound and included sophisticated filtering to simulate this. The result wasn't an exact duplicate of a miked-up sound by any means, but it was good to listen to and musically useful.

Specialised guitar recording preamps are now available from a variety of manufacturers, many models being programmable and with MIDI program control selection. The quality has improved over the years and the best of today's units can emulate a selection of big name guitar amplifiers very accurately. In fact the only effect they don't capture, unless you turn the studio monitors up very loud, is the way a real guitar amplifier feeds back.

speaker emulators

Another approach to DI'd guitar is to use your regular amplifier but replace the speaker with a speaker emulator or simulator. These often take the form of a dummy load allowing the amplifier to perform just as it would with a speaker, and they include a filtering network to emulate the coloration produced by a typical guitar speaker. The output signal is reduced to a level which the mixing console can accept, usually in the form of a balanced mic level signal. Cheaper models are available without the dummy load, but that means your guitar amp speakers must be left connected or you must use a separate dummy load. Most transistor amplifiers will work happily just with the speakers unplugged, but valve amplifiers could sustain damage.

In general, speaker simulators give a reasonably convincing rock sound, but they still don't quite capture the effect of loudspeaker breakup or the sense of being in a real space. The addition of a little reverb or ambience improves matters enormously and you have the advantage that the basic character of the amplifier being used is retained.

re-miking

One method of working that has proven to be very useful is to treat DI'd sounds by feeding the guitar track through a guitar stack or combo during the mix, miking this up and then feeding the mic output back into the mixer. If the guitar is recorded unprocessed, this gives the engineer the option of producing virtually any type of sound subject only to the availability of a suitable guitar amp. It has been known for these to be set up in bathrooms or concrete stairwells to achieve a very convincing, live sound. Of course there's no reason not to do this with a recording preamp – record the guitar clean via a DI box, then patch in the preamp when you come to mix. In fact these days the preamp doesn't even need to exist – it may come as a software plug-in for your computer audio system.

interference

Finally, be aware that electric guitar pickups are very susceptible to induced noise due to magnetic fields from studio equipment and computer monitors. Humbucking pickups are the least susceptible, but it's always a good idea to move the guitar as far away from potential sources of interference as possible. In some situations, it may be possible to switch computer monitors off while recording the guitar. Solid state LCD computer monitors should produce far less interference than regular CRT models, so for serious work in a computer-based studio, one of these may be a good investment. There's also a range of high quality replacement humbucker pickups available that sound very much like the single-coil models they replace, but with far less susceptibility to hum and noise.

drums

Recording a drum kit can be one of the most satisfying experiences an engineer can enjoy, but it also brings with it a unique set of problems. There are several ways of approaching the job and because music is so varied, it's impossible to say that one method of miking a drum kit is the best. But before we even think of reaching into the microphone locker, we have to get the drum kit itself sounding right.

Unlike most other instruments, you can't just take a drum kit that has been tuned for live use and then expect it to sound good in the studio. In a live situation, some of the unwanted characteristics of the drum sound will go unnoticed or be covered by other instruments: rattles, buzzes, metallic rings and that sort of thing. In the studio, these artifacts show up more clearly so some time must be spent tuning and damping the kit before any mics are set up. And don't forget to oil squeaking bass drum pedals and stools.

Depending on the type of sound required, the drums should be set up in a slightly live environment so that they produce an exciting sound in the room. Some forms of music demand a very live environment which usually means a large room with a lot of hard surfaces, but the smaller studio can create some of this ambience by using artificial reverb at the mixing stage.

single heads

The easiest kit to record is the one that uses single-headed toms and a bass drum which has had a large hole cut in the front head. Some players simply remove the front head but this can put uneven stress on the drum shell and may cause a loss of tone or even physical distortion of the shell. The hole should be as large as is practical to prevent the remaining material from ringing and being picked up by the mics.

For most contemporary work, a wooden bass drum beater gives a better defined sound than a cork or felt beater and a patch of mole skin or hard plastic taped to the head where the beater hits will add more of a click to the sound. There are specialist drum products for this application.

If the toms are double-headed, the bottom heads can normally be removed without problem though you may find that the nut boxes start to rattle. If this is the case, stop the rattles by pushing Blu-Tac or plasticine into the nut boxes or, better still, make up a set of heads with large holes cut in them so that the tuning components are kept under tension.

If a double-headed tom sound is required, then the miking technique is much the same, though more care has to be paid to tuning and damping. Whatever the kit, it should be confirmed that the heads themselves are in good condition. Just because a head isn't broken doesn't mean it's okay – old heads stretch unevenly and the surface becomes dented and worn causing a loss of tone.

snare

Snare drums come in many sizes and are usually provided with metal or wooden shells. Wooden shells give a less ringy sound than metal ones and a deeper shell generally equates to a deeper tone. Make sure that the snares themselves are in good order and properly adjusted to minimise rattling and buzzing.

Every drummer has his own preference for tuning but in general, the snare head should be just slightly looser than the batter head. The heads should be tensioned evenly so that tapping around the edges produces the same pitch note all the way around the head. If the batter head is tensioned too tightly, then the tone will become tubby and unpleasant. Conversely, if it is tuned too slack, the sound will lack body. There is a range between these two extremes where a variety of usable tones can be coaxed from any reasonable quality drum.

damping

A kit with no damping will usually sound very boomy and the individual drums will sustain too long. The choice of heads affects the damping and a thin, hard head will give a bright tone with a long sustain. Thicker heads or those utilising a double layer of material will give a slightly fatter sound with a shorter decay while some of the very heavy oil-filled heads sound just like hitting suitcases, even before damping is applied!

Too much damping can leave the kit sounding lifeless and it is as well to keep in mind the fact that the ringing and over-long sustain will sound less pronounced in the context of a mix where other instruments are playing.

Toms may be damped by taping tissue or cloth to the heads near the edges and it should be ensured that these damping pads aren't likely to be hit by the drummer. Similarly, try to keep the damping pad away from the area of head where the mic is likely to be pointing.

The way in which toms are tuned affects their tone and decay characteristics and a perfectly evenly tuned head may not always give the best sound. One popularly used trick is to tune the head evenly, then slacken off just one of the tuning lugs slightly. This gives a slight pitch drop after the drum is struck and is very popular in rock music.

Many drums are fitted with internal dampers, but unless these are quite sophisticated, they are unlikely to give good results. The main problem is that they apply pressure to one point on the head and upset the tuning.

The snare drum may be damped in a similar way but no damping is normally applied to the snare head as this would dull the tone of the snares. As with the toms, don't overdo the tuning and err on the side of too little rather than too much.

Damping the bass drum is best achieved by placing a folded woollen blanket inside the drum so that it rests on the bottom of the shell and touches the lower part of the rear head. Further damping is unlikely to be necessary though noise gates are often used to sharpen up the decay of the sound.

miking options

The simplest and perhaps most honest way to mic a drum kit is to position a stereo pair of mics around five feet from the ground and between five and fifteen feet in front of the kit. Figure 12.1 shows how this may be set up in practice. These mics will capture the live sound and stereo imaging of the kit as played in that particular room very accurately, but they will also pick up spill from any other instruments that happen to be playing at the same time. More importantly, the accurate live sound of the kit is seldom the objective in pop music production.

The stereo pair approach is probably best suited to jazz work but even here, the snare and bass drums often benefit from a little extra help. To achieve this, close mics are used on the bass and snare drums and the stereo pair positioned several feet above the kit on extended boom stands. These overheads may be set up as a coincident pair but it is more common to use spaced omnis. Capacitor mics are normally used for this task as their high end response is needed to faithfully reproduce the cymbals and the attack of the drums, though good results can be achieved using budget PZM mics which use electret capsules.

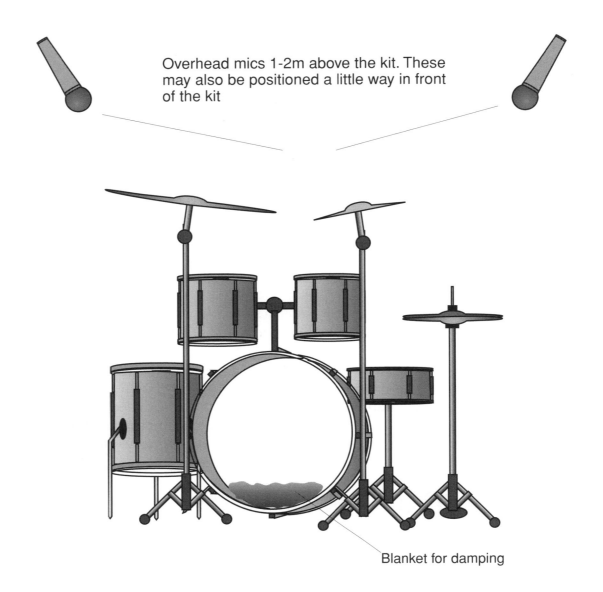

Overhead mics 1-2m above the kit. These may also be positioned a little way in front of the kit

Blanket for damping

Figure 12.1: Miking a drum kit using a stereo pair

snare mic

The snare mic may be either a dynamic or a capacitor type depending on preferences and budget. Either type will give a useful sound, but the character will be different. As you might expect, the capacitor will give a crisper sound. Either directional or omni pattern mics may be used – in either case, the close proximity of other drums means that some spill is inevitable and even though omnis will pick up a little more spill, it will be tonally correct. Off-axis spill into a cardioid mic is likely to sound less bright than the on-axis sound.

Ideally the mic should be placed a couple of inches from the drum head and positioned to one side where the drummer is unlikely to hit it. The mic may be tilted so that it points towards the centre of the head and it should be positioned so that it isn't pointing directly towards an adjacent drum which would worsen the spill situation.

bass drum mic

Bass drum mics are usually mounted on boom stands so the mic can be positioned inside the drum shell. The exact position of the mic within the shell will influence the tonal character of the sound and a good starting point is with the mic pointing directly at the point on the head where the beater hits at a distance of between two and eight inches from the head. Moving the mic to one side or other, or angling it slightly, will emphasise the overtones produced by the drum shell so there is a lot of leeway to change the basic sound without recourse to equalisation.

Large diaphragm dynamic mics tend to be favoured for bass drum work and either figure-of-eight or cardioid models are the usual choice. Extremely high sound pressure levels are generated inside bass drums, so a mic capable of working at these levels must be used. Because of the low frequencies involved, a mic with a good bass response is essential if the sound is to have any body to it. Many specialist bass drum mics, such as the AKG D12, have a low frequency boost at around 80Hz to emphasise the thump of the drum and their later D112 also includes a degree of high end boost to accentuate the click of the beater hitting the head. Figure 12.2 shows a kit miked with stereo overheads plus separate kick and snare mics.

multi miking

In contemporary music recording, drums are nearly always miked individually enabling the engineer to finely control the balance of the drums within the kit. Furthermore, close-miking gives a more immediate sound, which is popular when a larger than life sound is called for. And in the case of pop or rock music, we nearly always want a drum sound that is more powerful than that of an acoustic kit played without amplification.

The approach to miking the bass, snare and overheads is the same as before except we now add further mics to cover the toms. An additional mic may be needed for the hi-hat, especially if the snare mic is going to be gated, to improve separation.

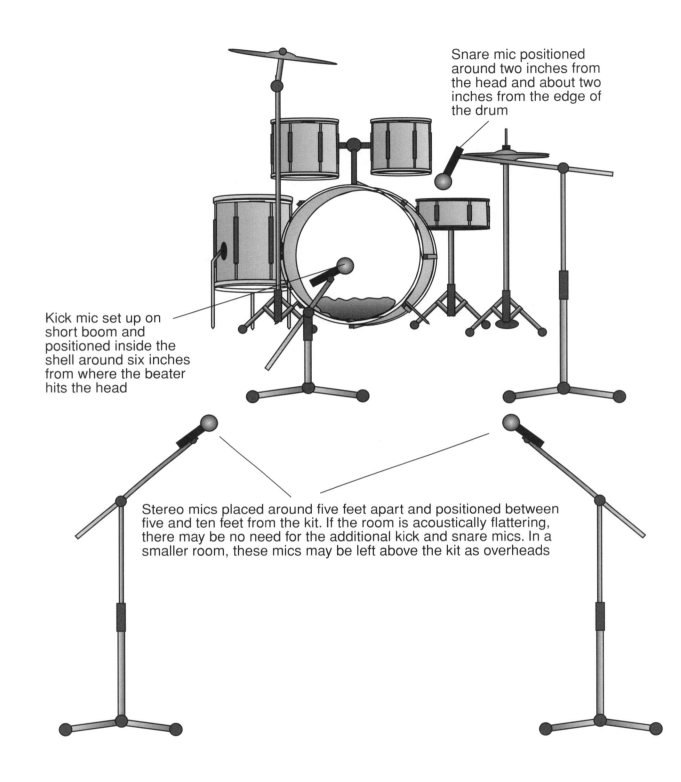

Snare mic positioned around two inches from the head and about two inches from the edge of the drum

Kick mic set up on short boom and positioned inside the shell around six inches from where the beater hits the head

Stereo mics placed around five feet apart and positioned between five and ten feet from the kit. If the room is acoustically flattering, there may be no need for the additional kick and snare mics. In a smaller room, these mics may be left above the kit as overheads

Figure 12.2: Overhead pair plus close bass and snare mics

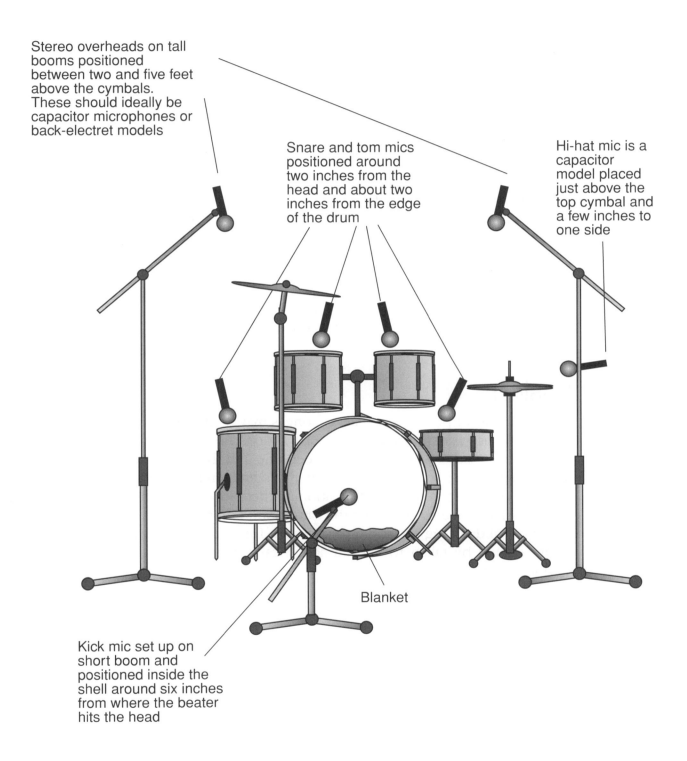

Stereo overheads on tall booms positioned between two and five feet above the cymbals. These should ideally be capacitor microphones or back-electret models

Snare and tom mics positioned around two inches from the head and about two inches from the edge of the drum

Hi-hat mic is a capacitor model placed just above the top cymbal and a few inches to one side

Blanket

Kick mic set up on short boom and positioned inside the shell around six inches from where the beater hits the head

Figure 12.3: A fully miked kit including hi-hat mic and overheads

toms

Positionally, the tom mics are set up similarly to the snare mic and once again, the mics may be dynamic or capacitor – cardioid or omni. A great many British engineers use dynamic cardioids such as Shure SM57s or Sennheiser 421s but there is a swing towards the use of capacitor mics because of their improved transient handling capability. This leads to a better defined drum sound. The argument for using omnis rather than cardioids so that any spill will at least sound tonally correct is also valid.

The overheads and hi-hat mics should be capacitor mics to preserve the transient detail of the cymbals, but depending on the setup of the kit, you may find a separate hi-hat mic unnecessary because the snare mic and overheads will pick up all the hi-hat level you need. Take care in positioning separate hi-hat mics so that they don't get hit by a blast of air every time the hi-hats are closed as this will spoil the sound. A position a few inches from the edge of the cymbals and angled from above or beneath is usually adequate though always experiment with different positions if you feel you can get a better result. Figure 12.3 shows a fully miked kit including hi-hat mic and overheads.

percussion

Other forms of percussion such as congas may be miked from overhead in either mono or stereo, and unless separation is a problem, the mic distance may be increased to anywhere between one and three feet from the drum head depending on how much of the room ambience you wish to capture. If in doubt, keep in mind that positioning the mics close to the performer's head will capture more or less the same sound that he hears while playing. Additional damping is seldom required on Latin and ethnic percussion but care should be taken to find an acoustically sympathetic environment in which to work.

chapter 13

the piano

With so many excellent and inexpensive MIDI piano modules currently on the market, you might wonder why anyone bothers to go to the trouble of recording the real thing – or at least, you might if you haven't already listened to the difference between a good piano and its sample-based emulation. The truth of the matter is that a piano is a living, breathing instrument full of resonances and vibrations that are far too complex to emulate with absolute accuracy. For example, whenever you play a note on a real piano, the other strings also vibrate in sympathy, but in different ways depending on which note you've played and how hard. If you play two notes at a time, the pattern of sympathetic resonances gets more complex, but because of the way in which most electronic pianos are sampled, the best you can hope for is that each note will be accompanied by the sympathetic resonances that occur when that note is played in isolation. And unless each separate note is sampled (as opposed to one note being transposed to cover several keys), the resonances will also be transposed depending on the note you play.

There's also the way the timbre of a real piano changes with dynamics to consider. Velocity crossfading between a few discrete samples or using a velocity-controlled filter is never going to capture the subtle nuances of a real piano played by a virtuoso performer, and while a MIDI piano might be fine as part of a mix, few piano players feel entirely comfortable using them for solo performances or prominent parts. In such cases, there's no alternative but to get out the mics and record the real thing.

the piano sound

When it comes to recording, the acoustic piano isn't without its problems – like most acoustic instruments the sound doesn't just emanate from one convenient point but from the strings, the soundboard and the casework of the instrument – it's only when all these vibrating parts make their contribution that a true sound can be captured. To further frustrate the recording engineer, there are various mechanical noises such as the pedals and dampers that must be minimised, and while a change in playing style is sometimes all that's needed, it's not uncommon to have to wrap the pedals in cloth to stop them thumping. And, of course, unlike the MIDI piano, there's acoustic spill and room acoustics to worry about.

Most important piano recordings are made using a grand piano unless the musical style specifically needs the sound of an upright, and it's generally thought that the larger the piano, the better the sound, especially at the bass end. Before getting into mic positions, it's necessary to think about the sound of the instrument and the type of mics that will be needed to do that sound justice. The piano spans the entire musical spectrum, from deep bass to almost ultrasonic harmonics, so a microphone with a wide frequency response is a must. A good capacitor or back-electret microphone is the preferred option, though you can exercise a degree of artistic choice in deciding to go for a ruthlessly honest small capsule model or a more flattering but less accurate large diaphragm mic. Aside from their excellent frequency response, capacitor mics are very sensitive, which means they'll be able to capture the dynamic range of the instrument without introducing unwanted noise, even when you're recording from several feet away. For demo work, good dynamic mics will produce acceptable results, but capacitor models are really the only choice for release-quality recordings.

Pianos are most often recorded in stereo and any of the standard stereo mic techniques may be applied. You can use spaced omnis, coincident cardioids, MS pairs or PZM mics, though if you're worried about mono compatibility, you may feel safer sticking to a coincident mic setup rather than a spaced arrangement as spaced mics, by their very geometry, introduce phase effects which may cause the sound to change for the worse when you hit the console's mono button. On the other hand, spaced microphones do allow more control in balancing the upper and lower registers of the instrument, especially if you opt for a close-miking approach.

Some engineers habitually use three or more mics but this runs the risk of more serious phase problems, so unless you've got plenty of time to experiment, it may be safer to stick to a stereo pair. The only exception to this rule is when using spaced omnis at a large distance from the piano as this often leads to a lack of definition in the centre of the soundstage and an additional centre mic can help to hold the sound together.

mic positions

Before deciding on a mic position, decide on the sound you want. Pop recordings may require a bright, up-front sound where accuracy is less important than getting the right type of sound, while for classical and jazz

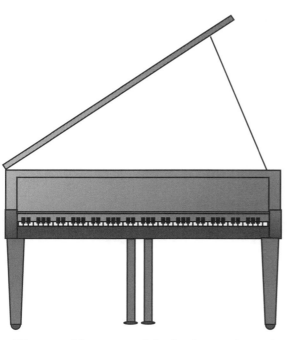

Spaced or coincident microphone pair placed between six and ten feet from the piano. Spaced mics may be around six feet apart, but experiment to get the best result

Piano with open side facing microphones

Figure 13.1: Stereo miking of a grand piano

work, you will probably want to capture the instrument as accurately as possible including a little ambience from the environment.

Assuming that the room is sympathetic to the piano and that spill from nearby instruments isn't a problem, a simple stereo pair positioned between six and 10 feet from the right hand (opening) side of the piano may be all that is needed. If the sound is becoming clouded by room ambience, you can move in closer, whereas if the room is making a positive contribution to the sound, you can afford to move the mics further out. Choosing cardioid mics means that you can work further from the piano than with omnis for the same amount of spill or room ambience, so if the room really isn't helping the sound, using cardioids or even hypercardioids might help.

Keep the mics at a height such that they're aimed about half way up the inside of the open lid. If the room acoustics dictate that the mics have to be brought in very close, it may be advantageous to add a little artificial reverb afterwards, though this should be used sparingly because the sympathetic resonances of the piano's own strings and soundboard provide a type of reverb. Figure 13.1 shows a suggested position for both coincident and spaced mics.

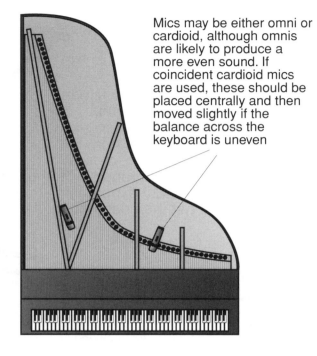

Mics may be either omni or cardioid, although omnis are likely to produce a more even sound. If coincident cardioid mics are used, these should be placed centrally and then moved slightly if the balance across the keyboard is uneven

Figure 13.2: Close-miking the grand piano

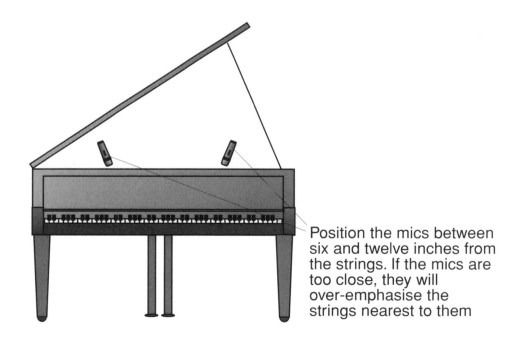

Position the mics between six and twelve inches from the strings. If the mics are too close, they will over-emphasise the strings nearest to them

For pop work, close-miking is often employed to create a more cutting, 'in-your-face' sound and one popular technique is to position the microphones inside the open piano lid between six and 10 inches from the strings, close to the position where the hammers strike the strings. Though cardioids may be used, omnis might be a better choice as they have a more accurate off-axis response which tends to produce a more even tone across the strings. One covers the higher octaves and the other the bass end, and though this doesn't produce an accurate stereo recording, it does sound good in stereo. Having said that, it may not be wise to pan the two mics to the extremes as you could end up with a piano that sounds about 20 feet wide! Trust your ears on this one and use just enough panning to create a convincing end result.

Close-miking has the additional benefit of reducing spill from other instruments, and if even greater separation is necessary, blankets may be draped over the piano lid so as to cover the opening. With any method involving spaced mics, whether close or distant, it's as well to do a mono compatibility check by running through scales using the whole keyboard. Any unduly loud or quiet notes, or groups of notes, that may be attributable to phase addition or cancellation should be quite evident, and if the mono compatibility has suffered too much, try changing the spacing between the mics slightly and ensure that there is at least three times (and ideally five times) the distance between the two mics as there is between the mics and the strings. Figure 13.2 shows a typical close-miking arrangement.

Having suggested a few mic positions based on experience and common practice, don't be afraid to experiment, because nearly all initial mic setups can be improved upon or fine tuned simply by trying new positions. For example, if you need a more mellow tone or a fuller sound, think about putting a mic under the piano to capture more of the sound from the soundboard. Similarly, if the room is too live or coloured, improvise screens around the piano using bedding or sleeping bags.

boundary mics

Some engineers like to use PZM or boundary mics for recording piano, and the underside of the piano lid makes a perfect baffle. Simply tape the two mics to the underside of the lid with one mic favouring the high strings and the other the low strings. Warning: use adhesive tape that can be removed without damaging the finish, especially if you're dealing with a concert grand! Though the popular Tandy/Radio Shack PZM mics don't turn in anything like the performance of professional studio PZM or boundary mics, they can yield unexpectedly good results when used in this way.

upright piano

Though this description is likely to offend the purists, the upright piano can be thought of as approximating a grand piano turned up on end – when it comes to miking it up. The soundboard is now at the back rather than underneath, and because there's no single, large lid covering all the strings, the only way you can close mic it properly is to remove some or all of the front panelling.

The upright piano has a noticeably different tone to the grand, especially in the bass register where it produces a less rich sound, but you can still get a good miked up sound with a little perseverance.

A stereo pair, either coincident or spaced, can be positioned on boom stands above the instrument with the top of the piano left open. Check for an even tonal balance right across the range of the instrument and move the mics if there are any obvious dead or hot spots. Spaced mics are easier to use as they can be moved independently to balance the high and low ends of the instrument, but the down side is, as ever, the potential for audible phase problems. Figure 13.3 shows a typical miking arrangement.

Standing the piano close to a solid wall can help to beef up the bass end by getting the boundary effect on your side, and if the room suits the piano sound you're after, you can move the mics back to a few feet behind the player. A room with a tiled, wooden or stone floor will help maintain a bright, lively tone whereas carpet will tend to rob the sound of some of its sparkle. If you're struggling to get a mic position that works, it's always worth remembering that an instrument nearly always sounds okay to the person playing it, so try setting up the mics to 'look' over his or her shoulders.

When close-miking the upright piano so that the mics are pointing directly at the strings, you can choose to mic either the section beneath the keyboard or the section above it, the main concern being to get an even level across the keyboard and to check for mono compatibility.

Because upright pianos are often set up in imperfect rooms, and because a great many of them are indifferent instruments, a little equalisation may be useful in shaping the sound to your needs. Keep EQ to a minimum; use gentle slopes or cuts rather than harsh boosts, and to add sparkle, add a little boost at around 6kHz or use an exciter/enhancer (sparingly). An indifferent upright played in a carpeted room may benefit from both high end EQ and a little artificial ambience or reverb, plate settings being the most flattering.

Mics should be facing into the open top of the piano. However, if it is possible to remove the front covers as well, this may help to produce a bigger sound. Adjust the mic positions to get an even level across the strings

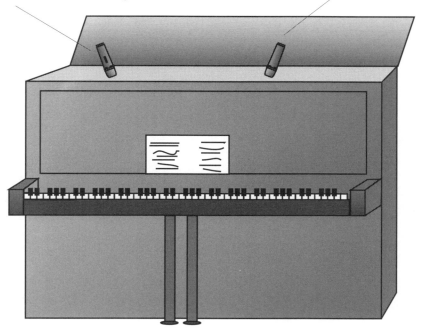

Upright piano

Figure 13.3: Miking the upright piano

There's no real black art to recording the piano, you just need to apply a little logic and be prepared to experiment. If you're on a tight budget, a couple of cheap PZMs (sadly now discontinued) from your local Tandy/Radio Shack shop will work far better than they could reasonably be expected to, given their price, and with the current preponderance of good quality, inexpensive capacitor mics, even doing the job seriously isn't prohibitively expensive. Don't be afraid to give it a try – providing the mics are half-decent and the piano is in tune, you're almost certain to end up with a usable recording.

the piano as reverb

As a novel alternative to reverb, use an effects send to drive a small instrument amplifier or hi-fi amp and speaker placed underneath a grand piano or behind an upright piano. Close-mic the piano strings, jam down the sustain pedal using a convenient brick, and use the sympathetic resonance of the strings as a reverb substitute. This works particularly well on plucked or percussive sounds. Similarly, an electronic piano recording can be played back into a real piano via a loudspeaker to add a little sympathetic vibration.

chapter 14

stringed instruments

Most bowed instruments produce a relatively limited volume of sound, but are capable of a wide range of expression and playing dynamics. They also produce complex harmonics extending to the limit of human hearing, which means a high quality capacitor microphone is the most logical choice. Some engineers, however, prefer to use ribbon microphones because of their smooth character and these are likely to produce a more mellow tone. However, because of their reduced sensitivity when compared to capacitor microphones, they may need to be used relatively close up to avoid noise problems.

The choice of microphone pattern is determined largely by the acoustics of the studio or venue, and the need to minimise spill and for this reason, cardioids are often used. As in most other applications, a good omni will give the most natural sounding results – room acoustics and spill considerations permitting.

single instruments

A solo violin, viola or cello may be miked using a single microphone positioned between three and five feet from the soundboard and pointing directly towards the instrument. Because of the playing position of violins and violas, a tall stand will be necessary to hold the mic above the soundboard unless ceiling suspension can be arranged. Note that the mic shouldn't be placed too close to the ceiling as unwanted reflections may be picked up.

Cellos and double basses may be miked using a short floor stand or a boom folded back on itself, and in the case of the double bass, a microphone with a frequency response extending down to 40Hz or below is necessary if the low notes are to be recorded faithfully. Figure 14.1 shows how the mics might be arranged in practice.

Double bass played 'rock 'n' roll' style often lacks power when miked conventionally, so the use of contact transducer pickups attached to the bridge is quite common. Generally the sound of the pickup will be added to

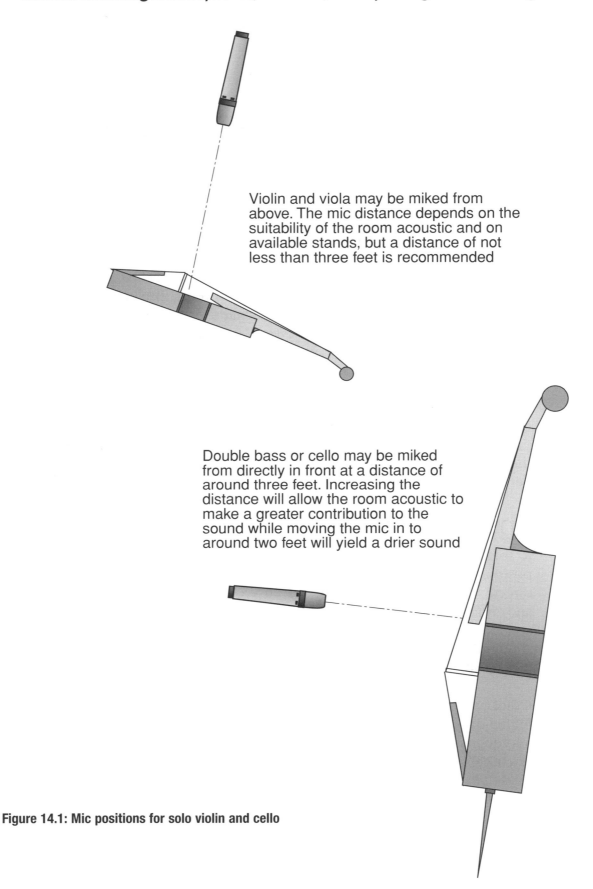

Violin and viola may be miked from above. The mic distance depends on the suitability of the room acoustic and on available stands, but a distance of not less than three feet is recommended

Double bass or cello may be miked from directly in front at a distance of around three feet. Increasing the distance will allow the room acoustic to make a greater contribution to the sound while moving the mic in to around two feet will yield a drier sound

Figure 14.1: Mic positions for solo violin and cello

Mic aimed at the back rows of the section, mounted high enough to be roughly equidistant from all the performers being covered

Figure 14.2: Individual mics used to record each section of a large ensemble or orchestra

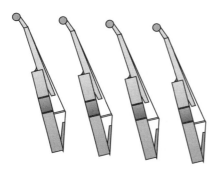

Mic aimed at the front rows of the section. This should be around three feet above head height and far enough in front of the section to be roughly equidistant from all the performers being covered

Main stereo mics for whole orchestra ambience

the miked sound, but check both positions of the microphone phase switch to see which produces the most bass. Alternatively, a good dynamic mic wrapped in cloth and placed inside the instrument via the sound-hole will often do the trick. In this latter case, a degree of equalisation may be needed to obtain a satisfactory tone and so an external graphic or parametric equaliser should be patched in if one is available. A viable alternative to this is to tape a mic behind the overhanging section of fingerboard.

multiple instruments

Individual miking isn't necessary for larger string ensembles, and even for smaller ensembles such as string quartets, one of the stereo mic techniques discussed elsewhere in this book will yield the best results in a suitable room. For example, a stereo pair of microphones placed a few feet above or in front of the ensemble will usually work well. If the acoustic is too dry, some artificial reverberation may be added at the mixing stage.

For the large ensemble, either one or two mics can be used to cover the individual sections: first violins, second violins, violas, cellos and basses. One mic can be placed at the front and to the centre of each group, preferably above head height in the case of violins and violas, and if a second microphone is needed, this can be positioned over the centre of the section angled downwards towards the back row. Figure 14.2 illustrates a practical arrangement.

The outputs from the separate groups of strings should be recorded onto separate tracks if possible, or if this isn't possible, they should be balanced with the other sections and panned to their natural positions within the sound stage. A pair of ambience mics further back in the room may be used to capture the natural, stereo reverberant field of the venue and this may be added to the panned mix to homogenise the sound. These may be a coincident stereo pair, spaced omnis or boundary mics, either spaced or mounted either side of a baffle end-on to the performers. The boundary mic technique is described more fully in the chapter on boundary microphones. Be aware that combining close and distant mics will introduce some phase shift, and in some situations, this can affect the overall sound. It is possible to reduce this effect by delaying the ambience mic signals by around 1ms for every foot of distance between them and the close mics.

Stereo pair recording is only suitable for recording large ensembles in acoustically good venues because of the high proportion of ambient sound picked up. In this case, the engineer must monitor the output from the microphones and adjust their distance from the musicians until the balance of direct and ambient sound is considered correct. In some cases, it may be necessary to move whole groups of musicians backwards or forwards if they are too loud or too quiet in the overall mix.

harp

Harps produce a very low acoustic output so the distance you can work at is limited mainly by mic noise and spill considerations. A cardioid capacitor microphone perpendicular to, and about two feet from, the sounding board should give a fairly accurate result, and if the sound is bass heavy due to the close proximity of the microphone, then a little low EQ cut may be necessary to compensate.

The mic should 'look' through the strings towards the soundboard and be positioned at the opposite side of the instrument to the player.

Other plucked string instruments may be miked in a similar way to the acoustic guitar.

chapter 15

soundproofing

I f you're making music using a computer and a few synthesizers, you can work with headphones if you want to work at antisocial hours, but working with acoustic instruments can be a problem, especially if you have close neighbours and thin walls. For most home studio operators, this means installing some sort of soundproofing in order to maintain the peace. I'd like to make it clear very early on that soundproofing is quite a separate subject from acoustic treatment, which deals with the acoustic quality of the room from a listener's point of view. I'd also like to establish a few basic physical facts and to point out that in some situations, there will be no complete solution, no matter how much money or work you throw at the problem.

the great egg box myth

The story still circulates that sticking egg boxes to walls will work as soundproofing, but this is quite simply not true – I tried it in my college days, and though it makes some improvement to some aspect of the room's acoustics, it has virtually no effect at all on sound leaking out or in. The purpose of this section of the book is to see what practical measures can be applied to improve the sound leakage situation in a typical project studio using methods that do work!

In most situations, the phrase soundproofing is rather misleading and the best you can hope for is to improve the situation – eliminating all sound leakage is virtually impossible, even with a custom-designed building. A more realistic approach is to see how sound leakage can be reduced to the point where it is acceptable to those around you. Most of the practical measures described are within the scope of a competent DIY enthusiast and nearly all the materials are available from your local builders' merchant. However, there are some specialised materials that must be purchased from speciality suppliers, so you may need to refer to *Yellow Pages* or to the classified ads in the back of your favourite recording magazine.

sound theory

Sound is essentially a form of energy that propagates by mechanical vibration through gases, liquids and solids. Energy cannot be destroyed, only converted to another form, so to 'lose' sound energy, you have to make it do work that will convert it into heat. The reason sound doesn't simply continue forever is twofold: firstly, there's something called the inverse square law, which means that sound reduces in level the further it travels from the source (simply because it is being shared over a larger area), and secondly, because it is progressively absorbed (and converted into heat) by any surfaces that it encounters and by the air that it passes through. Because we don't need a lot of acoustic energy to produce a subjectively loud sound, the heating effect of sound absorption in a typical studio can be considered negligible.

The challenge in designing effective soundproofing is to attempt to convert as much of the unwanted sound to heat as possible. The simplest way to attenuate sound is to put a solid wall in its way, and one of the fundamental rules that you should try to remember is that every time you double the mass off a wall, you'll roughly halve the amount of sound transmitted. This means that to halve the sound leakage through an existing solid wall, you'd have to double its thickness.

sound reduction index

Another keystone of acoustic theory is that as the frequency is reduced, the isolation provided by a structure also falls. In fact for every octave drop in pitch, the sound isolation is halved. From this, it's easy to see that soundproofing against high frequencies is not too much of a problem, but deep bass is very difficult to contain. You only have to walk past a music club to hear the amount of bass that can escape through solid brick walls! Because attenuation is frequency dependent, the effectiveness of a particular sound absorbing partition design or material is generally measured in dBs for a range of frequencies averaged over the range 100Hz to just over 3kHz, and this figure is called the Sound Reduction Index or SRI. A single brick wall might, for example, have a quoted SRI of 45dB while a double thickness wall made of the same material might be rated at around 51dBs. This is a lot of attenuation, but if you are producing levels of around 100dB on one side of the wall, that still leaves around 50dB making it through to the other side, and remember that this will be worse at the bass end. If you are directly adjoining a neighbour and have just a solid brick wall between you, it is unlikely that the degree of isolation will be adequate if you monitor very loudly – or play the drums.

It's possible to work out the approximate Sound Reduction Index or SRI of a single solid wall if you know the mass per square metre of the wall material. The answer is frequency dependent, which is why frequency has to be fed into the formula. This particular formula uses metric measurements because it works out easier that way.

$$R = 20 \log(fm) - 47dB$$

f is the frequency of the incident sound
m is the mass of the wall measured in kg per square metre
R is the Sound Reduction Index (in dBs), we are trying to calculate.

Materials that aren't completely solid behave differently from solid ones and actual measurement is often the only reliable way of checking actual performance. Furthermore, the isolation you get between one room and another depends on the area of the dividing wall.

Lightweight partition walls or breeze block will fare rather worse. To give an example of typical SRIs, a light panelled internal door has an average SRI of around 15dB or less and at low frequencies, it will be significantly worse. On the other hand, a brick cavity wall, plastered on the inside, can have an average SRI of better than 50dB. How troublesome sound leakage is depends on the ambient noise at the other side. During the day, traffic noise and other sounds help mask low levels of leakage, but at night, especially in the countryside, even the slightest sound will be audible. Often the only workable solution is to combine some soundproofing treatment with a reduction in the noise that you make in the first place.

double benefit

If a single wall can reduce the sound leakage by 45 or 50dB, what happens if we use two walls separated by an air gap? You might, not unreasonably, think that 45dB for one wall added to 45dB for the next would give a 90dB figure, which would be terrific. However, the maths doesn't work out quite so simply – unless the walls are separated by a considerable gap, air loading between the walls reduces the efficiency of the isolation. The wider the gap, the better the isolation. Approaches to sound isolation based on multiple barriers separated by air gaps tend to be the most successful, and a double structure will invariably perform significantly better than a single layer barrier of similar mass.

problem areas

I'll come onto the construction of soundproof walls in due course, but in most real-life situations, the walls are the best-designed parts of the room from a sound isolation viewpoint, so it's no good trying to improve them if the doors and windows leak like sieves. Even double-glazed windows offer only a limited amount of sound isolation compared to a solid wall, though they are far better than single-glazed units. DIY improvements in this area might include extra internal glazing with a large air gap and heavy glass, or if you don't need the light at all, you could fill the window space with sandbags and board it up. Heavy curtains are a minor help, but the difference they make isn't great, especially at low frequencies.

If you don't need to open a window, you can at least make it airtight very quickly by using a mastic gun and some frame sealant, but doors have to open and it's surprising just how much sound gets through and around a typical internal door. Because of the lightness of modern interior doors, significant improvements can be made by increasing the mass of the door, either by replacing it with a heavier one or by adding material to one or both sides, and by fitting good door seals. However, even the heaviest single door will perform significantly worse than a double door structure with an air gap between.

floors and ceilings

Concrete floors are good news from a sound isolation viewpoint because of their mass, but wooden floors can be a real problem. Even if you build a 'floating' floor above the original, the leakage will still be worse than that through a solid brick wall. Without major structural work, it's very unlikely that you will be able to use a real drum kit in a wooden floored room without causing serious disturbance to those below. This can be a real problem in commercial premises or flats, especially if there isn't room to accommodate the additional floor height, but in your own house where some noise leakage may be acceptable, there are strategies that can be used to improve the situation without too much structural upheaval.

If floors are difficult, ceilings are ten times worse, because whatever soundproofing material you add, you're going to have to find some way to hold it up there – at least with floors, gravity is on your side! Short of suspending woodwool or sandbags over your head, or building a substantial false ceiling below the original, there's not a great deal you can do that's really effective, but a couple of layers of thick underfelt below the carpet in the room above can make a worthwhile improvement.

the pro approach

One studio designer I know told me the story of a guy who didn't want to spend much on soundproofing because he only used cheap musical instruments in his studio. Sadly, physics is no respecter of budgets, and 110dB of sound obtained by hitting a dustbin is just as loud as 110dB from a top-of-the-range Boogie amplifier.

Just to illustrate how difficult the problems can be, a professional studio design would usually involve building a completely separate inner room inside the existing room, isolated from the original floor by blocks of neoprene rubber. Aside from the obvious cost factor, most home studios simply don't have the space to do this, but just in case you are in a position to try it, I'll be covering the basics of 'room within a room' construction in Chapter 18. A further advantage of this system is that adding internal acoustic treatment is often simplified as a properly designed inner shell makes the acoustics more predictable. Having said that, it's quite impractical for most project studio owners.

overview

The laws of physics are most definitely on someone else's side when it comes to keeping sound in or out, but don't let that put you off. Various sound isolation methods lend themselves to a low cost, DIY approach, and it could be that tackling just the weakest areas brings about sufficient improvement. By taking a common sense approach to applying the principles outlined in this book, you should be able to make noticeable improvements at minimal cost. Before doing any work, the first step is to check out the walls, floors, ceilings, windows and doors to see where the worst leakage occurs. That way you can concentrate your resources on the weak areas. If you have just one ill-fitting door or window in a whole room, it will allow sound to leak out, rendering the rest of your efforts useless.

At its most basic, you need structural mass and air-tight seals around doors and windows to achieve good sound isolation, but you also need to consider structure-borne sound and find ways to avoid it. This is important because sound travels very efficiently as mechanical vibrations through solid structures, such as wooden joists or steel girders. There's little point in getting everything else right if your soundproofing is rendered ineffective by an ill considered structural feature.

breathing!

A soundproof room generally means an airtight room, so you also need to think about how you'll get fresh air into your studio. Can you get by with opening the doors between takes, or will you have to install an air conditioning system? Simple air conditioners just cool and recirculate the existing air, but a serious studio air conditioner that brings in fresh air from outside needs silencer baffles, large ducting, anti-vibration mountings and so on. This is likely to cost more than most complete home studios, so a compromise approach is most likely.

choosing premises

Most of this section of the book refers to private studios in the home, but the same physics applies to commercial studios. If you're looking for premises to set up your studio away from home, you can save yourself a lot of time and money by taking particular note of the existing structure of the building. You also need to think about its location and any noisy industrial activities that may be taking place close by. If at all possible, pay an acoustic consultant to do a report on the premises before you sign anything – it could save you a lot of money.

Perhaps the easiest location to deal with is a ground floor premises in a solidly-built brick or concrete building with a solid floor. However, if the ceilings aren't heavy, you'll need to know what is going on above, and whether this may change to something less studio friendly in the future. Also listen for low frequency rumble from traffic or trains – even with a solid concrete floor, you may have to resort to building a floating floor to keep outside noise to a minimum, and if this is the case, does the room have the necessary height to accommodate the alterations?

In the event you're looking at an upstairs room, find out what is happening above, below and to either side of you. Some businesses may close down at night when studios are traditionally busy, but can you afford to have your hours restricted, and are any of the neighbours likely to go in for sudden extended overtime? If you are planning to do any serious acoustic treatment or build a 'room-within-a-room' inner shell, you must allow plenty of space for the acoustic treatment. Even a simple inner shell will need a couple of feet of free space above it to work effectively. A simple floating floor may be between three inches and six inches deep depending on how you build it, so most rooms will stand this. However, if you're putting in a false ceiling, you need to allow almost as much room as for an inner shell room, and in any event, not less than about 18 inches.

pragmatism at home

For most home studio owners, major construction is out of the question, so you'll need to rely on uprating what already exists. You may also need to compromise on the amount of noise you make. If you can't get the noise down as much as you want by soundproofing, you may have to find a compromise that keeps all parties happy. For example, the majority of private studio owners record part time, so it may be possible to record drums or other loud instruments when the neighbours are out, or at any rate, not at night when they are trying to sleep.

sound leakage

As I hope I made clear in the previous chapter, you can make significant improvements to sound isolation using DIY techniques, but you shouldn't expect the impossible. Unless you already have a very solid building with massive walls, you shouldn't expect to be able to contain the sound of a drum kit or a serious studio monitor system turned up full bore without doing major structural work. What you can expect is a useful reduction in the level of sound leaking into and out of your studio, and most of the leakage that occurs in a typical home studio does so via floors, ceilings, windows and doors. Lightweight partition walls are also less than ideal sound isolators, though a properly constructed one may be reasonably effective.

Because ceilings and wooden floors are significantly less massive than the walls of a typical room, they tend to be amongst the weak spots when it comes to sound isolation. Perhaps the best low cost measure when dealing with floors is to fit thick hair underfelt in your studio room, and if possible, also beneath the carpet in the room above. The combined weight and thickness of the carpet and underfelt provides both absorption and damping, so buy the heaviest grade possible. Foam underlay isn't nearly as good as the matted felt type from an acoustic viewpoint.

However, the greatest improvement can usually be made by uprating doors and windows, so I'm going to tackle those first. If you don't have double-glazed windows, then your windows will almost certainly be the biggest cause of sound leakage. Even double-glazed units are only of limited use, and will leak sound far more than the surrounding walls, so additional internal glazing behind the original windows is strongly recommended. If, on the other hand, you are working in a room with regular single-glazed windows, secondary double-glazing should be considered essential unless you are prepared to block the window aperture up altogether using a shutter or sandbags. DIY secondary double-glazing kits are fairly cost effective, and because the space between the original window and the secondary glazing is usually quite large compared to the glass spacing in a regular double-glazed window, you'll generally find that the amount of sound reduction is rather better. It also helps to use the thickest glass you

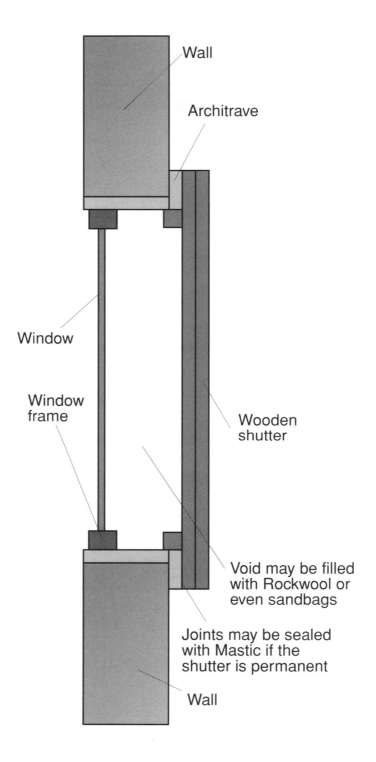

Figure 16.1: Window shutter

can find for the internal glazing as more mass translates into less leakage, especially at lower frequencies.

window shutters

If you are prepared to forego the luxury of daylight, then the cheap and cheerful solution is to block off the window using a heavy wood or MDF shutter screwed over the window opening as shown in Figure 16.1. Fasteners can be used if you need to take the shutter down between sessions, but if you don't need to remove the shutter, stuffing the void between the window and the shutter with mineral wool insulation will improve matters further. Any gaps can be sealed with acrylic frame sealant applied using a mastic gun. Heavy curtains hung over the shutter or internal glazing will also make a small improvement.

doors

A typical lightweight internal door with plywood skins and a cardboard honeycomb filling probably provides around 15dB of isolation at best. If there's a gap under or around the door, the figure will be even worse, so the very minimum you should do is fit a heavier door. Even the heaviest door will provide far less attenuation than a solid wall, but you should be able to improve on 15dB! Using a solid timber door and then gluing on an extra layer of three quarter inch ply can work well, but only if the door makes a virtually airtight seal to the frame.

If you intend to build your own doors from two layers of thick ply or chipboard, leave a gap between the two layers and use mineral wool or fibreglass to stuff the remaining space. This will help to deaden any vibration of the panels and also to absorb a proportion of the sound trying to radiate from one panel to the other. Because chipboard is not a structurally strong material, hard wood insets need to be used to take the hinges. Plywood is much stronger, and though more expensive, it makes the job a lot easier. Figure 16.2 shows the general principle of construction.

It's important to make the door as nearly airtight as possible, so use heavy duty seals around the edges, not forgetting the threshold below the door, and if you can afford it, fit a compression latch (similar to those fitted to industrial freezers), so that the door is squeezed more tightly shut as you pull the handle down. These are mechanically simple latches that work by running up a tapered plastic wedge screwed to the door frame, so the door is forced harder against the seal as the handle is closed. Figure 16.3 shows how door seals are fitted – the seal material is available from most good studio materials suppliers. The simplest type is a foam neoprene strip with

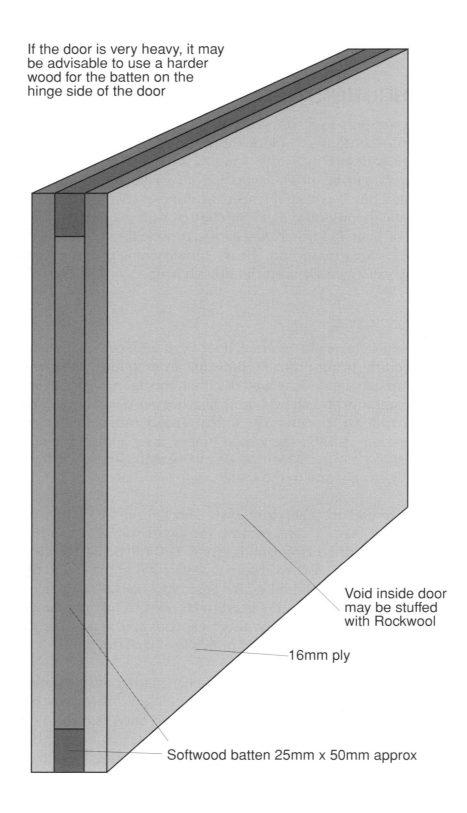

If the door is very heavy, it may be advisable to use a harder wood for the batten on the hinge side of the door

Void inside door may be stuffed with Rockwool

16mm ply

Softwood batten 25mm x 50mm approx

Figure 16.2: DIY door

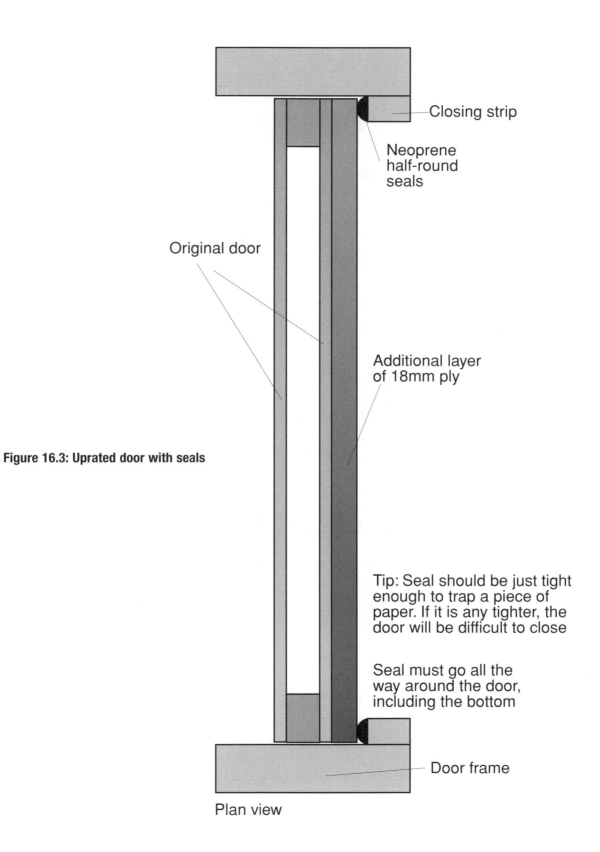

Closing strip

Neoprene half-round seals

Original door

Additional layer of 18mm ply

Figure 16.3: Uprated door with seals

Tip: Seal should be just tight enough to trap a piece of paper. If it is any tighter, the door will be difficult to close

Seal must go all the way around the door, including the bottom

Door frame

Plan view

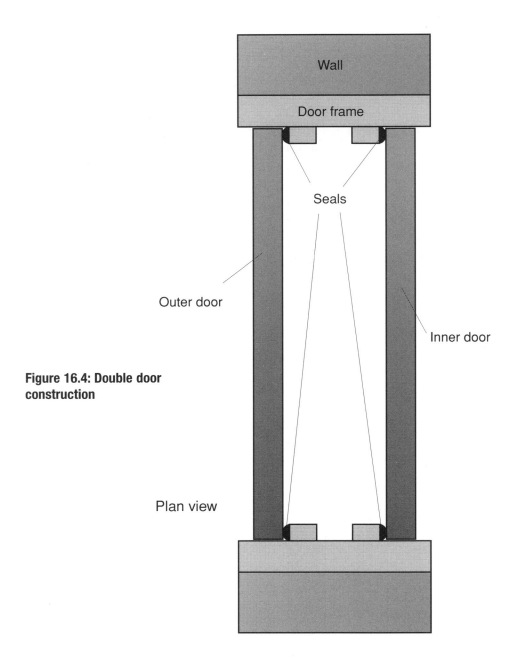

Seals

Outer door

Inner door

**Figure 16.4: Double door
construction**

Plan view

a semi-circular cross section, and it can be stuck in place with any good contact adhesive. The simplest way to fit the seals correctly is to hang the door in the frame first, then stick the seals to the wooden closing strips before you nail them in place. With the door closed, pin the strips in place one at a time so the seal is just touching the surface of the door – if you try to make the seal compress more than a little, you'll have great difficulty closing the door again, especially if you don't have a compression latch. Some studio designers say that the seals should just be tight enough to grip a piece of paper when the door is closed. Once you're sure the door is fitting correctly, you can screw the closing strips permanently in place.

double doors

No matter what you do to a single door, the law of diminishing returns makes it far easier to fit a double door in situations where a lot of isolation is needed. In most rooms, it's possible to fit doors to either side of the wall, leaving an air gap the thickness of the walls between them. This is shown in Figure 16.4. Both doors should be fitted with seals, but only one needs to have a pressure latch – the outer door can have a spring closer or a conventional latch. In professional studios, the inside of the door frame may contain elaborate sound traps, but for most DIY purposes, sticking a layer of one inch thick fireproof furniture foam around the inside of the inter-door space should be enough.

It's best where possible to use separate doorframes rather than one wide one when building a double door, but this may only be practical when building from scratch. This is to prevent vibration travelling from the first door, along the frame and directly to the second door. To this end, frames are often isolated from the surrounding brickwork and from each other using neoprene sheeting. This might be a little extreme for home use, but is worthwhile if building a studio from scratch or converting a garage. Gaps may be filled using expanding foam filler or mastic.

patio doors

Commercial patio doors provide a convenient means of dividing the studio and the control room because they double as both viewing window and door. However, to achieve adequate sound isolation, two sets of double-glazed patio doors with an air gap between them are required. Ideally, the air gaps should be nine inches or more, otherwise the low frequency isolation will be compromised. A larger gap also helps compensate for deficiencies in the door seals.

The walls within the cavity formed by the two sets of doors should be lined with fabric-covered mineral wool or acoustic foam. Figure 16.5 shows a practical example of patio doors used to divide live and recording areas.

practicalities

Ultimately, how much soundproofing work you can do will be tied to your budget and to the available space, but hopefully this introduction has given you a realistic idea of what is involved. To keep the rules simple, doors need

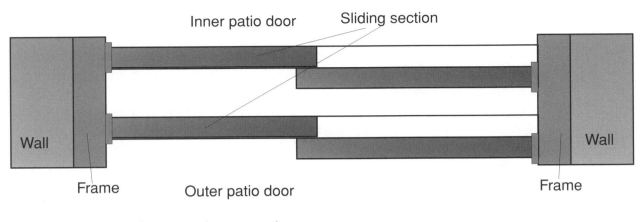

Inner patio door   Sliding section

Wall

Wall

Frame   Outer patio door   Frame

The wider the gap between the two patio doors, the better the sound isolation

Figure 16.5: Double patio doors

to be as heavy as possible, they must be airtight, and a double door assembly will always out-perform a single door. Sound travels well through solid materials, so neoprene sheets can be used to isolate structures such as door frames, studding wall frames and suchlike from the main structure. Mineral wool stuffed into air gaps will help by providing both absorption and damping, while aerosol polyurethane foam is useful for filling small gaps. Mastic or frame sealer can be used for filling smaller gaps.

For windows, double- or triple-glazing is invariably the best answer unless you can afford to block the windows entirely, and in any event, the window frames must be airtight. The glass panes should be isolated from their respective frames using neoprene or foam rubber glass mounting strip if the best isolation is to be achieved, though even when all these steps have been taken, the sound leakage through the doors and windows is still likely to be greater than that through the walls. At low frequencies, simple mass forms the only really effective barrier. Though you're unlikely ever to achieve your goal of a totally soundproof studio, a little carefully planned DIY work can make the difference between a studio that is workable and one that isn't.

chapter 17

walls, floors & ceilings

n the previous chapter, I covered some fairly simple methods of improving the sound isolation of a typical solid-walled room, but sometimes this isn't enough. For example, you may have a room with very thin floors or ceilings, or the walls themselves may be too light to offer a useful amount of sound isolation. Fortunately, there are still DIY solutions, and providing the required treatment isn't too drastic, you can do most or all of the work yourself to keep the cost down.

the studding partition

The first area I'd like to cover is the studding partition wall, because if you need to divide a large room into two to create a separate playing area and control room, the only real alternative to permanent masonry is to use plasterboard and studding. Even so, concrete blocks will always be more effective than studding, so use them if at all possible. Lightweight studding walls don't have the necessary mass to act as effective sound isolators, especially at low frequencies, so we need to fall back on the two mainstays of soundproofing – a double barrier and as much mass as possible. If you have the space, two separate studding walls are best, but if you don't want to lose too much space, a simple four inch thick frame with several layers of plasterboard on each side can be quite effective. However, you have to be careful how you fix this in place as sound energy travels quite happily within solids. You need to find some way of isolating the frame from the rest of the structure so that vibrations don't travel to or from the floor, the walls or the ceiling. This isolation can never be perfect as the frame needs something to rest on, but providing you use something resilient, the improvement will be worthwhile.

Perhaps the best option is to use quarter-inch neoprene rubber sheet between the frame and the floor, and also where the wall touches other walls and the ceiling. Alternatively, use thick rubber car mats cut into strips. Try *Yellow Pages* for rubber, foam and plastics suppliers if you don't know where to find neoprene. Some energy leakage is inevitable via the fixing screws, but this probably won't be too serious in the case of a studding wall.

Once the frame has been constructed, it must be panelled on each sides

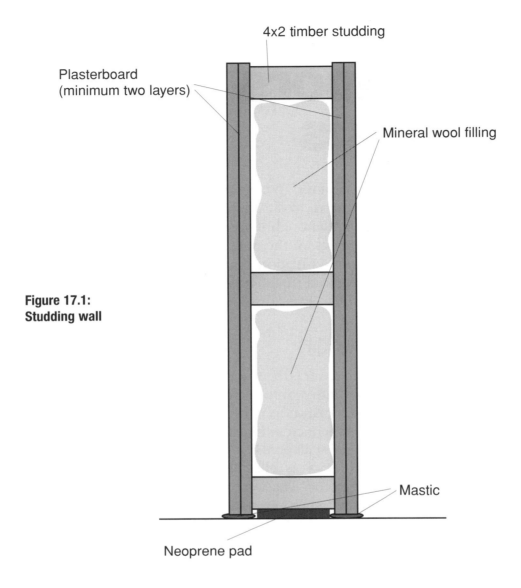

4x2 timber studding

Plasterboard
(minimum two layers)

Mineral wool filling

**Figure 17.1:
Studding wall**

Mastic

Neoprene pad

with at least two layers of plasterboard, and use the thicker 12mm (half inch) grade if you can get it to keep the mass as high as possible. Ensure the boards are staggered so the seams don't coincide, and use temporary spacers made from hardboard or wood off-cuts to ensure the plasterboard stops just short of touching the existing walls, floor or ceiling. Putting a layer of lightweight fibreboard between the two layers of plasterboard can improve the damping of the wall without adding much to the mass. Having the surface skimmed with plaster on completion will also help, but try to keep that small gap around the edges. When the plaster is dry, you can seal the gap with frame sealer using a mastic gun. Figure 17.1 shows how a studding wall can be constructed.

double studding wall

Though simple to build, the basic studding wall suffers a little because the frame itself can conduct vibrational energy from one surface to the other. To improve on this, you could nail the plasterboard to the frame via rubber or felt spacers, but perhaps the best approach is to build a double frame structure as shown in Figure 17.2. Here the timbers are staggered to fit between each other so that the wall isn't much thicker than before. In either case, stuffing the void between the two sides of the wall with mineral wool loft insulation will help absorb any energy trying to pass through the void.

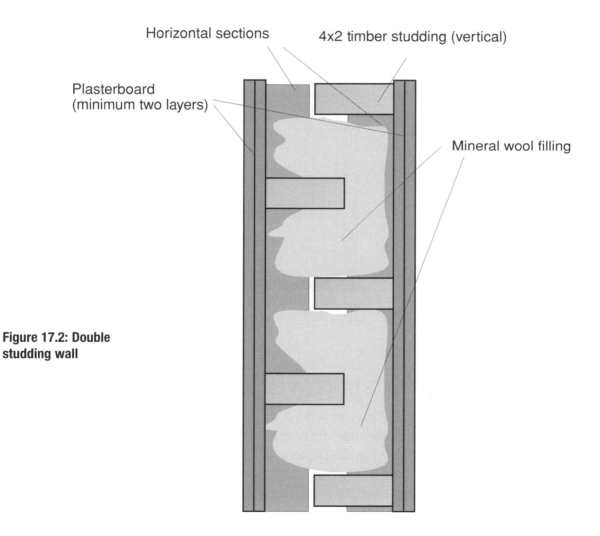

Horizontal sections   4x2 timber studding (vertical)

Plasterboard
(minimum two layers)

Mineral wool filling

Figure 17.2: Double studding wall

Plan view   Both the horizontal and vertical studs are staggered to prevent contact

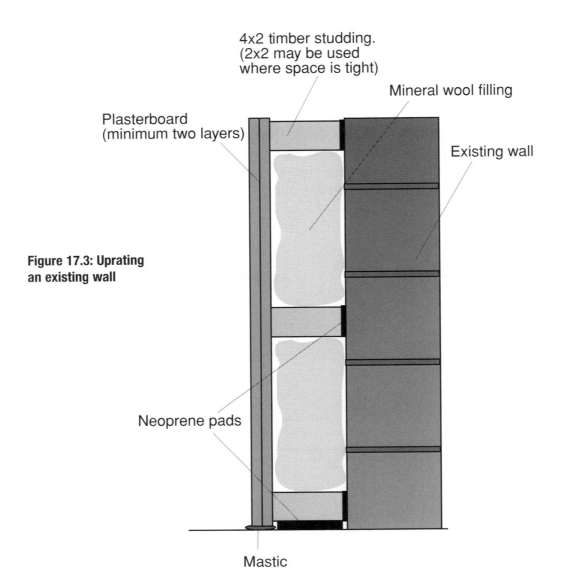

4x2 timber studding.
(2x2 may be used
where space is tight)

Mineral wool filling

Plasterboard
(minimum two layers)

Existing wall

**Figure 17.3: Uprating
an existing wall**

Neoprene pads

Mastic

improving an existing wall

You may have a situation where an existing wall doesn't provide enough isolation, either because it is too thin, or because it is made from a lightweight building material such as breeze block. Such walls can be lined with studding and plasterboard using similar constructional techniques to the freestanding studding wall just described, except you only need to cover one side of the frame. Ideally you should leave a small gap between the frame and the existing wall, again best achieved by using neoprene spacers, though screwing the studding to the wall via compressed mineral wool also works. The cavity can be filled with mineral wool before the plasterboard skin is nailed in place.

As before, two or more layers of plasterboard are required to build up a worthwhile mass, and a fibreboard middle layer may also help. Layering different materials creates an acoustic mismatch, reducing transmitted vibrational energy and damping out resonances. Figure 17.3 shows an existing wall being uprated by adding a studding/plasterboard layer. In all multilayer walls where two or more layers of board are being used, it helps to seal the gaps between boards using a flexible mastic or frame sealer before fixing the next layer. It also helps to use dabs of plasterboard adhesive between adjacent layers of plasterboard to prevent the panels resonating independently, and if you can afford the space to add even more layers of plasterboard, that's all to the good providing your existing wall and floor can take the weight.

Unless you use many layers of plasterboard to create a very heavy wall, the attenuation at low frequencies will probably be less than that offered by a solid brick or concrete wall, but the improvement should still be significant. If you do need to build an internal wall, then look at the ratio of the height, width and length of your newly created rooms to see if you might be inviting acoustic problems. As a rule, having equal dimensions for width, height and depth is the worst possible case as you'll end up with strong room resonances at specific frequencies, and you should also avoid one dimension being an exact multiple of either of the other two for the same reason. Keep the ratios as random as possible, and if you can slope one wall slightly to avoid having parallel surfaces in the room, this will help minimise flutter echo. However, don't worry if you can't avoid parallel walls as the acoustic treatment needed to kill flutter echoes is fairly simple. If you're in the situation of having to decide on the size and shape of your studio at this point, it's worth skipping ahead to the chapters on acoustic treatment before starting work.

floors

If you have a concrete floor, then you're probably starting from a reasonably good position, but if the studio is in a bedroom with a wooden floor, you're going to have problems. Not only is a typical domestic floor a relatively poor sound isolator, most of the noisy gear, not to mention tapping feet, will be in contact with the floor, which only makes things worse. Because of this latter consideration, structurally-borne sound needs to be tackled, and the cheapest first step is to fit heavy felt underlay beneath the studio carpet. Once you've done that, try to get noisy gear off the floor by using speaker stands for your monitors (placing the speakers on blobs of Blu-Tak on top of the stands), and try putting things like guitar amps on blocks of thick foam rubber. Drum kits are more problematic, and it's unrealistic to expect any DIY approach to provide anything like complete isolation. The most effective way to reduce drum kit noise is to make a shallow plinth or raft on which to set up the drum kit and isolate this from the floor by standing it on thick foam rubber. If this doesn't provide adequate isolation, the next step is to consider a complete floating floor.

floating floors

Professional floating floors can be massive and complex affairs, but for the smaller studio, you can build your own quite simply. A floating floor is just a false floor mounted on acoustic isolators above your existing floor with resilient material around the edge so that it doesn't come into direct contact with the walls. A commercial floating floor may be cast from reinforced concrete, several inches thick, and may be supported over a void several feet deep, the weight being borne by springs or machine rubber mountings, but clearly this is impractical for most bedrooms!

There are less massive floor designs based on studding and chipboard, or you can even buy a specially made floating floor material comprising chipboard with mineral wool bonded to the underside. This type of structure won't be too heavy for a typical domestic floor to support, and though it won't work as well as six inches of concrete on springs, it will make a very noticeable difference. One such commercial material is known as Lamella, flooring grade chipboard backed with a tightly packed mineral wool material where all the fibres are perpendicular to the board, rather like the bristles on a scrubbing brush. To fit the floor, a felt strip would be fitted around the room, somewhat like a felt skirting board, then the Lamella boards laid on top of the existing floor. Once the floor is down, a second layer of flooring chipboard is glued and screwed to the top with the joints staggered. This adds strength and rigidity to the floor as well as preventing the individual panels from drifting apart. Figure 17.4 shows a Lamella floating floor in place.

This type of flooring may also be used as a base on which to build a small studding/plasterboard room-within-a-room type of studio so long as the weight of the inner room isn't so great as to cause the floor to bow under its weight. While building a room within a room isn't usually an option in a bedroom studio, it may be practical if you're converting a large garage, so I'll cover this type of construction in the next chapter.

An alternative to Lamella is to build a wooden 2x2 or 2x4 inch frame and cover it with two layers of flooring chipboard. This may be separated from the original floor by blocks of neoprene, though the most usual approach is simply to cover the existing floor with mineral wool loft insulation, then place the studding raft on top of that. Observe the rules on isolation by

Figure 17.4: Floating Lamella floor

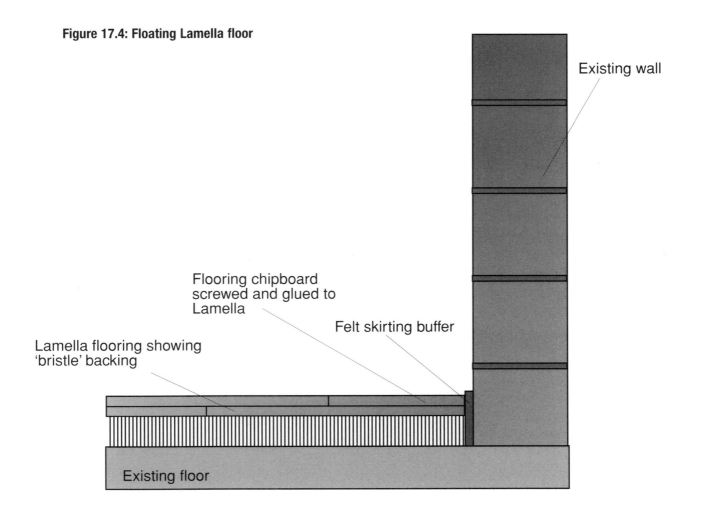

not allowing the floor to touch the existing walls at any point and fill any gaps with mastic to ensure the floor is airtight. Figure 17.5 shows a studding floor.

ceilings

Ceilings have all the problems associated with floors, but as pointed out earlier, you don't have the benefit of gravity to help you keep your sound isolation treatments in place. Acoustic foam tiles stuck to the ceiling might look good, but in practice they'll keep out very little sound. A professional studio designer would probably specify a false ceiling, probably quite a heavy one involving lead or sand, but in the home studio, you have to be a little more pragmatic. Your first step should be to fit underfelt to the

Figure 17.5: Floating framework floor

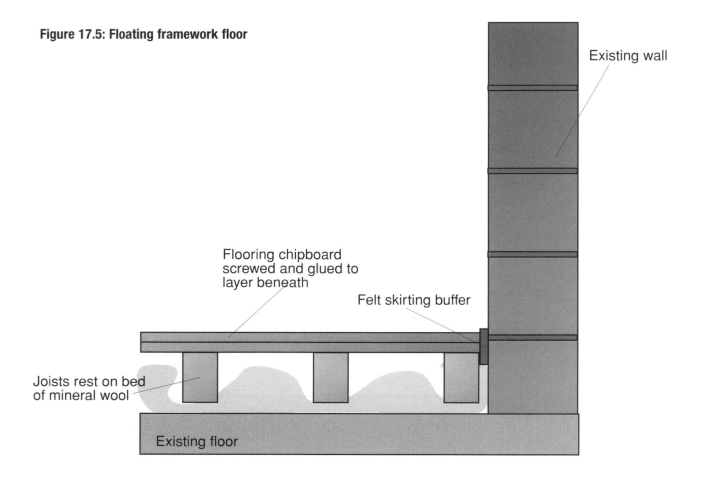

Existing wall

Flooring chipboard
screwed and glued to
layer beneath

Felt skirting buffer

Joists rest on bed
of mineral wool

Existing floor

room above your studio – even if this room belongs to someone else, offer to pay to have it fitted.

If you're serious about going further, you need to know if the floor above is made from floorboards or chipboard. Chipboard floors are reasonably airtight, but floorboards may well have gaps, in which case you'll need to remove the ceiling plaster or plasterboard to expose the joists. This will give you access to the undersides of the floorboards of the room above. Start by filling all the gaps with mastic, but to do the job properly, also fit barrier mat between the joists as shown in Figure 17.6. Barrier mat is a heavy, flexible material that has many uses in studio construction, but you're unlikely to find it anywhere other than at a studio materials suppliers. Barrier mat employs a mineral loaded plastic construction and looks rather like a black, flexible linoleum, but is much heavier. It may be fixed in place using a powered staple gun or flat headed roofing nails, but you'll need somebody to help you take the weight until you've got enough staples in to hold the material up.

Once the barrier mat is in place, the gaps between the joists can be stuffed

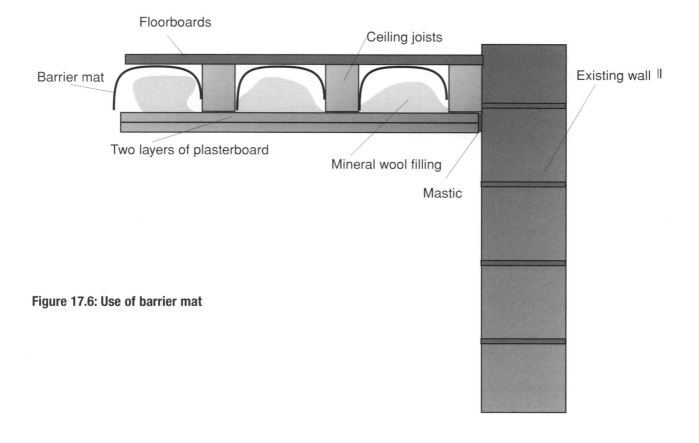

Floorboards

Ceiling joists

Barrier mat

Existing wall

Two layers of plasterboard

Mineral wool filling

Mastic

Figure 17.6: Use of barrier mat

with loft insulation grade mineral wool and the underside of the joists covered with at least two layers of 12mm plasterboard. Get a plasterer to skim the plasterboard for you and you have a smooth new ceiling, as well as reduced sound leakage.

suspended ceilings

If you have height to spare, fitting a false ceiling can help, but if you don't know exactly what you're doing, this is a job for a professional builder as the size of the joists needed depends on the length they are required to span. The approach is shown in Figure 17.7 and still requires the old ceiling to be stripped of plasterboard and treated as per the previous example before you start. Notice that the joists for the new ceiling are fixed in between the existing ceiling joists to minimise height loss, though if you have plenty of headroom, you can simply leave the original ceiling untouched and build the new one beneath it. The void between the original ceiling and the suspended ceiling should again be stuffed with mineral wool, otherwise it may resonate.

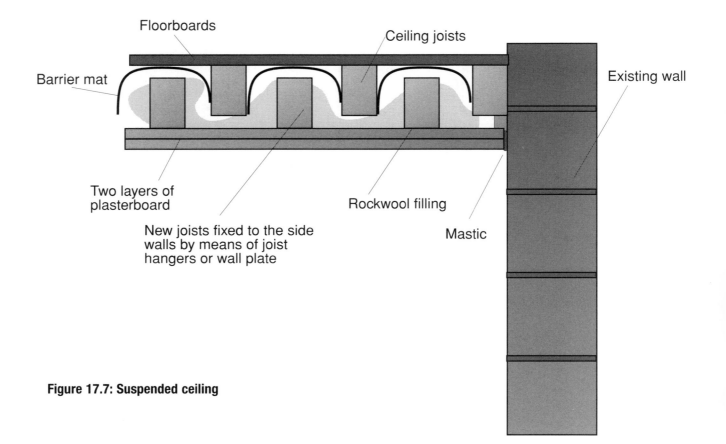

Figure 17.7: Suspended ceiling

A suspended ceiling is built from joists and plasterboard in much the same way as a studding partition wall. It is supported by wooden wall plates fixed to the original walls, so the original walls must be of solid construction. The heavier the false ceiling, the better the isolation, but you can introduce a layer of lightweight insulation board between the plasterboard layers without incurring much of a weight penalty. Whether or not you isolate the edges of the ceiling from the existing wall is up to you, but as there is no sound producing equipment in direct contact with the ceiling, the difference will not be nearly so significant as it was with the floor.

WARNING Commercial studios may have up to four inches of plasterboard and chipboard screwed to the ceiling, but don't go to these extremes without proper architectural advice.

chapter 18

room within a room construction

The methods so far described in this book for improving the sound isolation of doors and windows are based on the same fundamental principles as those used in professional studio installations, but the methods I've discussed for uprating floors, walls and ceilings would almost certainly be inadequate for use in a large commercial studio where high sound levels are involved, unless the studio happens to be located well away from neighbours or sources of external noise. The ideal way to build a studio is to start off with a sufficiently large, solid-walled building and then construct additional rooms inside. These inner rooms should be self-contained structures built upon a suitable floating floor, and should not be in physical contact with the main shell of the building other than via the supports for the floating floor or neoprene isolation blocks. The greater the space between the inner room and the outer shell, the better the low frequency isolation – an eight-inch gap should be considered a minimum.

The reasons why the room within a room approach is so effective is apparent from the preceding chapters – by building one room inside another, we have created a double-walled construction and, at the same time, have virtually eliminated structurally-borne sound by isolating the inner room from the outer shell. The degree of isolation achieved depends largely on the type and construction of the floating floor. As a rule, the more massive the floating floor, and the greater the space between it and the 'true' floor below, the more effective it will be at low frequencies. In mechanical terms, the inner room can be considered as a mass supported by a spring, and if the resonant frequency of the system is lower than the lowest sound frequencies being generated, the degree of isolation can be extremely high. While lightweight floating floors can be approached by the DIY enthusiast with relative safety, the kind of massive concrete floor on springs used in a large commercial studio requires the services of a specialist architect and builder and is inappropriate for all but the most serious commercial studios.

a practical solution

For smaller studios, edit suites or video-post facilities fortunate enough not to have acute problems with outside noise or nearby neighbours, a relatively lightweight inner room construction is often adequate and follows the same general principles as the double-skinned studding wall described earlier in the series. The timber framework for the walls is made from 4 x 2-inch timber built directly onto the floating floor and the ceiling joists are fixed to the wall frames. Ceiling joists may need to be 2 x 6 inches or deeper depending on the span to be covered, but it is advisable to consult an architect or experienced builder over the constructional details before starting work unless the room is fairly small.

An alternative form of ceiling construction favoured in broadcast is to use pre-screeded, channel-reinforced woodwool slabs which are plastered on the underside after construction. Woodwool slabs are made from strands of compressed wood mixed with cement and, because of the air trapped during manufacture, the material is relatively light and quite strong; it's also highly fire resistant. It is manufactured in panels, with interlocking metal channels fixed to the edges, enabling a wider ceiling to be assembled. The channels also provide a degree of rigidity. Once again, your supplier or builders' merchant should be able to provide information as to how wide a span can safely be covered by this method. Where more sound isolation is required, two layers of woodwool slab may be used with an air gap between them.

If the walls are to rest directly on the floating floor, it is vitally important that the floating floor is properly supported and is rigid enough to take the weight of the walls and ceilings. Failure to ensure this will result in the floor 'crowning' as the floor edges are pushed down, leaving a bulge in the centre. Proper support of the floor often involves using more support material around the edge of the floor, neoprene isolation blocks being a popular choice for smaller installations. If you intend to use a proprietary floating floor material such as Lamella, it is advisable to discuss your requirements with the supplier, who should be able to advise on loading and support. It helps if several layers of flooring chipboard are screwed and glued over the basic floor structure before the wall construction starts, as this will increase both the mass and stiffness of the floor. Figure 18.1 shows a room within a room built directly onto a floating floor.

An alternative approach, and one that I consider to be more straightforward from a DIY point of view, is not to build the wall frame directly onto the floating floor at all, but instead, to support it on felt or neoprene strips laid on the true floor. The floating floor may then be built inside the room with felt or neoprene isolation strip between the edges of the floor and the wall partitions. This approach is less prone to problems where the room size dictates heavy ceiling joists. Although the theoretical isolation is compromised to some extent because of the increased coupling between the walls and the true floor, this tends not to be serious, though it is wise to ensure that sound-producing

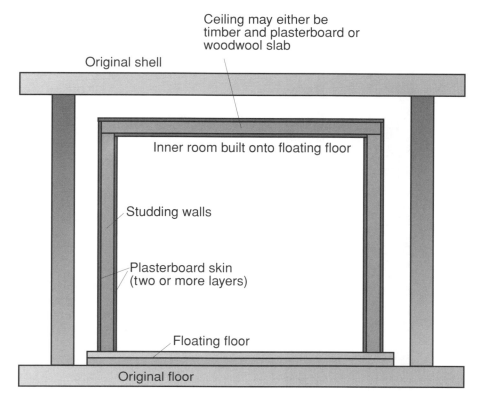

Ceiling may either be
timber and plasterboard or
woodwool slab

Original shell

Inner room built onto floating floor

Studding walls

Plasterboard skin
(two or more layers)

Floating floor

Original floor

This is the most difficult type of
construction as all the weight of the inner
room rests on the floating floor

Figure 18.1: Room within a room built onto a floating floor

equipment is mounted on the floor rather than being in direct contact with
the walls. Figure 18.2 shows this type of construction. If the underlying floor
is not solid, it is imperative you consult an architect to determine whether the
floor will safely carry the weight of your inner room.

floating concrete

Though a Lamella or 'board upon mineral wool' floor may again be used in
a room of this type, if the underlying floor is solid, it is possible to build a
concrete floating floor by using a layer of 1¼" (30mm) mineral wool (around
150kg/cubic metre density) covered by 2¾"-3" (70mm) of lightweight,
reinforced concrete, a polythene membrane being laid over the mineral
wool before the concrete is poured. The floor may be finished using a layer
of concrete screed, as shown in Figure 18.3. This is relatively cheap to build
and has a higher mass than most simple chipboard floors, which helps

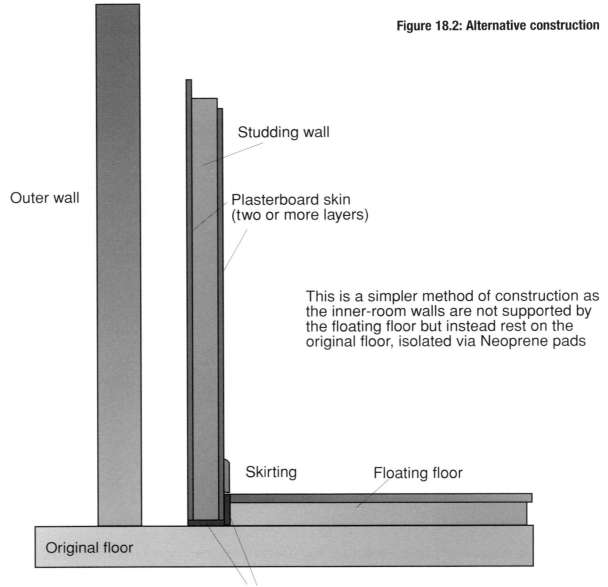

Figure 18.2: Alternative construction

Studding wall

Plasterboard skin
(two or more layers)

Outer wall

This is a simpler method of construction as the inner-room walls are not supported by the floating floor but instead rest on the original floor, isolated via Neoprene pads

Skirting

Floating floor

Original floor

Neoprene or dense felt

improve low frequency isolation. A further advantage is that plastic ducts can be set into the concrete to carry cables from one side of the room to the other. I would suggest using wire reinforcement mesh within the concrete to prevent cracking.

doors

Where a doorway is required, there is an obvious weak spot in the sound isolation. A double door construction is essential to maintain the isolation of a room within a room, one door in the inner room and one in the outer shell.

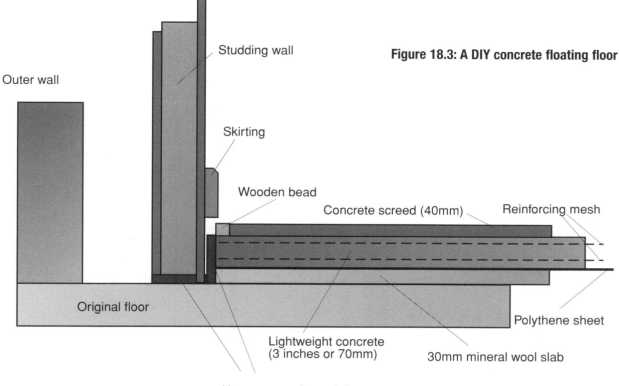

Figure 18.3: A DIY concrete floating floor

Outer wall

Studding wall

Skirting

Wooden bead

Concrete screed (40mm)

Reinforcing mesh

Original floor

Polythene sheet

Lightweight concrete
(3 inches or 70mm)

30mm mineral wool slab

Neoprene or dense felt

It is also advisable to use barrier mat to help isolate the space between the doors from the void between the inner and outer rooms. Figure 18.4 shows how this may be achieved. Either one or both of the doors should be fitted with compression latches and proper door seals fitted. The heavier the door construction, the more effective the sound isolation is likely to be. Similar precautions should be taken when building windows – the inner and outer frames may come close to each other but it is essential that there be some gap between them to prevent vibrations being transmitted from the inner shell to the outer wall. Figure 18.5 shows a practical way of arranging this.

further considerations

Building a room within a room need not be beyond the scope of the DIY enthusiast, but professional consultation is advised at the planning stage, to ensure the structural safety of the new room as well as of the floor upon which it will stand if the existing floor is not solid and on ground level. The wider the gap between the inner and outer rooms, the better the low frequency isolation, and if you can integrate any corridors into the studio design in such a way that they also double as air gaps, isolation can be improved even further.

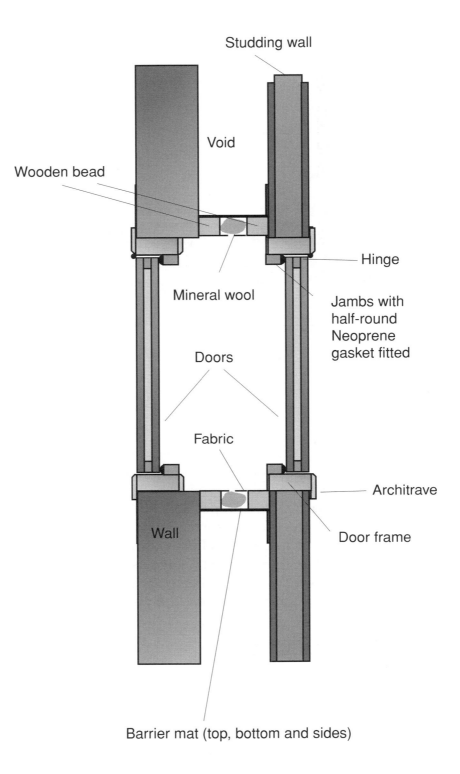

Figure 18.4: Fitting a door

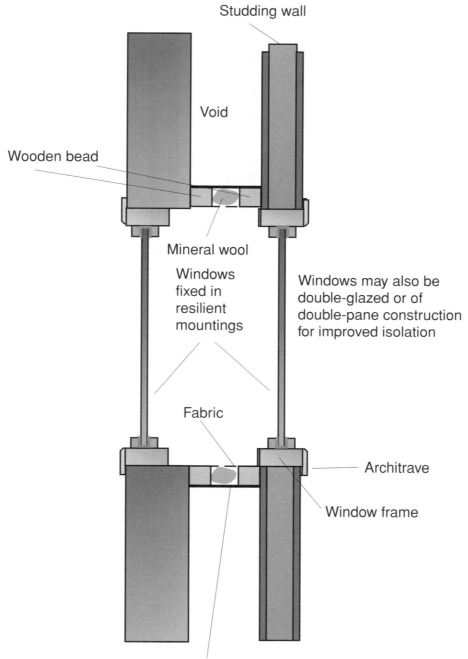

Studding wall

Void

Wooden bead

Mineral wool

Windows fixed in resilient mountings

Windows may also be double-glazed or of double-pane construction for improved isolation

Fabric

Architrave

Window frame

Barrier mat (top, bottom and sides)

Figure 18.5: Fitting a window

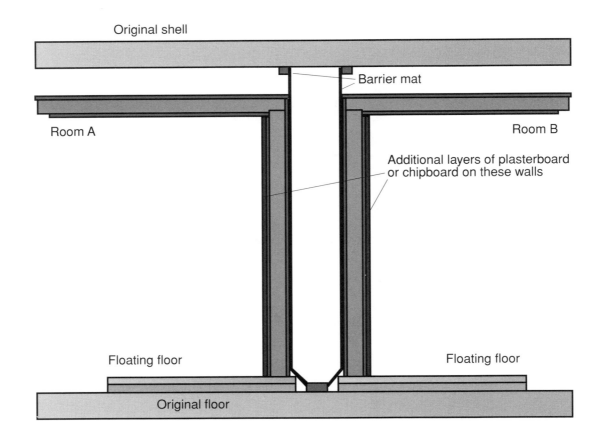

Figure 18.6: Inter-room isolation

Where two inner rooms are to be built inside the same outer room, sound leakage from one inner room to the other can be a problem. One solution is to use an airtight curtain of barrier mat between the rooms to provide a degree of isolation between the void surrounding one inner room and the void around the other. An alternative approach is to use barrier mat to seal off the void at the point where the two rooms meet, as shown in Figure 18.6. Adjacent walls may also be uprated with extra layers of plasterboard or chipboard to improve inner-room isolation.

What is important is not that any of the ideas discussed are carried out to the letter, but that you understand the basic principles involved in sound isolation. Most studio designs incorporate a mixture of practical ideas and methods to achieve their aims, but the laws of physics always remain the same. Once you have sketched out your initial design, inspect it to find out where the weak spots are, and the chances are that you'll be able to adapt one or more of the techniques explained in this section of the book to improve the situation.

practical acoustic treatment

So far I've looked at the basics of sound isolation, but there is often some confusion between what is meant by soundproofing and what is meant by acoustic treatment. Soundproofing is, essentially, concerned with reducing the amount of sound getting into or out of a room, but the degree of soundproofing in no way defines how the room behaves as a space for listening to music. Indeed, it is very unlikely that a heavily soundproofed room will function as a good listening or performing environment without further treatment.

A good listening room needs to be not too live sounding or too dead, and to achieve this, it's usual to combine sound absorbing materials with scattering surfaces to break up strong reflections. Both these subjects will be covered in more detail after putting the problems into perspective.

pragmatism in acoustics

The accurate acoustic treatment of a room cannot be undertaken based purely on theory, because, as we'll see later, the formulas (where you decide to use them at all) are notoriously imprecise for small rooms, and the building materials involved may not have the same acoustic properties as stated in the tables of standard values you sometimes find in textbooks and materials catalogues. Furthermore, the acoustic properties of a room depend to a large extent on what you put into that room.

Professional studio designers use a combination of maths, measurement and experience to arrive at a satisfactory solution, and the measuring equipment, which tends to be expensive, requires specialised operator knowledge.

If you interpret this as advice not to tackle the job yourself, you'd be both right and wrong. A high budget commercial studio needs to be designed by a professional acoustic engineer, but fortunately, it is possible to make significant improvements to a listening space by applying a few basic rules. What's more, because home recording tends to rely heavily on nearfield monitors, the contribution of the room's acoustic isn't as significant as it would be in a larger room with the monitors positioned further away from the listener.

The secret is to improve the room by doing as little as possible to it. Fortunately, most carpeted domestic rooms with just a few items of furniture are already pretty close to being acceptable listening environments. The purpose of this section of the book is to examine some of the basic principles of acoustics so that you know what you're dealing with, and hopefully also to dissuade you from doing anything that might make the situation worse. For example, it has been known for people to carpet the entire wall area of their studios, usually with disastrous results. Once you've learned the basic rules, you'll know exactly why this might be the case, and you'll have a number of options to try that have a far higher probability of success.

studio area

While a control room should be designed to provide the best possible environment in which to listen to and evaluate the music being recorded and mixed, the performing area or studio may have quite different acoustic properties. These might be dictated, as much as anything, by current fashion. For example, there are stone or wooden live rooms, rooms with variable acoustics, neutral rooms, and, occasionally, fairly dead rooms. Of course, some kind of compromise has to be reached in the project studio, where the recording and mixing is often carried out in the same room.

dead acoustics

A relatively dead recording environment excludes nearly all natural room ambience, enabling the engineer to start with a clean slate when it comes to adding artificial effects. Most leading engineers and producers would agree that instruments that require a live acoustic setting invariably sound better in a sympathetic live room than when processed with artificial ambience from a digital reverb unit or echo plate, but it's probably fair to say that a reasonably dead room is more useful than a very live one if it's the only room you have.

Separate live rooms remain popular for drums or certain other acoustic instruments, and a typical live room might consist of an untreated stone or tiled room with an exposed concrete or wooden floor. If space permits, it is possible to create a more general purpose recording room by designing an area that is live at one end, but damped at the other. Acoustic screens that are reflective on one side and absorbent on the other may then be used to create localised areas with the desired acoustic characteristic as well as providing some separation between instruments. Movable carpets or heavy drapes may also be used to deaden a naturally live room. Such studios should not be confused with live end/dead end control rooms, which will be discussed later.

control rooms

While studio acoustics may vary depending on the type of music to be recorded, the control room must provide a controlled environment in which recordings may be evaluated and in which valid musical decisions can be taken. However, because of the multiplicity of different monitor speaker systems and the widely differing design philosophies of control rooms, the aim of creating anything approaching a universal standard has yet to be realised. Indeed, it was once said that if you were to take a sample of domestic living rooms and compare their acoustic performance, the results would be more consistent than a similar survey of studio control rooms. That may be an exaggeration, but it serves to show that virtually all studio control rooms sound different – though it's also true that most acoustic designers agree in broad terms what constitutes a good listening room. Before looking at the possible solutions to acoustic problems, it's helpful to look more closely at their causes.

reflections

The first thing to appreciate is why a room should have a sound in the first place when it's the speakers you're listening to. Sound bounces or reflects off all solid surfaces, so that when a sound source, such as a loudspeaker, stops producing sound, the reflections continue for a period of time until the energy is absorbed. In effect, the room functions as an energy store, returning some of the acoustic energy to the air at some point after the initial event.

Because of the presence of these reflections, we don't just hear the direct sound from our monitor loudspeakers, we also hear an appreciable amount of reverberation as the sound bounces around the room. In a good listening room, the reverb time will be too short to be perceptible under normal circumstances – although you'd still notice a big difference if it were absent altogether. However, different materials and structures reflect different parts of the audio spectrum more efficiently than others, and the dimensions of the room cause resonances or modes to be set up (more on these later), so the reverb we hear is 'coloured' – in other words, it doesn't have a flat frequency response.

The ideal listening room needs a touch of reverb to help increase the perceived loudness of the monitors and also to prevent the room sounding unnaturally dead. But the reverb time also needs to be roughly equal at all frequencies across the audio spectrum if coloration is to be avoided. Reverb times of between 0.2 and 0.4 seconds are normally chosen for control rooms, though it is also common for the very low frequency reverb time to be slightly longer, other than in very sophisticated designs, where elaborate bass-trapping techniques have been used.

An even reverberation time can only be achieved by the careful deployment of different types of sound-absorbing material and structures, and formulas exist that enable the areas of treatment to be calculated. However, as stated in the introduction, relying purely on calculations is likely to lead to inaccurate results, not only because the formulas work best for large spaces, but also because of variables in the performance of the materials. Add to this the effect of reflective and resonant studio equipment introduced after the design is complete, plus the presence of people in the studio, and you can see why making accurate predictions is virtually impossible. It is also likely that the existing building has acoustic properties that can't be accurately calculated. It's for this reason that professional studio designers use very sophisticated measuring equipment and not just simple spectrum analysers to calculate room acoustics both before and after treatment. Once construction is complete, it's commonplace to make further fine adjustments to ensure the measured result matches the target figures.

control room compromise

Much of today's recording is done in the control room rather than in the studio proper, so the control room design may end up being a compromise between ergonomics and acoustics, especially when equipment is regularly being moved in and out of the studio. However, once the most serious problems have been ironed out, such changes generally make less of a practical difference than you might imagine.

Once the room performance has been brought within acceptable parameters, the choice and location of loudspeakers can still have a dramatic effect on the overall monitoring accuracy of the room. This subject will be covered later.

modes

Rooms suffer from reflections and resonances. The frequencies at which a room resonates depend on something called room modes, which cause the spectrum of the reflected sound to vary at different points in the room. Assuming you have solid walls, room modes are directly related to room dimensions and, because the same physical laws apply, they will affect both control room and studio acoustics. If a sound wave is generated that has exactly the same half-wavelength as the longest dimension of a room, it will be reflected back and forth from the facing walls in phase with the original, thus reinforcing it – a phenomenon known as a standing wave. Accepting the value for the speed of sound as being roughly 1100 feet per second, an 11-foot room would correspond to a half wavelength at 50Hz, the result being a strong 50Hz mode.

Any sound reproduced in the room would, therefore, undergo an artificial reinforcement or coloration of sounds at, or around, 50Hz and its multiples. Introducing sound into the room at any of these multiple frequencies will cause standing waves, resulting in a potential trouble spot for every 50Hz increase in frequency.

This is only in relation to one room dimension. The width and height of a room also give rise to their own series of standing wave frequencies. Because they are related to the three axes of the room (length, width and height) modes caused by standing waves between parallel room surfaces are known as axial modes. There are other more complex modes caused by sound bouncing off more than one wall and travelling round the room: these are known as tangential and oblique modes. Because the sound bounces off more surfaces to produce these modes, some of the energy is absorbed or scattered, so the intensity of the modal peaks is less than for axial modes. To be more precise, tangential modes produce half the energy of axial modes whereas oblique modes produce one quarter of the energy of the axial modes.

These modes decay at different rates, so to damp a mode (in order to reduce its decay time), absorbing material must be placed in an area of high pressure. For example, to damp a mode produced by two opposite walls, the absorbent material must be placed on one of the walls, rather than on the floor or ceiling.

optimum dimensions

Unless you make at least one of every opposing pairs of surfaces completely absorbent across the entire audio spectrum, modes will exist – if a room has dimensions, it has modes, though the absorbency of the walls will influence the intensity of these modes. The problem is how to reconcile these resonances with a flat reverb spectrum? The answer is that if the modes are fairly evenly distributed and not too widely spaced, there should be no drastic peaks or dips in the room's response. In practice, modal problems are most serious at lower frequencies, and unfortunately, smaller rooms tend to be worse affected than larger rooms because the low frequency modes are often strong, with little happening between them. One approach is to use tuned absorbers to damp down the energy peaks at the main modal frequencies, although some problems can be avoided at the planning stage by picking room dimension ratios that produce the most evenly spaced modes. Furthermore, nearfield monitors with a restricted bass response may be used to avoid exciting low frequency room modes.

To learn a little more about the best shape for a room, consider the worst possible shape – a cube. Inside a cube, all three axial modes will occur at exactly the same frequencies so reinforcing each other to create noticeable peaks in the room response. Non-cuboid shapes are obviously more suitable, but if one dimension turns out to be exactly twice one of the others, then modes will still occur at the same frequencies. Even apparently unrelated dimensions can cause modal pile-ups at some frequencies purely by chance. Much research has been undertaken in the past to find sets of ratios that minimise these undesirable peaks and it's also possible to buy acoustic analysis software that will plot out the modes for any given room dimensions. This is certainly easier than calculating each one manually.

Large gaps between modes create problems because the room response will dip noticeably in these places. In practice, you might find that musical notes coinciding with these inter-mode gaps sound quieter compared with the rest of the spectrum. Clearly this is a bad thing because it will upset your perception of what you're hearing over your monitors, leading to a less accurate mix.

In most rooms, once you get above 300Hz or so, the modes become so closely spaced that there's no need to worry unduly about peaks or gaps. Below this frequency though, the ideal situation is not to have gaps between modes of more than around 20Hz. At the same time, you should avoid closely packed or coincident modes. In a typical studio, the modal resonances tend to be around 5Hz wide, and the more reverberant the room, the narrower the modal bandwidth. Unfortunately, if a room is below a certain minimum size, it is impossible to arrive at dimensions where the low frequency modal behaviour is ideal because the modes are too widely spaced – and most project studios fall into this category.

An approximation to the modal behaviour of a room can be arrived at by plotting just the three axial modes against frequency and ignoring the tangential and oblique modes. Calculating the tangential and oblique modes is much more complicated, which makes analysis software even more attractive. Figure 19.1 shows how the axial modes may be calculated for each opposing pair of surfaces in a room. By substituting the numbers one, two, three, and so on for the value of n, a whole series of modes can be

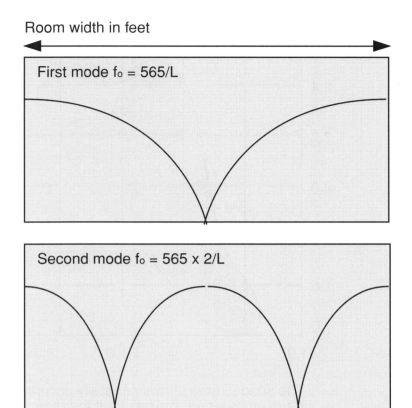

Room width in feet

First mode $f_0 = 565/L$

Second mode $f_0 = 565 \times 2/L$

$f_0 = 565n/L$ where L is the distance between opposing surfaces in feet and f_0 is the frequency of the mode in Hertz. n is the order of the mode (1, 2, 3 etc)

Figure 19.1: Calculating room modes

calculated, though the most significant fall below 300Hz.

As modal problems invariably have an adverse effect on the quality of speech in a room, much can be deduced about a room's mid-range performance simply by holding a conversation in it and checking the intelligibility of the speech. As a rule, if a room sounds good for speech, it will sound good for music, though there may still be low frequency problems below the natural frequency range of the human voice.

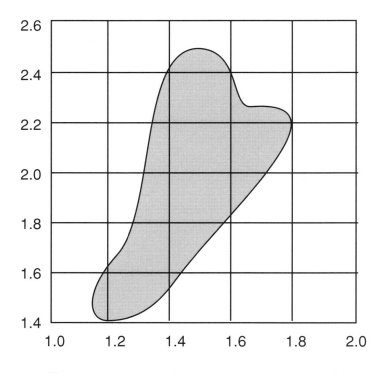

The shaded area shows generally acceptable room ratios where the height of the room is 1. However, not all values within this graph are ideal, and not all those falling outside it are unsuitable, so always recalculate the room modes after choosing dimensions

Figure 19.2: Bolt's graph of room ratios

wall angles

It is a common misconception that building non-parallel walls will improve the low frequency standing wave situation. Low frequency modes will develop much as they did in a parallel sided room based on the mean distance between walls. Even so, splaying the walls by as little as 1:10 or even 1:20 will help reduce high-frequency flutter echoes caused by mid- and high-frequency sounds bouncing between two facing walls or floor and ceiling. In fact commercial studio designs make extensive use of angles to make sure that reflections are directed away from the listening position. In the project studio, flutter echo problems between parallel walls can be solved quite easily by using relatively small areas of acoustically absorbent material, such as acoustic foam, at either side of the listening position.

One architectural feature to avoid where possible is any form of concave structure such as a bay window or curved wall. These tend to focus reflected sound into one place, just like a parabolic reflector, which can seriously affect the room's acoustic performance when you're anywhere near the focal point. Convex or irregular surfaces, on the other hand, are generally desirable, as they help to diffuse high frequencies leading to a more even sound field.

Bolt's ratios

If you don't have a room acoustics analysis software package and you don't fancy spending time with a calculator, you might be interested in Bolt's graph (he presented a paper on the subject in 1946), where the shaded space denotes acceptable room ratios. This graph, shown in Figure 19.2, isn't foolproof though, as some 2:1 room ratios fall into Bolt's area and some perfectly good rooms fall outside it – a lot depends on how large the room is. It does, however, give a good indication providing you recheck the modal performance of any room dimensions you arrive at. Several sets of preferred ratios have evolved which work well practically as well as theoretically. Three of these are:

1 : 1.14 : 1.39
1 : 1.28 : 1.54
1 : 1.6 : 2.33

In practice, most project studio owners will have little control over their room sizes, but an unfavourable set of ratios need not be disastrous so long as the monitors are chosen and positioned with care.

design trends

Ever since recording moved beyond the foyer of the record company offices, a number of control room design philosophies have enjoyed popularity. For example, early studios were often constructed like padded cells with mineral wool-lined walls covered with hessian. But we now know that this treatment produces a very dead acoustic, often with inadequate absorption at very low frequencies. The result is a room that booms at low frequencies, but sounds unnaturally dead to speech.

Then we had the flirtation with the so-called 'live end, dead end' approach, where the end of the studio with the monitors was made to sound dead using a combination of absorption and geometry, while the back of the room was allowed to contribute some reflections. We've also seen rooms with carefully designed scattering surfaces, virtually anechoic rooms (ie those having virtually no reverberation) with huge monitoring systems... and just about everything in between. Today's control room tends to incorporate a number of techniques with the aim of producing a better-balanced result, and no doubt the design fashion will change again as more studios equip themselves for surround sound mixing. Most project studios work fine with a little carefully placed absorption, and if the room is slightly bass heavy, some basic bass trapping.

chapter 20

acoustic treatment

There's little you can do about an uneven modal response if your room is already built. Fortunately, by taking a pragmatic approach, combined with the use of sensibly chosen nearfield monitors and properly placed acoustic absorbers, you can produce well-balanced pop music in a relatively unsophisticated room. Further worthwhile improvements can often be made by placing suitable acoustically absorbent materials at particular points within the room.

In the studio area, there's usually a lot of close miking employed, and even then much of the sound subscribes more to fashion rather than to pure fidelity. It's really in speech, vocal or acoustic instrument work that well behaved acoustics are most important in the studio, and if the room is less than ideal, local acoustical spaces can be set up using acoustic screens or improvised absorbers.

absorbers

Having introduced the leading rogues of the acoustic world, it's now time to check out some of our allies. Absorbing mid and high frequencies is not much of a problem, there are several proprietary acoustic tiles, foams and heavy drapes that can effectively soak up frequencies above 300Hz, but the bass end requires more tenacity. Low frequency sounds have long wavelengths and a purely absorptive bass trap needs to be at least one eighth of a wavelength deep to do any good. At 50Hz, that's approaching three feet, and there aren't many home studios that can afford the space to cover one or more walls with a three foot thickness of (150 to 175 kg/cubic metre density) mineral wool (such as Rockwool). In its favour, this type of trap has the advantage of working equally well at all frequencies down to its lower cut-off point, but in most small studio situations, it isn't a realistic solution.

The other, and understandably more popular, approach is to build a damped resonant structure that will absorb a significant proportion of a specific frequency band by converting it to heat via frictional losses. Fortunately, the resulting temperature rise may be considered insignificant.

resonant traps

There are two trap designs commonly used in commercial studios, both of which are easy to build: the panel absorber and the Helmholtz resonator. However, you have to know precisely where your problem frequencies are and you have to build these traps accurately to ensure that they work at the right frequency. I've really included them for academic interest as in a nearfield monitoring situation, you can generally solve your worst problems by less complicated means. Both types of absorber take up a large area but have the advantage of being only a few inches deep. Even so, you must bear in mind that these are tuned traps and so are useful only to reduce specific resonances – they are not suitable for use as broadband absorbers unless you construct a panel trap using a highly damped, limp membrane, such as barrier mat or roofing felt.

panel absorber

The panel absorber is the easiest and most predictable bass trap to design and build, consisting of a simple wooden frame over which is fixed a thin, flexible panel such as plywood, hardboard, barrier mat or roofing felt. Fibreglass or mineral wool is often fixed inside the frame to help damp the system by absorbing energy – the more the trap is damped, the wider the frequency range it works over, but the less absorption it has at its centre frequency. The resonant frequency is a function of cavity depth and mass per square foot of the panel material, so it's easy to calculate the dimensions using the simple formula:

$F = 170/\sqrt{MD}$ where F is the frequency you're aiming to absorb, M is the mass of the panel in lbs per square foot and D is the depth of the air space in inches.

The metric equivalent is: $F = 60/\sqrt{MD}$ where the mass is in kilograms and the unit of length is metres.

The surface area of the trap doesn't make any significant difference to the operating frequency, but obviously the more absorption you need, the larger the area of panel you'll need in any given room. To better understand the effect of a given area of absorber, consider that a perfectly efficient full-range trap would affect the sound in the same way as an open window of the same size, but without the associated problems of sound leakage.

Filling the cavity with fibreglass or mineral wool tends to lower the resonant frequency by up to 50% and can double the effectiveness of the trap. It also lowers the Q of the trap so that it is effective over a wider frequency range. A typical panel-type trap is effective for frequencies around one octave either side of the centre frequency, so you don't have to be deadly accurate to get results. Because the centre frequency and the Q of the trap vary depending on how much damping is used inside the trap, it is difficult to precisely predict the performance of a home-made panel trap. You can, however, find the resonant frequency by fixing a cheap contact mic to the panel's surface, then plugging the mic into a preamp or mixer with a VU meter. Via loudspeakers, play a test tone from an oscillator or test tone CD and vary this around the frequency the trap is designed for until you get a maximum meter reading. This will be at the trap's resonant frequency. The approximate bandwidth of the trap can be estimated by finding the two frequencies either side of the centre frequency where the meter reading falls by 3dB. The difference between these will be the bandwidth.

Higher frequencies may be reflected from the surface of the panel and curved panel traps have been constructed to simultaneously absorb bass frequencies and diffuse higher ones. However, it may be easier to cover the front face of the trap with a layer of acoustic foam to extend its usefulness to the mid and high end of the audio spectrum. Figure 20.1 shows the constructional details of a conventional panel absorber.

damping

An undamped panel trap using a rigid membrane will radiate some energy back into the room after the incident sound has ceased – clearly an undesirable state of affairs, so some degree of damping is generally included. Though panel traps are normally considered to be tuned absorbers, the use of a heavy, well damped panel material lowers the Q of the trap so much that it may be considered a broad band device, especially when combined with plenty of internal damping.

There are specialist materials such as mineral-loaded vinyl barrier mat, or even lead-loaded materials that are heavy, flexible and highly damped which lend themselves to wide band bass trap design. Good results may also be obtained from a mineral wool-filled trap, between eight and 12 inches deep, with a simple roofing felt membrane, though roofing felt tends to change its properties with age, so barrier mat is a better if more costly solution. Apparently the BBC used to use roofing felt, but now they've replaced the traps with more up-to-date designs except where the budget doesn't permit, and in those cases, the recommendation is to cover the fronts of the traps with carpet to reduce reflections and to increase the low frequency absorption (I assume the carpet also acts as a

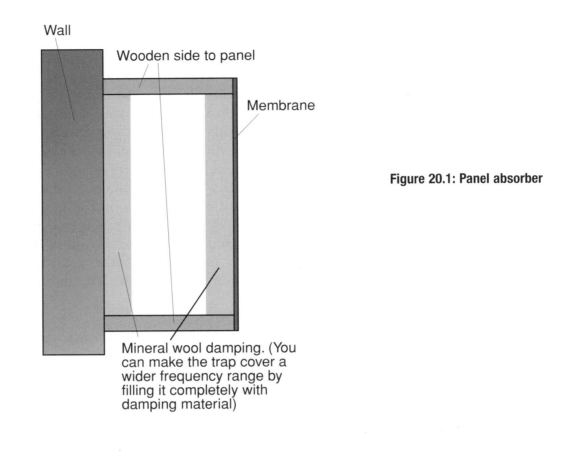

Wall

Wooden side to panel

Membrane

Figure 20.1: Panel absorber

Mineral wool damping. (You can make the trap cover a wider frequency range by filling it completely with damping material)

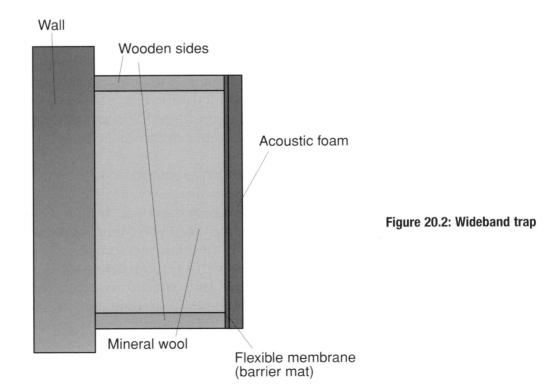

Wall

Wooden sides

Acoustic foam

Figure 20.2: Wideband trap

Mineral wool

Flexible membrane (barrier mat)

membrane in conjunction with the roofing felt?). It's also worth experimenting with heavy vinyl floor covering as a membrane.

With such a high degree of damping, the action of the trap is less like a resonant panel and more like a 'floppy wall' – the sound energy is expended in trying to vibrate the limp membrane which is so well damped that the energy is largely absorbed. Because the Q of such traps is low, the depth of the trap becomes far less critical. A broadband trap is shown in Figure 20.2.

Many historic buildings feature wood panelling and often exhibit well controlled acoustical properties. That's because a panelled wall with an air space behind acts as a tuned bass absorber. To a lesser extent, studio construction involving plasterboard fixed to a frame also helps us in that it acts, to some extent, as a trap for bass and mid frequencies depending on the depth of the air space behind it.

When it comes to acoustics, it is generally easier to treat a room that has a lightweight construction, as opposed to one that has solid walls, because a large proportion of the bass energy passes straight through lightweight walls instead of being reflected back. Unfortunately, what is helpful as regards acoustic treatment is, in this case, totally at odds with what is desirable for good sound isolation. If you have plasterboard walls, you can again try the sweep oscillator and contact mic approach to establish the actual resonant frequency. If the walls are too resonant or resonate at the wrong frequency, adding a second layer of plasterboard, ideally a different thickness to the first, will damp the resonances and change the frequency of absorption. The damping effect of a second layer of plasterboard is likely to reduce the Q of the structure to such an extent that it can no longer be considered to be tuned, especially if wall board adhesive is applied between the layers.

helmholtz traps

Another type of tuned trap, popular in broadcast studios and older recording studios, is the Helmholtz resonator, which works on the same principle as blowing over the neck of a bottle to obtain a tone. A bottle has a very narrow bandwidth but by introducing an absorbent material such as fibreglass or mineral wool into the neck to reduce the Q, the operating range can be widened. You don't see many studios full of bottles (at least not used as bass traps), and in any event, a few tuned bottles would make very little difference, but it is possible to simulate the effect of hundreds of tuned bottles by fixing a perforated panel over an air space into which some damping material has been introduced.

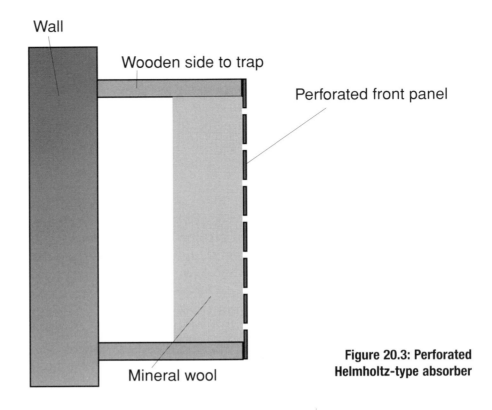

Figure 20.3: Perforated Helmholtz-type absorber

By fixing a perforated wooden or hardboard panel over a frame and putting an absorbent material such as mineral wool inside the space thus created, a resonant bass trap is formed where each perforation acts as a single bottle in our virtual bottle array. As you might expect, a fairly simple formula can be applied to determine the operating frequency:

$$R = 200 \sqrt{P/DT}$$

Where R is the resonant frequency, P is the percentage of perforation (total hole area divided by panel area times 100), T is the effective hole depth in inches (thickness of panel plus 0.8 of the hole diameter) and D is the depth of the air space in inches. It's easy enough to convert this to metric, but the numbers are more straightforward if you stick to imperial measurement.

Figure 20.3 shows the construction of the Helmholtz trap. By varying the perforation percentage, the design can be applied to both the bass and mid-range. Predicting the performance of these traps, however, is difficult

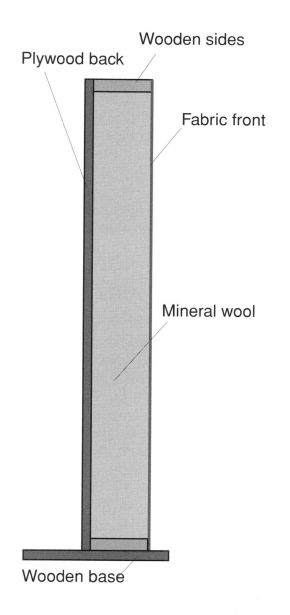

Figure 20.4: Simple acoustic screen

because the Q or bandwidth varies depending on the amount of internal damping. The other problem is getting the right perforation percentage. Common pegboard is usually used in mid traps rather than bass traps. For example, pegboard having 3/16 inch holes on a one inch matrix has a perforation percentage of 2.75%. Fixed over a four inch air gap, this gives a resonant frequency of a little over 400Hz. Boards of different perforation percentages may be available from specialist acoustic suppliers but are not readily available from conventional builders' supply merchants.

Like the panel absorber, adding an absorbent material lowers the resonant frequency slightly and broadens the resonant peak. Instead of using perforated board, it's theoretically possible to use a series of slats to create a slotted panel with the correct slot percentage, but the calculations for such an absorber don't always predict the result as precisely as might be desired. Helmholtz resonators were once very widely used in both broadcast and recording studios, but panel traps with limp membranes seem more widespread in modern designs.

Tuned traps should be placed on the walls corresponding to the room modes that you wish to attenuate and bass traps are traditionally placed in corners where there's an area of high pressure. Floor to ceiling modes may be tackled by placing a trap on the ceiling.

mid and high absorbers

One of the simplest absorbers for use at higher frequencies is basic open-cell foam such as that used in furniture. For safety reasons, the fire-retardant type should be used and expensive acoustic foam tiles are often only sculpted versions of this same material. The lowest frequency that will be effectively absorbed is dictated by the thickness of the foam, a one inch foam being most effective above 1kHz while a four inch foam is useful down to around 250Hz. The low frequency absorption can also be improved by spacing the foam away from the wall by a few inches on a wooden frame.

A similar absorber can be made from two inch mineral wool slab, fixed to a frame two inches away from the wall and covered with open-weave fabric to prevent the fibres escaping into the air (always wear a mask and gloves when handling mineral wool and install it in such a way that it is impossible for fibres to escape into the air of the room). A mineral wool trap made in this way should be effective down to 250Hz or so. A variation on this is the acoustic blanket used in broadcast work where layers of mineral wool reinforced with lightweight wire mesh are covered with fabric and hung from walls where needed. The greater the airspace behind the blanket, the lower the frequency it is effective to.

Carpet is insufficiently thick to be effective at anything less than the high frequency end of the spectrum and its absorbency drops off noticeably below 2kHz. There is a slight advantage to using a foam-backed carpet, and once again, mounting this with an airspace behind will extend its effectiveness down another octave or so. However, it is less than ideal as a wall treatment unless combined with another absorbent material positioned behind the carpet.

Variable absorbency in the mid and high frequency range can be achieved by hanging heavy drapes a few inches from the wall. These should be generous enough to allow the material to hang in folds rather than being stretched tightly, and if these are hung on a rail in front of a reflective surface, it's a simple matter to draw back the drapes to convert a dead acoustic into a live one.

movable screens

Portable acoustic screens are useful because they can be used to modify the sound of a small part of a room for the recording of, say, a vocal track, drums or acoustic guitar. These screens are generally built with a polished wood or synthetic laminate face on one side and a mineral wool or foam absorber about four inches thick on the other. They are supported by simple wooden legs and, by facing either the hard or the absorbent side to the performer, either a live or dead environment is created. These screens are only effective down to around 250Hz on their absorbent side but that's usually adequate.

Drum booths may be set up using a set of tall screens with another screen balanced on the top to form a roof. To aid eye contact, some screens are built with thick perspex windows in them. For drums, acoustic guitars and so on, the live side is normally faced towards the performer, and for vocals, the dead side. Figure 20.4 shows how a simple acoustic screen may be constructed.

summary

Absorbent traps can be useful in producing a more even acoustic environment, but only if applied intelligently so as to produce a nominally consistent reverberation time across the audio spectrum. The most common mistake people make when building their own studios is using too much trapping, usually at mid and high frequencies, and this serves only to further emphasise low frequency resonances that are more difficult to cure. In any event, it's probably unwise to do anything irreversible before the carpets and equipment are installed in the studio as these invariably make the room sound totally different to the way it did when empty.

Numerous advances in trap design have been made by specialists in the field, with the result that it's now possible to treat a completed room by adding just a few well chosen panels in the right places. It's also possible to build panels with variable absorbency so that they can be adjusted in situ. Understandably, the designers of the more sophisticated traps are reluctant to give too much away! Getting the performance of a room dead right involves a lot of calculation plus verification by measurement, and the next chapter looks at some of the calculation methods employed. Nevertheless, if you use nearfield monitors and are prepared to experiment with simple absorbers such as acoustic foam tiles, floppy traps and drapes, it's generally possible to arrive at an acceptable solution without too much difficulty.

chapter 21

doing the sums

Asuccessfully designed control room will use a combination of absorption, geometry and scattering to produce the desired acoustic environment, so it would be wrong to look at using absorbers as the sole solution to the design problem. However, absorbers are important in controlling the reverb decay time of the room, and for music mixing, decay times of a little over 0.3 seconds are typical with the time increasing slightly at low frequencies. Other surface treatments may be devised for the diffusion or scattering of sound in order to further randomise the reflections arriving at the listener and this important area will be covered later in the series.

Most of us will be familiar with reverberation both as an artificial and as a natural effect. It occurs in all normal rooms to the extent that music or speech sounds unnatural without it, but in a studio control room environment, the reverberation characteristics need to be controlled within fairly close limits if the end product is to be evaluated with any accuracy.

Reverberation is created whenever sound energy is fed into a room and the room modes discussed earlier are excited. When the source of energy is removed, the reverberation will decay at a rate determined by the geometry and absorbency of the room and its contents. Excessive low frequency reverberation related to one dominating mode can cause serious problems for the engineer. The danger is that you may attempt to correct your mix using EQ to compensate for the apparent bass boost, but then when you play back your mix on a properly balanced hi-fi system, the result sounds bass light. Furthermore, excessive reverb time at one frequency can cause notes to hang on, generally blurring the sound and making it more difficult to concentrate on fine details.

T60

In a simple space, reverberation dies away exponentially, so some way of defining the decay time in a repeatable and measurable fashion is required. Reverberation time is conventionally defined as the time taken for a sound to die away to one thousandth of its original sound level and the resulting figure is called T60 because the reverb time is measured to the point where the sound has decayed by 60dB. The ideal reverb time varies depending on the room size and the type of material being auditioned, though a control room is likely to be around 0.3 seconds. It is important to note though, that in small rooms, the sound reflections don't build up into an even reverberant field as they do in a large room, so any calculations can only be approximate.

In the studio area, an optimum reverb time for speech might be somewhere between 0.2s and 0.5s, whereas classical music might require between 0.6s and 0.8s of reverberation to add life and body to the performance. A typical living room has a T60 of around 0.4 to 0.5s and unless you're going to spend a lot of money on studio design, that's not a bad figure to aim for in a project studio control room. Some people would disagree with me on this point, but I feel that unless you're doing the job properly using qualified designers who have access to the correct measuring equipment, you can easily make the listening environment much worse by trying to do too much.

In a poorly designed control room, problems arise because the T60 tends to be different at different frequencies, though it's normally okay to accept a slightly longer T60 at lower frequencies – this is typical of a furnished domestic room. The main thing to bear in mind is that if the room isn't designed with low frequency reproduction in mind, it's invariably safer to use nearfield monitors with a limited low end response. Studio design ideals are subject to changes in fashion, and no doubt the renewed interest in surround monitoring will complicate the issue still further, but the current consensus seems to be that for small studio control rooms, we should aim for as constant a reverb time as possible up to 8kHz or beyond. Though a slight rise of RT at lower frequencies is permissible, it should not be excessive.

sabine

The maths needed to calculate reverb time or T60 is fairly straightforward using the formula devised by Sabine, though this is admittedly only accurate when applied to large rooms. There is a more accurate but rather more complicated formula attributed to Eyring, but in order to illustrate the basic principles, Sabine will serve quite adequately. Sabine states that:

$$T60 = \frac{0.05v}{ST \times Aave}$$

where T60 is the reverb time in seconds, V is the volume of the room in cubic ft, ST is the total surface area of the room in square feet and Aave is the average absorption coefficient of the surfaces within the room.

However, the metric equivalent is:

$$RT = \frac{0.161v}{ST \times Aave}$$

where the volume is measured in cubic metres, and the surface area in square metres.

If the room is to be furnished, the surface areas, volumes and materials of the furniture should really be included in the calculations, but unless you're putting a lot of furniture into a small room, it's easier to do your calculations based on the empty room and then assume that adding any soft furnishings later will only improve things. It's possible to obtain tables of absorption coefficients relating to all the commonly used building, decorating and furnishing materials (check a good builders' supply company and get leaflets on specific materials for details), but a few useful ones gleaned from various textbooks are included at the end of this chapter. Keep in mind that these can only be regarded as approximate as no two manufacturers' products are identical.

here comes the science

Multiplying the total surface area of the room by the average absorption coefficient for the surface materials tells us how absorbent the room is, and this figure is expressed as a number of absorption units called Sabines. Simply put, we can consider each area of different surface material separately, calculate the number of Sabines it contributes, and then add up all the Sabines for the room to give us the bottom line for the simple equation shown earlier. For example, assume that the absorption coefficient for concrete at 125Hz is about 0.01 which isn't very high. 500 square feet of concrete surface, such as a floor, would give us 500 x 0.01 = 5 Sabines of absorption. Add on the number of Sabines due to plaster walls, panel absorbers or whatever and you end up with the total number of Sabines for the room at 125Hz.

To complicate the issue slightly, the absorption coefficient for a given material varies with frequency, but it isn't practical to do a different set of calculations for every possible audio frequency. Instead, we rationalise the audio spectrum to six discrete frequency values at one octave intervals from 125Hz up to 4kHz. Even so, that means working through the formula six times with six sets of values to give us six T60 times, one for each octave. Once this has been done, the figures tell us at which frequencies we have either too much or too little absorption. Then it's down to pencilling in a trap, a carpet or a few acoustic tiles and then going through the sums again to see if things are better. Anyone capable of using a spreadsheet program should be able to automate this tedious calculation, but a simple calculator is quite adequate if you have the patience. However, an acoustic design software package makes this job infinitely less tedious.

limitations

One limitation of Sabine's equation is that it assumes a perfectly diffused soundfield, which small rooms invariably don't have, and it also ignores any sound absorption due to the air within the room. That's another good reason why any result arrived at on this basis should be treated as a guide rather than as a rigorous analysis. Acoustic consultants make a good living out of weighing the results of these and similar calculations against reality, then applying their experience and expertise to come up with something that will actually work.

distributed absorption

It is good practice to try to balance the properties of facing walls rather than calculate that you need X amount of trapping for the whole room and then stick it all in one place. What's more, tuned trapping designed to combat specific room modes must go on the wall relevant to that mode. For example, if you have a mode due to the length of the room, then the trapping must go on the end walls, not the side walls. When treating facing surfaces, it's most effective to distribute the absorptive material between them rather than putting everything on one wall and leaving the other reflective, and in the case of side walls, this is essential to maintain a nominally symmetrical listening environment. However, it's not always possible to treat opposing surfaces in exactly the same way, the floor/ceiling pair being the most obvious example. If the floor is carpeted, it will absorb the higher frequencies very efficiently but will hardly affect the bass or lower mid-range at all. One could, for example, mount bass traps in the ceiling designed to absorb the bass but to reflect back the mid and higher frequencies absorbed by the carpet. In practice though, it's often sufficient to place a foam absorber on the ceiling above the mixing console to soak up any ceiling-to-listener mid and high frequency reflections from the monitors.

The decisions on where to place absorbers will also be influenced by the underlying philosophy of the room. There are at least two types of LEDE

(Live End/Dead End) control room, there are rooms that rely heavily on scattering to diffuse reflections, and there are very dead rooms driven by huge monitoring systems. Ultimately, the only real criterion is that the room should work for creating mixes that sound 'right' when played on other systems outside the studio. Indeed, it is sometimes argued that as most music is listened to in a domestic living room, we should model our control rooms on living rooms, but the reality is that if we're to produce really good recordings, we need a monitoring environment that's a little better than that enjoyed by the end user. Whichever approach you take, the room must be as acoustically symmetrical as possible, the monitor system and any large windows in the side walls should be balanced by areas having similar acoustic properties on the opposite wall.

The design techniques are the same for the studio area as for the control room, though you may decide on a longer T60 for the studio depending on the type of music you wish to record. Speech requires a fairly dry environment whereas acoustic instruments thrive in a more lively setting.

doing the sums

Before getting down to working out the trapping for your room, you should decide on the basic room philosophy. Most small studios use a combination of diffusion and geometry to keep early reflections from the speakers away from the listening position combined with trapping and diffusion on the rear wall to prevent strong reflections from bouncing directly back to the sweet spot. However, this is not the only approach, and the ideal solution will depend to some extent on the shape and size of your room.

Once you've decided on a layout for your room, check the room dimensions to see if they fall inside Bolt's area. If they don't, plot out your main room modes and find out where trouble spots are likely to occur so you can employ some extra trapping if necessary. Even if the dimensions fall inside Bolt's graph, it's a good idea to calculate the room modes anyway as you can still end up with trouble spots, especially in small rooms where the low frequency modes are more widely spaced.

Next, decide what floor covering is to be used as this will have a significant effect on the overall acoustics due to the large area involved. Carpet is a good idea in control rooms as vinyl tends to be too reflective at high frequencies. At this point, you can use Sabine's formula to work out the approximate T60s for the room as it stands at the standard frequencies of 125Hz, 250Hz, 500Hz, 1kHz, 2kHz and 4kHz. This will probably reveal an excessively long T60 at 125Hz, though if the walls are hard and reflective, you'll probably find the room is very live in the mid-range too.

With the help of Sabine and a table of absorption coefficients for your room materials, you should be able to arrive at the areas of treatment you need to get your T60 close to your target figure at all six frequencies. The best way to handle the calculations is to work out how many Sabines you need to provide at each frequency and then distribute them according to the room philosophy and the most dominant room modes. Any surfaces not occupied by doors, shelves, windows, equipment and suchlike may be used to distribute your acoustic absorbers, but don't panic, because in a typical domestic room, the amount of acoustic treatment needed isn't usually that great – it's not as if you have to cover all the available wall space with traps.

The procedure of calculating the amount of absorption required at each of the six standard frequencies sounds more complicated than it is, but as already mentioned, it can be time consuming. What's more, the result is only going to be an approximation due to the limitations of Sabine's equation when applied to small rooms, not to mention the uncertain absorption coefficients of various materials. Furthermore, the overall effect of the same area of absorbent material will be different depending on whether the material is all in one place or distributed around the room. As a rule, distributed absorption works more effectively and careful listening or specialised measurement is the only real way to tell if you have a successful result.

flutter echo

Flutter echo is a distinctive ringing sound caused by echoes bouncing back and forth between hard, parallel surfaces following a percussive sound such as a hand clap. To minimise flutter echoes, which can plague even a studio having a perfect T60 across the band, certain precautions should be taken. If you're building from scratch, facing walls can be made out of parallel by at least 1 in 10, but if this isn't possible, some form of mid/high absorber can be applied to the side walls to reduce the problem. In many cases, a pair of acoustic foam tiles fixed to the side walls, just forward of the engineering position, is all that's needed. Note that some of the absorbers discussed earlier, such as the panel trap, the Helmholtz resonator and the slatted absorber, have flat surfaces which are reflective at mid and high frequencies. Consequently, when positioning these, it is a good idea either to face them with acoustic foam or not to have them facing each other across a parallel room. Alternatively, panel traps can be constructed with a sloping surface, where the average depth is maintained by making the half-way depth equal to the calculated value. Padded door surfaces can also be beneficial and one of the popular methods is to fit two inches of foam to the door covered with upholstery quality vinyl or fabric, fixed by tacks to give a quilted appearance.

some useful absorption coefficients

These figures have been gleaned from a number of different materials catalogues so the dimensions are presented in either imperial or metric, as originally published.

MATERIAL	125HZ	250HZ	500HZ	1KHZ	2KHZ	4KHZ
50mm Acoustic Foam	0.08	0.25	0.6	0.9	0.95	0.9
100mm Acoustic Foam	0.2	0.7	0.99	0.99	0.99	0.99
50mm Mineral Wool (Medium Density)	0.2	0.45	0.7	0.8	0.8	0.8
Plaster on brick	0.013	0.015	0.02	0.03	0.04	0.05
Cotton Drapes draped to half area. 15oz/sq yd	0.07	0.37	0.49	0.65	0.54	
Foam backed carpet on concrete	0.05	0.16	0.44	0.7	0.6	0.4
Heavy Carpet plus heavy foam underlay on concrete	0.15	0.25	0.5	0.6	0.7	0.8
Coarse Concrete	0.36	0.44	0.31	0.29	0.39	0.25
Painted Concrete	0.01	0.05	0.06	0.07	0.09	0.08
Wood Floor	0.15	0.11	0.10	0.07	0.06	0.07
Window Glass	0.35	0.25	0.18	0.12	0.07	0.04
Plate Glass	0.18	0.06	0.04	0.03	0.02	0.02
6mm Glass	0.1	0.06	0.04	0.03	0.02	0.02
Plaster on brick	0.013	0.015	0.02	0.03	0.04	0.05
9mm Plasterboard over 20mm air gap	0.3	0.2	0.15	0.05	0.05	0.05
Brickwork	0.05	0.04	0.02	0.04	0.05	0.05
Vinyl Flooring	0.03	0.04	0.05	0.04	0.05	0.05
Breeze Block	0.25	0.40	0.6	0.5	0.75	0.5
LF Panel Absorber	0.28	0.22	0.17	0.09	0.10	0.11
Perforated Helmholtz absorber using 4" depth with mineral wool damping, 0.79% perforation	0.4	0.84	0.	0.16	0.14	0.12
Perforated Helmholtz absorber using 8" depth with mineral wool damping, 0.79% perforation	0.98	0.8	0.52	0.21	0.16	0.14

Broadband absorber consisting of 1" fibreglass slab at mouth of 7" deep cavity	0.67	0.98	0.98	0.93	0.9	0.96
Padded Seat (unoccupied)	0.1	0.2	0.25	0.3	0.	0.3

pragmatism in design

Most of the mathematics in the preceding chapter was included mainly for academic interest. Few project studios are professionally designed, and even if you apply the basic formulae to calculate the amount of absorbent trapping you need to add, the results are unlikely to be accurate. Part of the problem is that materials never seem to behave exactly as their textbook values suggest, and it's also well known that the way in which absorbent material is distributed on the room's surface has a profound effect on the outcome. A mathematical analysis of the requirements should get you into the right ball park, but it is possible to create a workable listening environment without doing any maths at all.

Fortunately, you can tell a lot about the acoustics of a room by listening to speech and music in that room, and even if the design isn't quite as good as you might have hoped for, the human hearing system is capable of compensating for a multitude of sins providing it has some form of reference, such as well mixed commercial music played over the same monitors.

Though you wouldn't go about designing a professional studio using only instinct and listening tests, you'd be surprised by how much you can improve the performance of a typical home studio by adhering to a few simple guidelines. One of the reasons this works is because the smaller monitors used in project studios don't have the same extended bass as the main monitors used in typical commercial installations, so there is less low frequency energy produced to excite the room where its T60 is longer than might be desirable. What's more, smaller monitors can be used closer to the engineer so the ratio of direct to reverberant sound is higher, meaning that the room acoustics have less of an effect on the perceived sound.

the holistic approach

The source of all the wanted sound in your control room is the loudspeaker system, so it makes sense to start by considering what happens to the sound after it leaves the speakers. At mid and high frequencies, monitor loudspeakers have a reasonably controlled directivity, which means that, as a broad generalisation, most of the sound emerges as a cone of energy from the front

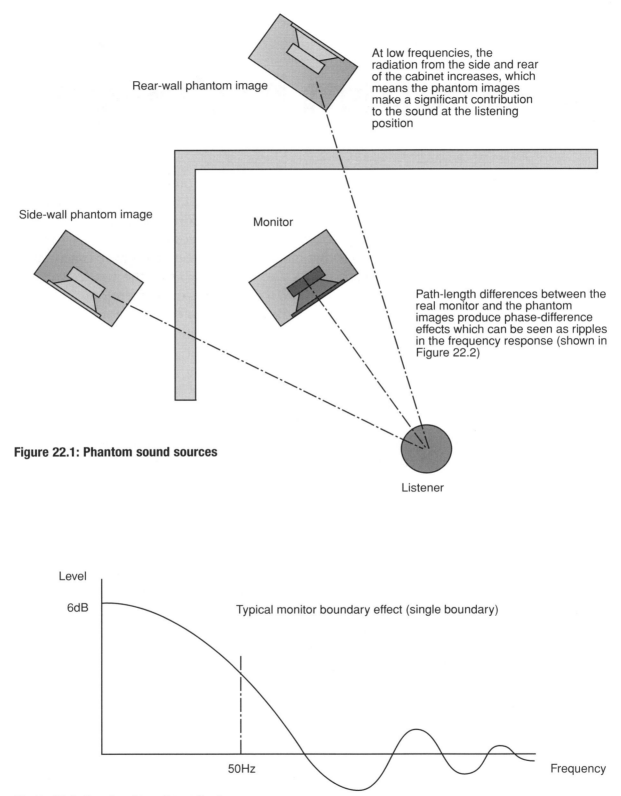

Rear-wall phantom image

At low frequencies, the radiation from the side and rear of the cabinet increases, which means the phantom images make a significant contribution to the sound at the listening position

Side-wall phantom image

Monitor

Path-length differences between the real monitor and the phantom images produce phase-difference effects which can be seen as ripples in the frequency response (shown in Figure 22.2)

Figure 22.1: Phantom sound sources

Listener

Level

6dB

Typical monitor boundary effect (single boundary)

50Hz

Frequency

Figure 22.2: Speaker boundary effect

of the box. Unfortunately, at lower frequencies, this cone widens until at very low frequencies, the speaker cabinet is effectively an omnidirectional source. However, attempting to absorb all the sound that misses the listener and instead hits a room surface is generally both impractical and undesirable. There are designs for studios that are virtually anechoic chambers, but most people find them oppressive to work in, and because so much energy is being absorbed, you need a very powerful monitor system to get the desired sound level. One of the reasons an anechoic or completely absorbent control room is unpleasant to work in is that speech within the room sounds very dry and quiet as there are no wall reflections to give it life.

In a normal music listening environment, sound coming from the speakers is reflected from the walls and other surfaces in ways that can be both musically constructive and destructive, so the secret of good control room design is to try to avoid the wrong type of reflections while encouraging and controlling the right type. A well diffused reverberation with an RT of around 0.3 seconds is generally considered to be about right for professional control rooms, though the project studio might get away with a slightly longer RT. Well diffused, spectrally neutral reflections arriving very shortly after the original sound tend to fuse with it and increase its subjective level. Even so, these reflections should be at least 10dB lower in level than the direct sound for the best results, which usually means avoiding reflections that originate from surfaces close to the speakers themselves. It also means avoiding reflections from materials that only reflect a part of the audio spectrum. Longer delays caused by reflections in larger rooms (over around 40ms) are audible as slap-back echoes and are clearly undesirable. This would correspond to a front-to-back room distance of around 20 feet or six metres.

highs and lows

It helps to understand what's going on if we split the audio spectrum into two bands. In a typical room, frequencies up to around 300Hz are mainly influenced by room modes and by the physical position of the monitors within the room while at higher frequencies, most of the problems are associated with multiple reflection paths. Looking at the loudspeaker position first, you can see from Figure 22.1 that if a speaker is positioned on a stand somewhere out in the room, sound from the back and sides of the cabinet will reach the side and rear walls of the room and then reflect back into the room. This is known as the speaker boundary effect. The best way to imagine what effect the reflected sound will have is to visualise the walls covered with mirrors. Everywhere you can see a reflection of the monitor, a phantom sound source will be created. Because the walls aren't perfectly reflective to sound, and because the sound radiating from the sides and back of the speaker is mainly low frequency, the phantom sources are effectively low-pass filtered so that only low frequencies come back. These low-pass filtered reflections combine with the direct low frequency energy from the front of the speaker as shown in Figure 22.2.

Because of the distance the reflected sound has to travel, it will never be exactly in-phase with the direct sound, but at very low frequencies where the wavelengths are long, they're sufficiently in phase to cause some constructive addition. In simple terms, this means that putting a speaker close to a solid wall will cause an increase in bass energy as some of the low frequency energy normally lost from the back of the cabinet is reflected back to the listener. As the frequency increases, the path length difference between the direct and reflected sound will correspond to a different number of wavelengths, so that at some frequencies the direct and reflected energy will add while at others it will cancel. That's why the graph shown in Figure 22.2 shows a series of ripples in the amplitude response.

If the speaker is placed close to a corner, reflections from both the rear and side walls combine to produce a greater bass rise and more pronounced ripples in the low frequency response, and if the floor reflections are also included, the bass rise can be very significant. While some users might view this as a simple way to get 'free' extra bass, the deep ripples in the low frequency response can lead to problematic hot spots and dead spots in the bass end. The only way to avoid this is to keep monitor speakers away from corners and to try to randomise the distances between the speaker cabinet and the nearby room boundaries. That's why in small studios, it's often best to place the monitors along the longest wall and away from the corners rather than along the shortest wall, nearer to the corners. If the speakers are placed exactly the same distance from the rear wall, the side wall and the floor, the bass boost can be up to 18dB at very low frequencies with huge ripples extending into the bottom couple of octaves of the monitor's response.

The only practical way to utilise the rear radiated energy from the speaker cabinet without incurring phase difference problems is to actually mount the monitor flush with the room boundary, which is why so many large studio monitoring systems are built into the front wall. This way all the low frequency energy is forced to radiate into a 180 degree space rather than being allowed to radiate into a 360 degree space, and because there is no distance between the monitor and the boundary, there is a near perfect doubling of low frequency efficiency with no ripples. To obtain a flat frequency response from flush-mounted speakers, the monitors themselves must be designed with a corresponding drop in low frequency efficiency so that the net result is flat. Speakers made for stand mounting, on the other hand, are designed on the assumption that the boundary will be some distance away, which is why many manufacturers include advice on the positioning of their monitors relative to walls. It's also for this reason that some active monitors include bass end tailoring controls to help compensate for the effects of positioning.

Because a stand-mounted speaker invariably produces some peaks and dips in the low frequency response curve, it can be helpful to use a studio design software program to determine the optimum speaker placement within the room, though in many situations, speaker placement is largely dictated by the position of the mixing console and of other equipment within the room.

geometry

Positioning speakers optimumly with respect to the room boundaries will minimise low frequency response anomalies, but it's also necessary to minimise the level of any early reflections due to the sound from the front of the speaker striking a nearby surface and reflecting back to the listener. In a professional studio with flush-mounted monitors, this is often done by combining areas of absorption with carefully planned wall and ceiling geometries designed so that any reflections that can't be avoided are deflected away from the listening position. This is rarely practical in the project studio, especially where stand-mounted monitors are in use, but it is possible to position areas of relatively simple mid/high frequency absorber on the walls and ceiling to intercept the strongest reflections. Figure 22.3 shows areas of foam acoustic tile on the side walls and ceiling that do this job very simply and cheaply. If you're not sure exactly where to place these, get a friend to hold a mirror against the studio wall. When you can see the reflection of the monitor in the mirror from your normal listening position, you have the location of the centre of your acoustic tile. An area of one square metre of tile per side wall is generally quite adequate, but use the thickest type you can get as it will be effective to a lower frequency than the thinner type. Something around 100mm thick is ideal. Do the same for the ceiling.

This approach to minimising strong early reflections is part of the so-called live end/dead end control room design philosophy which, despite a few changes, still prevails in modern control room design. The speakers are located at the dead end of the room (insomuch as the front of the room is designed to produce minimal early reflections), and the rear of the room is designed to scatter reflected energy back into the room in as random and well diffused way as possible. What you don't want is a solid, flat back wall that reflects the sound of the monitors back at you as a coherent echo. Commercial design strategies include angled sections of rear wall, semi cylindrical constructions and purpose made diffusors. In the home studio, you can break up the reflections by putting storage shelves on the rear wall, and if you can also put a soft sofa across the back of the room, you'll also add some welcome low frequency absorption.

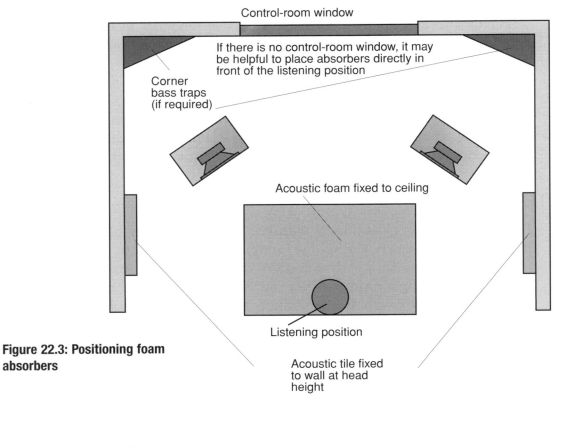

Control-room window

If there is no control-room window, it may
be helpful to place absorbers directly in
front of the listening position

Corner
bass traps
(if required)

Acoustic foam fixed to ceiling

Listening position

**Figure 22.3: Positioning foam
absorbers**

Acoustic tile fixed
to wall at head
height

Figure 22.4: A rear-wall trap

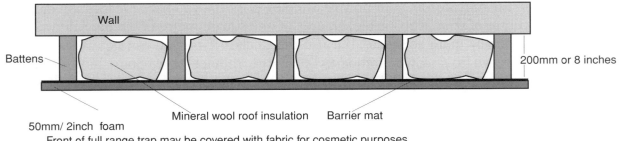

Wall

Battens

200mm or 8 inches

50mm/ 2inch foam

Mineral wool roof insulation   Barrier mat

Front of full range trap may be covered with fabric for cosmetic purposes.

small studios

This live end/dead end approach has to be modified further for small studios
as in rooms where there isn't a lot of front-to-back distance, it isn't generally
possible to break up the rear wall reflections sufficiently, and because of the
small distances involved, the reflections may be stronger than desirable. In
such cases, it's common to employ a mixture of heavy trapping and diffusion
on the rear wall. For example, a barrier mat covered mineral wool trap

around eight inches or 200mm deep may be constructed with a further layer of 50mm acoustic foam on the front surface to prevent high frequency energy reflecting from the barrier mat. This form of trap construction is shown in Figure 22.4.

To introduce some scattering, randomly spaced wooden slats could be fitted over part of the surface of the trap, though you could again fit some shelving to those parts of the walls that aren't being used as a trap. Shelving containing tapes, computer disks, manuals and so on breaks up reflections surprisingly well.

other trapping

When it comes to positioning other trapping that may be required, the main thing to bear in mind is to keep the room as acoustically symmetrical as possible. Bass traps tend to be fitted into corners as this is where the main room modes are anchored, and in a simple setup, two rear corner 'floppy membrane' traps may be all that's needed, with the area in between them taken up by scattering surfaces such as shelving. On the other hand, if you've decided to trap the entire back wall, you probably won't need any additional bass trapping.

If larger monitors are being used and the boundary reflections are causing problems, it may also be desirable to fit bass traps in the front corners or directly behind the monitors. Even so, in a typical project studio using suitably chosen nearfield monitors, it's often possible to get away with little or no bass trapping other than that provided by the furnishings.

more about scattering

Sound scattering, sometimes called diffusion, is the mechanism of breaking up reflected sound so that the energy is returned to the room evenly dispersed rather than as a solid, coherent echo. A properly designed diffusor will spread the reflected energy out over a full 180 degrees, though the effectiveness falls off at lower frequencies. As mentioned earlier, when you get down to around 300Hz, the room modes take over as the principle factors in room behaviour.

If you don't like the idea of covering your back wall with shelving, you can build purpose designed diffusors. Commercial designs are available comprising different depth wooden cavities where the depth and spacing of the cavities is determined by a mathematical formula based on something called quadratic residue (don't ask!). Several tests have been carried out that indicate the design of these diffusors is not as critical as the complex maths indicates they might be, and randomly chosen sizes seem to work perfectly adequately.

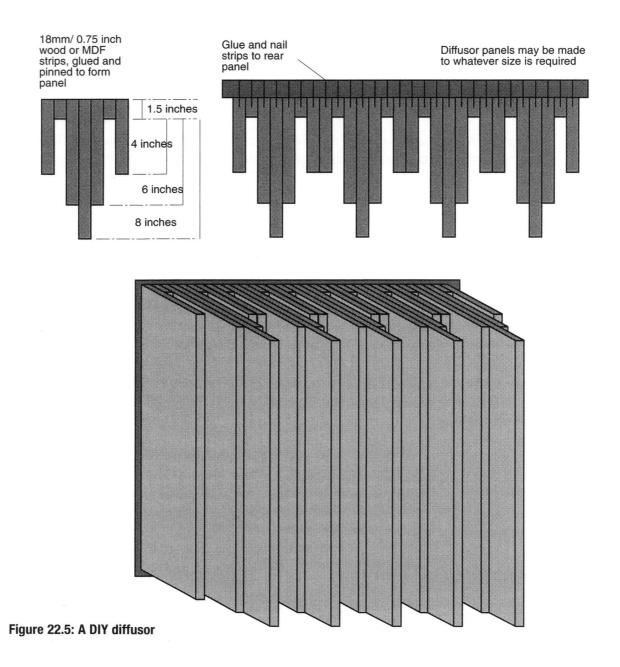

18mm/ 0.75 inch wood or MDF strips, glued and pinned to form panel

1.5 inches

4 inches

6 inches

8 inches

Glue and nail strips to rear panel

Diffusor panels may be made to whatever size is required

Figure 22.5: A DIY diffusor

Figure 22.5 shows a simple DIY diffusor that can be made from MDF or wood.

The way these diffusors work is that the reflections coming back from the differently spaced depressions return to the room shifted in phase with respect to each other, and this results in new wavefronts that propagate in different directions, rather like bending light through a prism. By contrast, a flat surface reflects a phase coherent wave that follows the 'angle of incidence equals angle of reflection' law. Properly diffused sound can help reinforce the sound from the monitors without compromising the overall monitoring accuracy or adversely affecting the stereo imaging.

chapter 23

acoustics and noise

The section of this book devoted to acoustics has been included to help you to appreciate the role acoustics play in creating a useful mixing environment, as well as to provide some guidance on improving your own listening space. Although some mathematical concepts have been introduced, I must stress yet again that any major studio-design work should be undertaken in conjunction with a good acoustic consultant, who will have the means to measure the actual performance of the room at various stages throughout the project. If you're working at home on a low budget or simply kitting out your garage as a studio, then by all means try applying the principles discussed so far, and if you intend to go through the maths, then consider buying some software to help you. Check the hi-tech music magazines or the Internet to see what's on offer.

In this chapter, I'd like to summarise the various stages you need to go through when designing a small studio, and accepting that relatively few structural changes can be made in most home studios, I'm also including a few alternative ways of working that might help you to avoid problems. Soundproofing is usually the first thing on the agenda, especially in residential areas, and while a complete cure may not be practical because of space or budget constraints, you'll almost certainly be able to make a significant improvement without having to rip the house apart or spend a fortune.

the source of noise

Accepting that you're unlikely ever to get perfect sound isolation in a typical house without major building work, you may be able to meet the problem halfway by generating less noise in the first place. The choice of monitors is important here, as this is where much of your noise will be coming from. Nearfield monitors are a good choice for the small studio for a number of reasons. Firstly, the overall monitoring level can be less loud than with a system located further away from the listener, so the effect of the room acoustic is minimised and the amount of sound generated in the first place is less. Furthermore, nearfield monitors generally produce less deep bass than large, full-range monitors, and while bass may be appealing, in a small or untreated room, it is likely to be very misleading. Far better to tailor the monitor's bass response to the room so that you get a more accurate picture of what's going on in the mix. As far as noise is concerned, low frequencies cause the most problems, so by cutting down on your bass output, you also cut down on the nuisance factor of your monitoring system.

If your system is still too noisy to allow you to work late at night, consider doing at least some of your recording using headphones and save the monitors for when you come to mix.

Noisy equipment invariably causes less unwanted sound leakage if it is isolated from the floor of the room, especially if the floor is made of wood. I heard a story where one frustrated project studio owner replaced his traditional drum kit with a set of electronic pads only to find that the physical thump of the bass drum pedal still sounded loud and clear in the room below. Try mounting instrument amplifiers on rubber foam or even inflated inner tubes to cut down structurally borne sound. Drum kits are a different matter, and though the amount of sound leakage can be reduced by positioning the kit on a plinth built like a section of floating floor, anyone expecting to get away with loud playing in a typical flat or apartment without upsetting the neighbours is doomed to a life of eternal disappointment!

Rock guitars may now be DI'd in a quite satisfactory manner using speaker simulators or dedicated recording preamps. Speaker simulators plug into the speaker outlet (or occasionally the preamp output) of an instrument amplifier and filter the sound in such a way as to imitate the coloration of the speaker. The output is a low-level signal which can be DI'd directly into a mixing console, and one of the great advantages of this approach, apart from the lack of noise, is that what you hear over the monitors is exactly the sound going to tape. While purists still prefer to mic their amps, some of the modern recording preamps are extremely good, especially those that use digital physical modelling. If you must use an amp, try a small valve practice combo as these often record better (and sound bigger) than a large stack as well as minimising noise and spill.

cheap and dirty acoustics

While soundproofing follows fairly predictable physical rules, acoustic treatment is less easily pinned down. As we have seen, although there are well documented physical laws governing the way sound is absorbed and reflected, there are so many variables in a typical room that precise calculation is virtually impossible. Perhaps this is why so many people consider acoustic design to be as much an art as a science. Even if you could be absolutely sure about the acoustic properties of all the materials making up your room, the acoustics would still change significantly once equipment and furniture was introduced into the studio.

There is also disagreement as to what actually constitutes the ideal monitoring environment, but ultimately we have to keep firmly in mind the fact that the end result of our efforts is likely to be a CD or cassette heard over fairly small speakers in a variety of imperfect domestic rooms or in cars. One thing you can be sure of is that few people will be listening in an acoustically perfect control room with monitors the size of cupboards. What's most important is that you have a symmetrical room in which the reverb time is well controlled and nominally even across the audio spectrum. Strong early reflections from the monitors should also be avoided.

choosing monitors

While it's important to listen to big-budget commercial mixes over full-range speakers to confirm what's going on right at the bottom of the audio spectrum, a pair of typical domestic hi-fi speakers may well miss out the lowest octave completely. Unless the control room is adequately large and properly designed to handle full-range monitors, the results are likely to be more misleading than simply relying on nearfield speakers. Even when a mix can be checked on a full-range monitor system, it's still wise to double-check that it sounds good on a typical domestic two-way speaker – hence the tendency to use compact, two-way devices as nearfield monitors. Yet another advantage of nearfield monitoring is that the weaker bass end leaves the vulnerable mid range more exposed so that any errors or distortions are easier to hear. This is a very important point, as the strong bass from full-range monitors can easily overpower and obscure the mid range.

Whatever the room and whatever the monitor system used, the way in which your ears evaluate music varies with time and with monitoring level, so it's essential that you have some sort of reference against which to compare your mixes. It's good practice to listen to some known recorded material over the system before mixing. It's well known amongst engineers that adding high-end EQ or processing the sound with an exciter will tend to make you less sensitive to the actual amount of top end in the mix, so if you don't do regular comparisons with some kind of standard, you could end up with a very oddly EQ'd track. Not all CDs are as well recorded as they should be, but it should be possible to pick out a few reference pieces that sound good and that cover the styles of music you tend to work on.

realistic aims

Commercial control rooms are designed to criteria simply not achievable in the smaller studio or home facility. They have inner shells designed with non-parallel walls, specially shaped ceilings and carefully calculated trapping. For those of us setting up a budget home studio or a small-scale commercial facility, many of these aims simply cannot be realised and we often have to adapt a rectangular room of less than optimum proportions. This isn't always as bad as it seems though, because that's exactly the description of a typical living room, and that's where most recorded music is listened to. In reality, most living rooms can be made to sound okay with the right speaker system installed.

There is a school of thought that suggests most of the acoustic problems of a studio are brought about by the physical needs of the studio space – in other words, a perfectly acceptable room is acoustically spoiled by emptying it of furniture and filling it with gear! This makes some kind of sense as soft furniture offers both diffusion and absorption while studio gear tends to have lots of hard, flat reflective surfaces.

With a little thought, many of these undesirable effects can be minimised. For example, carpeting the floor will help damp down ringing as well as shorten the overall reverb time while a soft sofa at the back will help soak up reflections and damp resonances as well as giving the clients somewhere to sit. Excess liveness can be cut down by hanging heavy drapes or rugs a few inches from the wall, but don't fall into the trap of overdamping the high end to leave the bottom booming out of control. Possibly the worst thing you can do is to carpet all the surfaces in the room because then you soak up all the upper mid and top leaving a room that sounds boxy and muddy.

Bass trapping probably isn't vital so long as you pick a pair of speakers with a smooth bass roll-off and keep some large soft furnishings in the room. Wooden floors and plasterboard-lined rooms also have the natural ability to trap out some of the bass. A monitor design that rolls off gradually below 80Hz or so will work far better in an untrapped room than one that uses heavily tuned porting to prop up the bass down to 50Hz or so but then cuts off rapidly.

There's one important aspect of studio performance that can't be designed in and that's your own hearing. A good engineer can make effective mixes on the most rudimentary equipment so long as he's aware aware of its limitations and he compares his work with a known reference recording from time to time. Try to avoid the temptation to monitor at loud levels for long periods as this not only clouds the judgment and changes the perceived musical balance, it can also cause permanent hearing damage. As a general rule, monitor your mix at the kind of level you expect it to be played at by the end listener, and restrict loud listening to short periods.

air conditioning

Professional studio air conditioning systems are beyond the scope of this book and in any event, they are not applicable to project studios because of the sheer volume of ducting, acoustic baffles and acoustically isolated pumping machinery required. Such professional systems can be hugely expensive as well as being bulky, and of course most need to be fitted at the studio building stage. Nevertheless, some fresh air is needed because a soundproof studio is also, effectively, air tight. Even so, the heat generated by a few racks full of gear in a well insulated room means that air cooling is actually a greater priority than introducing large quantities of fresh air. For small studios, where the doors can be opened from time to time to allow fresh air in, a heat exchanger air-cooling system may be quite adequate.

Basic air conditioning units come in two types: the 'through-the-wall' type and the split system. Both work on the same principle whereby a fan recycles the room air over a cooled element, the heat being dissipated outdoors. With a split system, the inner and outer units are connected by small bore pipework so you don't need to knock a big hole in the wall, but they tend to be more expensive than 'through-the-wall' models and need to be fitted by a qualified heating engineer.

Figure 23.1 shows a split system. By contrast, the cheaper 'through-the-wall' system is all built into one box which must be mounted half in and half out of the room via a large hole in the wall. These machines are not designed with sound isolation in mind, so if you do use one, it's a good idea to have a foam-lined cowl fitted over the outside of the unit, taking care to ensure there's no obstruction to the air flow. Figure 23.2 shows an all-in-one system with a DIY cowl fitted. Because of cost considerations, this is exactly what I did in my own studio and it works fine. What's more, unlike the split system, a 'through-the-wall' unit can be set to change some of the air in the room as well as cool it.

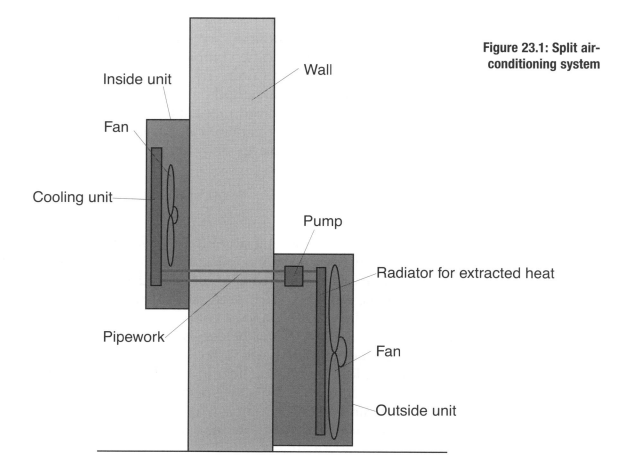

Figure 23.1: Split air-conditioning system

Though a split system always cools the same air, the fact that the inner and outer elements are physically separate and joined only by narrow bore pipes means that there's virtually no sound leakage. A further advantage of the split system is that one external unit can feed more than one internal unit so you could cool both your studio and control room. The actual power of the system depends on the size of room it is to cool and the amount of heat normally generated within the room, which you can estimate by adding up the power requirements of all your bits of gear. Don't forget to add on the power of all the lighting. Whoever supplies/fits your system will be able to calculate the power you need so long as you have these basic figures available.

Commercial studio air conditioning systems use large ducts and very low air velocities in order to keep the noise down. However, with a typical commercial air conditioning unit, the air velocity is comparable to that

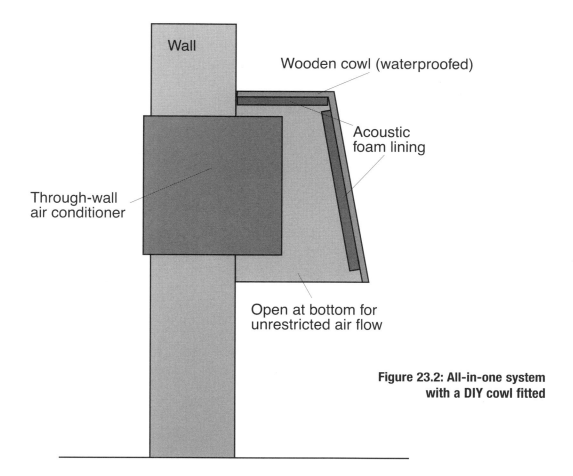

Wall

Wooden cowl (waterproofed)

Acoustic
foam lining

Through-wall
air conditioner

Open at bottom for
unrestricted air flow

**Figure 23.2: All-in-one system
with a DIY cowl fitted**

of a large fan heater, so don't expect it to be completely silent. You can always turn them off for crucial takes. The outside unit can also create fan noise so you should check the specifications of your intended purchase to make sure the air conditioning doesn't annoy the neighbours.

finding materials

Many of the materials used in sound isolation and acoustic treatment, such as mineral wool, fibre-glass, plasterboard, flooring chipboard, roofing felt, insulation-board and timber, can be found at regular builders' merchants. However, items such as barrier mat, half-round door gasket, compression latches, specially perforated peg-board, Lamella flooring, neoprene and acoustic foam is more specialised and so has to be bought via a specialist supplier of acoustic materials. Acoustic tiles are offered for sale in the classified ads of most music magazines, though your music store should be able to order them in for you. Other specialist companies may often be tracked down via *Yellow Pages*, music magazine classified ads or the Internet.

chapter 24

surround-sound concepts

Surround audio has been used for cinema soundtracks for many years, but the domestic audio market has only just started to take an interest for the first time since the ill-fated Quadraphonic (four speaker) surround system was launched over 30 years ago. Technology has since moved on, and large loudspeakers and complicated hardware are no longer necessary in order to enjoy surround sound. However, the main driving force behind surround sound for the home is not public demand for a more sophisticated listening experience but rather the popularity of home theatre – TV-based systems that can also play surround audio and stereo CDs.

The old Quadraphonic system used a conventional stereo pair of loudspeakers at the front and another at the rear, all four speakers being at 90 degrees to each other. By contrast, conventional stereo requires the loudspeakers to be positioned 30 degrees either side of centre, as this produces the best compromise between stereo width and image stability. While tape machines could be constructed with four tracks to reproduce Quadraphonic sound as discrete tracks, this wasn't possible with vinyl, which at the time was the main consumer audio format. To get around this limitation, *matrixing* was used to cram four channels of information into the two audio channels of a vinyl record so that the recording could be replayed in mono, stereo or Quadraphonic with a reasonable degree of compatibility. The ingenious sum-and-difference matrixing circuits that made this possible actually delivered pretty poor channel separation – something that's not a problem with modern digital systems.

A 5.1 sound system comprises three front speakers and two rear speakers (Left, Centre, Front, Left Surround and Right Surround), plus the LFE (Low-Frequency Effects) sub-bass speaker. Thus 5.1 audio requires six discrete channels of audio data.

Domestic resistance to the use of multiple speakers to reproduce surround sound still exists, but current speakers systems can be made physically much smaller than their predecessors. Because home theatre is designed for use with TV programs and DVD movies, exponents of audio surround have had to adopt the speaker system used for video rather than having the option to devise one that is optimised purely for music, but the positive side of all this is that home cinema is doing the hardware marketing on behalf of the audio industry.

Surround sound relies on using four or more speakers, whereas conventional stereo requires just two. Although there are some consumer systems based on psychoacoustic processing that claim to provide a surround experience from only two speakers, true surround requires multiple loudspeakers positioned around the listening position at specifically defined locations. Even though some of the 'fake' surround systems based on processing can sound impressive when listening to TV programs, I've yet to come across one that is sufficiently convincing for satisfactory music playback.

surround for music

Surround provides both technical and artistic challenges for the musician and record producer, although it certainly offers creative possibilities that could never be fully explored in stereo. Arguments rage as to the artistic merits of surround, particularly whether it is artistically valid to have instruments all around the room or whether the 'band' should remain at the front, with just room ambience and effects in the surround speakers. As you're likely to be part of the first generation doing any serious work in surround audio, I'll leave those choices to you! Whether or not you think surround is a good thing, either commercially or artistically, the record companies, film producers, television producers, computer-game developers and so on are increasingly expected to provide surround audio tracks as a matter of course, even though they may not be needed for release in that format initially. Furthermore, although the public demand for surround audio may be small at the moment, it will almost certainly increase on the back of the home theatre revolution.

surround monitoring

The 5.1 loudspeaker arrangement used in home theatre systems and cinemas comprises three speakers in front of the listener and two behind, all capable of handling full-range audio. These are augmented by a subwoofer fed from the LFE (Low-Frequency Effects) channel. As stated, 5.1 simply means that the system comprises five full-range speakers (ideally 20Hz and 20kHz) plus an LFE channel feeding a subwoofer. A surround mixing system is geometrically similar, but of course it fits into a studio control room, not a theatre.

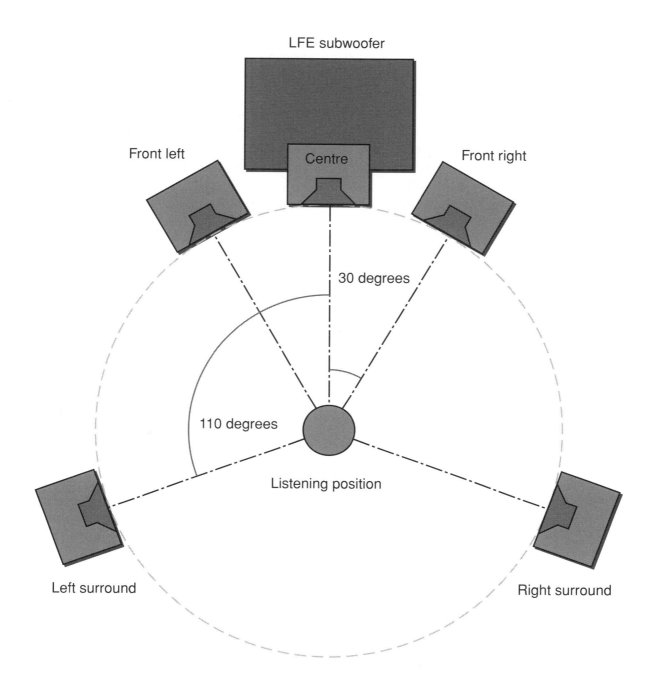

Figure 24.1: 5.1 speaker system

The physical positioning of the loudspeakers in a 5.1 monitoring system is defined by the ITU (International Telecommunications Union), which stipulates that the front three speakers are positioned with the angle between the left/right and the centre speakers, set at 30 degrees, as shown in Figure 24.1. Note that the left and right speakers in the ITU setup are also correctly placed for playing stereo mixes, so the same monitoring system can be used for both stereo and 5.1 simply by routing audio to the required speakers.

The three front speakers should be positioned on an arc centred at the listening position so that all are equidistant from the listener. In a professional installation where it isn't practical to set the centre speaker back by an adequate amount, a small centre-speaker delay (usually no more than a couple of milliseconds) is used to compensate, effectively making the speaker behave as though it's further away.

The rear speakers are also positioned at points on an imaginary circle drawn around the listener, as shown in Figure 24.1. These are set up at an angle of 110 degrees from the centre-front speaker, plus or minus ten degrees. Some surround amplifiers include variable rear-speaker delay, which permits the speakers to be mounted closer to the listening position than the ITU's recommended alignment while maintaining the correct time alignment. The rear speakers are known as *surrounds* and are generally abbreviated to as Ls and Rs.

video sound

Originally, matrixing systems such as Dolby Pro Logic were developed as a way to compact multiple audio steams into two (for delivery via systems originally designed to carry only stereo audio tracks), and there are some ingenious methods that can be used to minimise the inevitable effects of crosstalk caused by poor channel separation. However, for really high-quality surround audio playback, discrete audio channels are far more effective and, with modern digital technology, relatively easy to implement. Conceptually, a surround audio recording is much like a stereo CD, except that it carries separate tracks to feed each of the speakers. Because CD doesn't have the capacity to carry six streams of over an hour of high resolution audio, DVD is the playback medium of choice.

Dolby and surround

When films were first released on VHS video with Dolby-encoded soundtracks, the separation provided by early generations of Dolby decoder was also very limited, and although this system is still used for VCR soundtracks and some TV transmissions, DVDs now use discrete audio channels. Even so, a data-compression system is used to get the required amount of data onto the disc along with the picture.

DVD uses five discrete channels of audio plus a sub-bass channel, and this is known as the *5.1 format*, where *five* refers to the number of standard full-range speakers and the *.1* refers to the sub-bass speaker, traditionally used in movie theatres for handling low-frequency effects such as explosions, sci-fi noises, combat scenes and so on. More elaborate cinema installations may also use 7.1 systems, which provide separate surround channels for the sides and rear, but 7.1 has had little impact on music recording so far, and as it's hard enough to establish one surround system, it seems counter-productive to explore these other possibilities just yet!

It is possible to use just the audio capabilities of DVD video to provide music in a surround format, but this generally means using the data-compression system used for film soundtracks. Now that the final specifications for DVD audio-only discs (DVD-A) have been agreed and suitable players are being built, we also have the opportunity to enjoy a higher-quality, audio-only format based upon 24-bit/96kHz uncompressed audio.

DVD-A also includes options for 192kHz and even 384kHz sample rates, which is technically superior to CD and broadly equivalent to the Sony/Philips high-end audio SACD (Super Audio CD) format, as well as providing more audio channels than a stereo CD. The benefits of the 96kHz sample rate are questionable as far as the typical consumer is concerned, although as it becomes cheaper to work in this format it will probably become commonplace. I anticipate that a lot of DVDs released so far will be remastered from original multitrack recordings originally made for stereo release, or even 'folded out' from existing stereo masters, so the ultra-high-sample-rate argument is largely academic. However, if you're producing original music for DVD-A or one of the other high-definition formats, it's probably worth working at 96kHz wherever possible.

Conversely, if you're recording for stereo CD, it's often best to work at 24-bit/44.1kHz so that you can reduce the final recording to 16 bits at the mastering stage without having to convert to the same rate. This is particularly relevant with computer-based systems, where doubling the same rate also halves the number of plug-ins, audio tracks and storage time available. However, the main thrust of this section of the book is in dealing with mic techniques and monitoring, so I won't dwell on the delivery medium much further, other than to say that, at the time of writing, there's still relatively little inexpensive software around that allows you to master and burn your own surround DVDs that will play on commercial DVD systems. In fact, for the sake of compatibility, it may be wise to confine your original experiments in this area to producing your audio on DVD video discs, as the side-effects of data compression on these are relatively benign.

monitoring and mixing

Mixing in surround means employing a multi-speaker surround monitoring system and having access to mixing facilities that can handle surround and not just stereo. While stereo desks with enough busses can be coaxed into handling surround mixes, one of the new generation digital mixers or multi-output computer systems with surround capability built in as standard will make the job very much easier. Most modern sequencer packages are capable of handling surround mixing, as long as you have an audio interface with six or more separate outputs for monitoring purposes.

For accurate playback, the speakers in a 5.1 system must be set up in precise locations around the monitoring position in order to reproduce the intended listening experience. Even though the typical domestic user may not have their system set up optically, you need to mix on a system that's as accurate and as standardised as you can get it.

The LFE channel isn't strictly necessary for music use, as music rarely contains very low-frequency special effects, and surround music mix engineers disagree as to whether it should be employed or not. My own view is that most home cinemas are set up with the LFE channel far too loud so as to make explosions on film more impressive, so if the LFE channel was used for important musical information, the mix could end up sounding ridiculously bass-heavy. It's also true that placing key sounds such as lead vocals and solos in the centre speaker rather than in the front left and right – as we do for stereo – may cause problems if the end user's system is set up with the centre speaker too loud or too quiet, as this will affect the balance between the vocals and the music. Again, only experience will show what to mix into the centre and LFE channels, but I would advise caution.

In order to achieve accurate monitoring for film mixing, standard playback levels are used, although in music mixing this is less likely to be observed. The main criteria is that all five full-range speakers are set up to produce exactly the same level for the same magnitude of input signal and that the sub level is properly matched to that of the main speakers. Commercial surround amplifiers invariably have a built-in calibration system for achieving this, usually by sequencing bursts of pink noise around the speakers in a special setup test mode. If you buy the speakers and surround amplifier as a complete, matched package, there may also be a calibrated setting in place to provide the optimum main/LFE balance. Otherwise you may have to set the LFE level by ear while monitoring known material.

practical systems

Full-range speakers are specified for the five main speakers in a 5.1 monitoring system, but this is clearly impractical in many domestic installations and also in smaller project studios. The practical alternative is to use smaller speakers with a limited low-frequency range and then feed the missing low end to the subwoofer along with the genuine LFE information. This process is called *bass management*, and although it can compromise spatial accuracy at mid and low frequencies if taken to extremes, a well-designed system can give good results. In a typical studio system with bass management, it is unlikely that frequencies above 80Hz would be diverted from the main speakers into the subwoofer, as this would risk compromising the imaging of the system. The cut-off frequency of the LFE channel is defined as 120Hz for film mixing, although music mixing engineers sometimes set a lower value (typically 80Hz) for music-only applications.

choosing a 5.1 monitoring system

The simplest way to set up surround monitoring in the smaller studio is to use a powerful, commercial surround amplifier combined with passive speakers, as controlling the level of an active surround system is rather more difficult than handling a passive one unless your mixer has a dedicated surround-monitoring mode. It is crucial that all five main loudspeakers are matched, which means either using five identical speakers or, for the surround channels, using smaller speakers from the same family and with the same general characteristics (other than bass extension).

If you're working with a hardware mixer, the essential control requirements for surround panning are the ability to pan a track from front to back as well as left/right and to be able to adjust the width of stereo source material. If you're working with a stereo mixer that offers no surround support, you may need to improvise a little, and even where surround mixing is provided, you may find that there's no proper provision for surround monitoring. However, if you're prepared to adapt your working methods and do a bit of improvising, you can make effective surround mixes using a stereo console, provided that it has enough at least six output busses in order to carry the six elements of the surround mix.

At the channel level, you'll need some way of panning the signal left and right and between the front and rear busses. This, in effect, provides four-channel surround capability, but the centre speaker and sub can be fed from aux sends, so a full surround mix is possible. The trick is to use two mixer channels for each signal: one channel to handle the 'front' controls and one the surround. Here the two channels are fed from the same source (via a

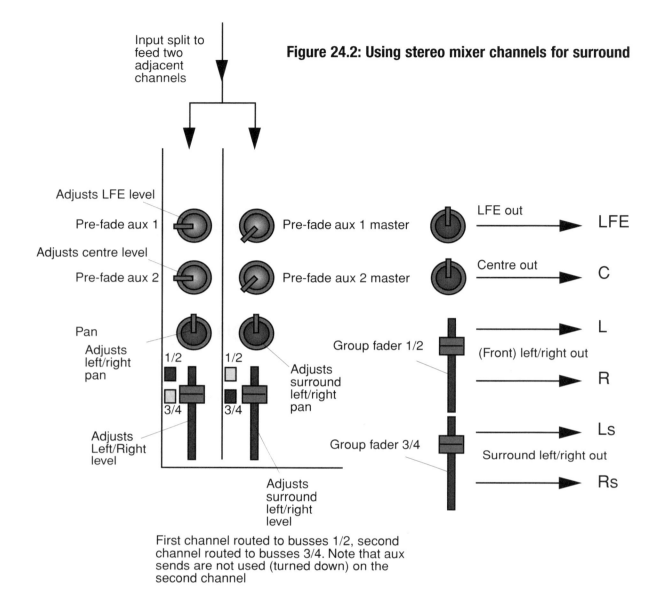

Input split to feed two adjacent channels

Figure 24.2: Using stereo mixer channels for surround

Adjusts LFE level

Pre-fade aux 1

Adjusts centre level

Pre-fade aux 2

Pan

Adjusts left/right pan

1/2

3/4

Adjusts Left/Right level

Pre-fade aux 1 master

Pre-fade aux 2 master

1/2

3/4

Adjusts surround left/right pan

Adjusts surround left/right level

LFE out

LFE

Centre out

C

Group fader 1/2

(Front) left/right out

L

R

Group fader 3/4

Surround left/right out

Ls

Rs

First channel routed to busses 1/2, second channel routed to busses 3/4. Note that aux sends are not used (turned down) on the second channel

split lead if necessary) where one channel is routed to the front left/right busses and the other to the rear (surround) left/right busses. Conventional panning can then be used to move the signals left or right in the mix, while adjusting the relative levels of the signal sent to the front and rear busses using the channel faders provides a means of controlling front/back positioning as well as enabling you to set the overall level of the sound in the track. The centre speaker and LFE channel are easily catered for by using two pre-fade sends: one to feed the signal to the LFE channel (which would be fed from the appropriate console aux out) and one to feed some of the signal to the centre speaker, as shown in Figure 24.2.

Numerous engineers have discovered that you can exploit the perceived difference between the centre speaker and the conventional phantom centre image by using both approaches in the same mix, depending on the sound being positioned. A typical example might be a double-tracked vocal which is mixed once in the centre speaker with the doubled version panned to the centre of the left and right speakers. The vocal line mixed to the centre speaker seems to sit slightly in front of the phantom image, which creates a sense of front/back perspective. To achieve this, you need only put the lead vocal in the centre speaker and the double-tracked vocals or the backing vocals in the left/right speakers.

A surround microphone can be as simple as five discrete directional mics, each picking up what will eventually be fed to each of the five surround speakers, although an arguably more sophisticated approach is that taken by British manufacturer Soundfield. Rather than used spaced mics, the Soundfield microphone captures directional information at a single point in space using coincident microphones, in much the same way as coincident middle-and-side microphones are used to capture stereo recordings. The B-format signals (see the section on 'Recording In Surround')may then be recorded directly to four tracks of an audio recorder if desired so as to allow for the greatest possible flexibility in post-production, but the B format is of no real use in its undecoded state and a decoder is necessary to convert it into 5.1 surround. Soundfield produce a hardware 5.1 decoder and also software plug-in decoders for a few of the high-end audio workstation platforms, but so far there is no low-cost VST equivalent.

Spaced stereo miking setups can employ either omnidirectional or cardioid mics, spaced apart in order to capture timing differences between the two channels that occur when sounds arrive from any direction other than directly on the axis between the microphones. By contrast, the coincident mic array only works when directional mics are used, as it relies entirely on amplitude differences.

In addition to using a Soundfield mic, it is also possible to adapt the conventional M&S mic technique for surround purposes by using two cardioid mid mics, one facing backwards and one facing forwards. Using a sum-and-difference matrix between the figure-of-eight side mic and the forward-pointing cardioid provides what is in effect a front stereo signal, while doing the same thing with the rear-facing cardioid and the figure-of-eight provides the rear-channel information. When all this is combined via a four speaker system, the result is true surround playback in the plane of the speakers. Furthermore, the forward-facing mic signal may also be used to feed the centre speaker in a 5.1 system, and by adjusting the M&S balance the ratio of centre signal appearing in the left and right channels

Front

Figure 24.3: Decca Tree
mic array

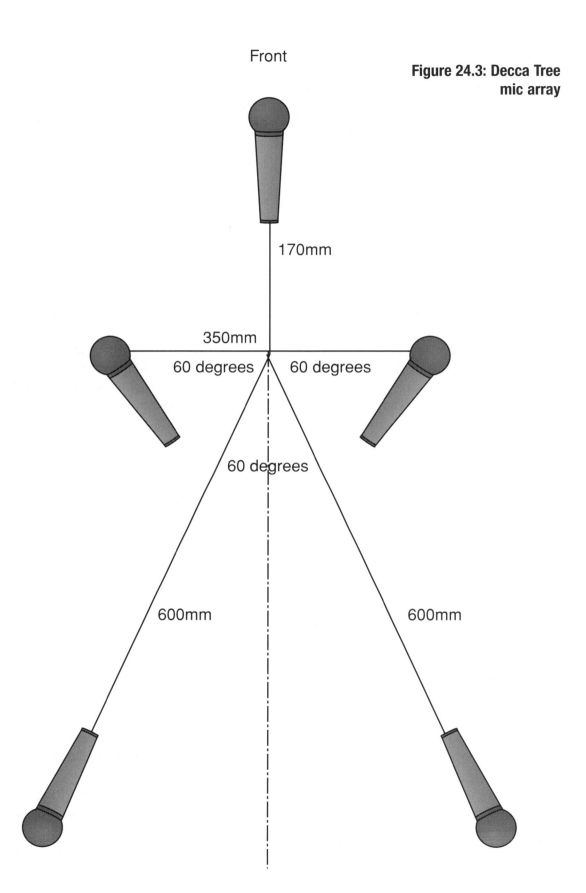

170mm

350mm

60 degrees 60 degrees

60 degrees

600mm 600mm

can be increased or decreased accordingly. This DIY point-source recording system can be set up using an analogue mixer with Phase Invert switches to do the necessary sum-and-difference operations, so no special decoder is needed to make use of it. (M&S mic setups are covered earlier in this book, where decoding using a simple mixer is described.)

spaced arrays

The most common spaced-mic arrangement for 5.1 recording is probably that based on the classic Decca Tree, which was originally developed for stereo recording. The 5.1 version comprises five spaced cardioid microphone capsules fixed to a frame consisting of a central hub with five arms fixed to it in the horizontal plane. A typical arrangement is shown in Figure 24.3. The front three microphones are arranged quite close together, while the two rear mics are located about 24 inches behind the hub and angled at 60 degrees to the axis.

surround mixing

If stereo is mixed using pan pots and stereo balance controls, how is surround handled? Essentially, the equivalent of a pan pot moves signals from front to back as well as from left to right. A further width control is also useful when working with stereo sources. Many of the better sequencers now include surround mixing as standard by providing multiple mix busses, virtual joystick surround positioning controls and separate sends for each mixer channel to feed the surround LFE channel. When using a sequencer that accepts processing plug-ins, a low-pass filter may be inserted into the LFE buss to roll off the audio signal above 80-120Hz, depending on the frequency setting you choose to work with. There also needs to be a way of determining whether centre-panned signals should be reproduced from only the left and right speakers (as in conventional stereo) or from the centre speaker. A variable Divergence control to set the balance between centre and phantom (left plus right) is the ideal solution, and again many software mixers provide this facility.

Where external MIDI sound sources are being used within a mix that's being handled by sequencing software, it's often better to record the external MIDI synths as stereo audio tracks so that they can be handled and positioned by means of the surround controls in the sequencer's mixer. This eliminates the need for an external hardware mixer with surround capability.

Positioning of the LFE speaker is less critical because of the low frequencies involved, but some experimentation may be required to find a position that gives a nominally even level of bass in any given room. Unfortunate positioning that coincides with room mode dimensions or their multiples can result in some notes being too loud and others too quiet.

Although accurate positioning of the subwoofer is best undertaken with proper room-measuring equipment (which requires a lot of expertise to use effectively), there is a very simple DIY method that yields good results. Start by standing the subwoofer in the place where your mixing chair normally goes, then play some material that you know has an even bass content. (You could create a series of bass scales using a MIDI instrument for this purpose.) Now move to the position where you you'd like the sub to be (usually under the mixing desk or somewhere close the centre front of the room) and listen to the playback, paying particular attention to any unevenness in levels between notes of different pitches. If you move your head around until you find a spot where the bass notes are all as even as possible, you can move the subwoofer to that position and the response will be just as even when you listen from your normal monitoring position.

artistic considerations

When we hear live music in ambient surroundings, much of what we hear is reflected sound coming from all the surfaces of the venue, not just from the musicians in front of us. In stereo mixing, digital reverberation is often used to try to create a sense of spaciousness, but it is always played back from speakers in front of the listener and so fails to create a convincing sense of being in the same environment as the performance. Surround helps in the creation of music that more effectively surrounds the listener, and in many respects the ability to convey a sense of three-dimensional room ambience is more important than being able to place instruments behind the listener.

In stereo recording, the individual music elements used to make up a mix may be mono or stereo, and in the case of mono, panning and the application of effects is used to give it a sense of stereo width or placement. Surround productions can also incorporate mono and stereo components as well as and full surround elements, the latter usually furnished by surround microphone systems such as the Soundfield (coincident point source) or an array of numerous discrete microphones. However, it's more likely that, for pop music production, surround mixes will be built up mainly from mono and stereo sources, just as when mixing for stereo. Positional information may be added by the use of 3D panning and effects, such as reverberation placed in the surround speakers, although, as we shall see, you don't have to use dedicated surround effects to create an effective surround mix.

Positioning a sound within the surround mix in this way is cumbersome but very possible, although doing any dynamic panning in this way is extremely tricky, as you need to adjust several controls at once. When positioning a sound manually on a console without surround panning, you generally need to operate at least two separate controls, and that's without considering what happens to the centre channel. If you have mix automation, you can program the more tricky multi-control moves and then edit them until they sound right, but it's probably fair to say that the easiest way to get into surround at the moment is to use a computer-based system.

surround effects

Effects are not really the focus of this book, but having gone so far down the road of surround monitoring, it's worth looking at some of the broader issues. Expensive surround processors with multi-channel outputs are available, but a number of professional engineers use processors designed for stereo without finding too many limitations. Perhaps the most important surround effects is reverb, and this can easily be achieved in a number of ways. At its simplest, a single stereo reverb can be panning to a surround position midway between the front and rear speakers, although it's usually more effective to use two stereo reverbs, one for the front speakers and one for the surrounds. Using separate reverb units (or plug-ins) gives you the option of delaying the rear reverb slightly or using a reverb with a slightly different character to create the desired impression.

The same is true of compression, and while you might feel intuitively that all five of the main surround channels should be treated using a linked compressor, experiments have shown that compressing the front and rear signals separately using separate compressors also works well, as long as the amount of compression isn't excessive. The same is true of limiters. The reason for using linked compressors is that, by applying the same gain reduction to all channels, there will be no unwanted image shifts that might otherwise occur if a peak in one channel resulted in significantly more gain reduction on that channel than on the other. However, as long as the front compressors are linked as a stereo pair and the surround compressors are also linked as a stereo pair, it seems that front/rear image shifts caused by not linking the compressors are less intrusive. Also, using a different compressor on the centre speaker shouldn't prove too much of a problem because no left/right image shifts will be caused by not having it linked to the left/right compressors. If you have a multi-channel compressor where you can link all the bands, it might be worth experimenting to see what the practical differences are between linking the front and rear channels as pairs and linking all the main channels.

surround mastering

A surround mix is saved as six discrete tracks of audio, so when working with a sequencer the end result is a bundle of six audio files. In a hardware studio, any suitable multi-channel recorder may be used to store the surround mix, such as an ADAT/DA88 digital tape machine or a suitable hard disk recorder. (Use a standard system for track management so that you know which part of the surround mix is on what number tape track.) The downside of surround mixing at this point is that, while you can play your surround mix back in your own studio, you can't play it back elsewhere until it is burnt onto a DVD, and the simplest way to do that is use a digital video editing/DVD burning package and save your work as a video disc with no picture.

Although DVD burners and media have fallen in price dramatically since their introduction, they are still rather more costly than the stereo CD-R equivalent and unforeseen compatibility issues often arise when trying to burn audio DVDs.

the professional viewpoint

I have been surprised by the number of differing views expressed by professional audio engineers on what is and what is not artistically acceptable in the context of surround mixing. Ultimately, the whole and only point of surround audio is to present the listener with a more interesting or more involving listening experience, and in that sense there are no rules. Having said that, there are things to consider, just as there are in stereo mixing. Perhaps the biggest area of disagreement is how far we should go in moving instruments into the surround speakers and away from their traditional front positions. There's no right and wrong here, so it's all down to the effect you want to achieve. If you want to create the effect of a band on stage, then keeping all the action near the front and the room ambience (real or generated) in surround is an obvious way forward, but then there are experimental bands with whom such constraints are less important. The same goes for orchestral music: do you want to hear the mix from the best seat in the house or do you want to hear what the conductor hears? Both are possible.

Another concern is more practical and involves the use of the centre speaker, which in film soundtracks generally carries the dialogue and any other sounds that need to be keyed to the centre of the visual image. After more than four decades of stereo, we're used to hearing stereo music with no centre speaker, so mixing with all the mono components coming from a centre speaker sounds quite different to what we're used to and many listeners feel the stereo width is diminished by doing this. Again, there is no right or wrong, and there are exponents of both ways of working. Putting centred sounds in the centre speaker means that their positions are less ambiguous if the listener isn't exactly in the 'sweet spot' between the speakers, but this has to be weighed against the less spacious result and the fact that any miscalibration of the centre speaker by an end user will lead to the wrong mix balance being heard.

The LFE channel (the .1 part) is not essential for normal music production, as the main speaker (or the main speakers plus the sub with bass management where the main speakers are of limited range) will cover the full music spectrum. One engineer said to me that it's fine to use the LFE channel for ultra-low bass sounds, but you should never put anything in there that will spoil the music if it goes missing, as you can't guarantee that all domestic systems will be able to reproduce those low frequencies effectively. This seems like good pragmatic advice. Normal bass will be reproduced even when small satellite speakers are being used, as the bass management will feed the low frequencies to the sub bass speaker.

recording in surround

Because surround audio can be mixed from mono, stereo or surround sources, recordings can simply be made using any of the established mono or stereo mic arrangements, as the recording can be positioned at the mixing stage, with or without additional processing. Of course, the result isn't true surround any more than panned mono recordings are true stereo, but where the mix is being assembled from numerous multitracked components (as is generally the case with pop music), it's perfectly valid. However, it's a different matter when recording a complete live event, and where that relies on acoustic instruments in a good-sounding environment, then true surround miking will produce the most satisfying end result.

The Soundfield system actually uses four directional microphone capsules arranged as a regular tetrahedron and spaced very closely together. This close spacing means that all audio formats can be extracted without running into phase problems, so the same recording can be used to create high-quality mono, stereo and surround mixes. A processor is then used to convert the outputs from the capsules into a four-channel signal (known as the B format) that can be used to generate any surround format, as all the horizontal and vertical directional components of the original event are encoded in the B-format signal. One way to describe the B format is as being equivalent to three sets of signals corresponding to three M&S mic pairs covering the three axes and where each of the figure-of-eight mics uses the same omni microphone as its 'middle' mic. These virtual 'omni output plus three figure-of-eights' are derived from the four capsules outputs using matrixing techniques and may later be recombined in different ways to reconstruct any desired microphone pattern or any surround format.

multi-mic surround

The other common approach to 5.1 surround recording is to use five discrete mics, each angled to pick up the signal appropriate for each of those five speakers, as described earlier in this chapter. These mics could be coincident or spaced, although spaced arrays seem to be the most popular as they tend to emphasise the spatial aspect of the recording, albeit sacrificing a degree of mono and stereo compatibility.

Computer-studio users who have no external sound sources may opt to use the outputs from the audio interface to drive the monitors directly, although this can be risky as, in the event of a computer crash or other software malfunction, it is possible that very high levels of signal will be fed to the monitors. For this reason, using a surround amplifier as a master level controller is a good idea, as it means that at least you have something to turn down when there's a problem.

room considerations

Implementing surround monitoring need not be difficult or expensive, but some consideration must be given to the room layout and acoustics in order to obtain the best results. In a traditional stereo studio, side wall absorbers are used to prevent reflections from the speakers from reaching the listening position, and as more speakers are added, there may be more wall areas that need treating. The simple test is to use a mirror held flat against the wall at different positions. Ever time you can see a reflection of a speaker in the mirror indicates that the mirror's current position is a potential source of unwanted reflections, and so the wall at this position should be treated, if possible.

Where active speakers are employed, these must be used either with a mixer that provides surround monitoring control or with a separate surround monitoring controller. Currently, these tend to be expensive, so a cheaper option may be to buy a commercial surround amplifier that provides line-level outputs (post-volume control) as well as amplified feeds for passive speakers, as shown in Figure 24.4. If you plan to record your

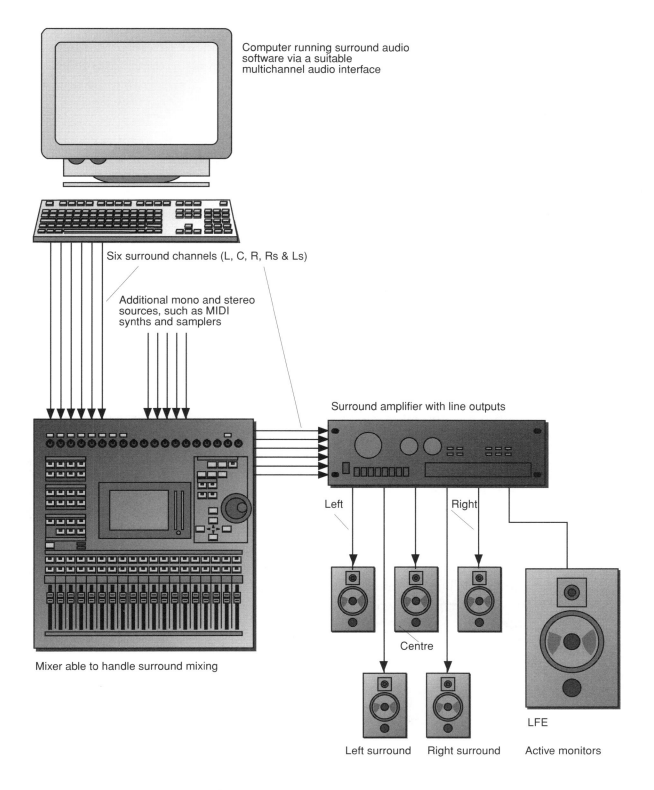

Computer running surround audio software via a suitable multichannel audio interface

Six surround channels (L, C, R, Rs & Ls)

Additional mono and stereo sources, such as MIDI synths and samplers

Surround amplifier with line outputs

Left

Right

Centre

LFE

Left surround

Right surround

Active monitors

Mixer able to handle surround mixing

Figure 24.4: Surround amplifier as a controller

surround mix to an external recorder (as opposed to recording it internally in the computer), the signal output from your mixer must be split to feed both the multitrack recorder used to record the six discrete channels of the surround mix and to feed the controller/surround amplifier. If everything is being mixed inside the computer, then you may be able to dispense with a hardware mixer altogether.

Any spaced surround mic technique requires special attention when it comes to creating mono and stereo compatible 'fold-down' mixes, as the physical spacing and the consequent inter-mic delays give rise to phase problems when the signals are combined. The greater the separation between the mics, the more serious this problem is likely to be, although there is always the option of using only some of the mic outputs to create the mono and stereo down-mixes. A discrete spaced system like the one described here is the simplest to handle at the mixing stage, as no decoding is necessary. Each of the five mics feeds directly to one of the five main speaker channels and the sub-bass signal can be derived by filtering.

summary

Surround sound for recorded music is still in its infancy, but once you've installed a surround monitoring system, it isn't difficult to have a go. Even though it's no trivial matter to burn surround audio CDs at the moment, it's inevitable that it will eventually become as simple as burning regular stereo CDs, so you might want to start saving surround versions of your mixes as well as regular stereo versions so that you can transfer them to DVD when more practical options of doing so become available. Because these are early days, it's also a great time to experiment with different ways of making music sound good in surround, and already we're seeing sequencer plug-ins become available in surround versions as well as basic mono and stereo. As with the early days of stereo, there will be excesses and there will be mistakes, but eventually surround audio will shake down into something that we can all enjoy and that everyone will take for granted, just as we do now with stereo.

voice channels & recording preamps

Since this book's first incarnation, the use of separate preamplifiers for recording has increased dramatically, due in no small part to the proliferation of computer-based studios where the types of mixers used may not be suitable for simultaneous high-quality recording and monitoring. Furthermore, much of the recording done in project studios is done one track at a time, so it makes sense to buy one really good mic preamplifier and use that for everything rather than rely on the perfunctory mic amps in a typical budget mixer. While stand-alone mic amps are still available, it is the so-called voice channel that has really taken off, as it combines mic and line preamplifiers with facilities such as EQ, compression, de-essing, limiting and enhancement. Not all models offer all of the above features, and the preamp section may or may not include an instrument-level input with a high-input impedance suitable for use with electric guitars and basses. However, most offer compression and all serious models have balanced outputs with level controls that can be fed directly into either a conventional mixer, soundcard or recorder.

digital outs

Some amplifiers also feature integral (or retrofittable) digital output options that allow them to be connected to the AES/EBU or S/PDIF digital input of any suitable recording system, and the better models support high sample rates as well as the more common 44.1kHz and 48kHz. Having a digital output is useful as matching the analogue output levels of a preamp to the requirements of a digital recorder can be tricky sometimes. Digital recorders tend to be calibrated differently and so require preamps that can deliver very high peak levels without distortion.

Because one good voice channel may cost more than an entire multi-channel budget mixer, you need to know that it's going to give you better results. There are several reasons why a well-designed voice channel can help you make better recordings.

signal path

Even a well-designed mixer has a fairly long and convoluted signal path, where the signal from the mic preamp passes though the channel strip (and in some cases the EQ can't be bypassed), through the routing busses and mix amps, and finally through the output stages of the mixer. The more circuitry a signal encounters, the greater the risk of adding noise and distortion, and so, all else being equal, a shorter signal path will always deliver a more pure signal than an unnecessarily long one.

Furthermore, as a voice channel has only one preamp section, this is often more sophisticated than you'd expect to find in a project-studio mixer, where the design of the mic amp has to be compromised due to cost restraints. A good voice channel may, for example, have a much wider audio bandwidth, better noise performance, lower distortion and more headroom. Some models also feature tube stages or transformer coupling that may add a musical warmth to the sound. On a purely practical level, there's less likelihood of introducing crosstalk or ground loop hum when you just have a single voice channel patched into your recorder, especially if the recorder has balanced inputs. Furthermore, because a voice channel includes other processing sections, it is possible to treat the signal prior to recording, although excessive pre-processing is generally not a good idea as it's very difficult to reverse if you later discover that it doesn't work in the context of the rest of the mix.

How much pre-processing you do depends to some extent on the type of recording system you have. For example, in a retro-style studio based around an analogue mixer and analogue tape machine, it's generally safest to record the signal completely flat or with just a small amount of compression, as analogue tape is fairly forgiving of overloading. The same applies to EQ – by all means add a little gentle brightening or other subtle change, but if you go too far you may end up with a result that you can't treat further in the way you'd like.

In a digital recording situation, where overloads are not permitted, most of the previous advice still applies, although if your voice channel has a separate limiter, you may want to use this to ensure that the recorder can never be overloaded by unexpected signal peaks. Few limiters are completely transparent in operation, but they all sound a lot better than digital clipping. Ideally, the limiter shouldn't come on at all during normal use – it's just there to catch unexpected loud peaks. You can use a variable-ratio compressor to emulate limiting by setting the compressor to its highest ratio and then adjusting the threshold so that compression occurs just before digital full scale on the recorder's meters. Limiting requires the fastest attack time combined with a release time of less than 100ms, and unless your compressor is very fast, some brief moments of clipping may still occur at the start of fast transients, but hopefully they will be too brief to be audible.

pre-processing

When working with a PC-based studio, the question of whether to process or not is a little more complex, especially when you consider that most of the processing needed can be carried out by plug-ins – in theory, at any rate. As a rule, I feel that the processing available within an analogue voice channel is subjectively better than that provided by most low-cost plug-ins – although some of the more serious plug-ins are exceptionally good. Gentle compression prior to A-to-D conversion will help make the most of the available digital headroom, and this can be particularly relevant for those still recording at 16-bit resolution rather than 24-bit. It's also a technically proven fact that analogue limiting has fewer detrimental side-effects than digital limiting because, unless a digital limiter works at a very high sample rate, the sudden changes in gain imposed on the signal can create audible aliasing artefacts.

As a rule, it's safest to use slightly less compression and EQ than you think you might ultimately need, as you can always call upon your plug-ins for fine-tuning when you come to mix. The comments about limiting also apply, so if your unit has a separate limiter, use it to prevent overloads. Similarly, if you don't need traditional compression when recording and you don't have a separate limiter, then use the compressor as limiter as described above. If your computer system has separate outputs feeding a conventional mixer, or if you have enough ins and outs to route a track via an external hardware processor, you can save your processing until the mixing stage and feed the track back through the line input of your voice channel.

The easiest time to use external processors is when you're working with a conventional analogue mixer to mix the outputs from your audio interface, as you can patch in the processing section of the voice channel via the mixer insert points. Most mixers have unbalanced insert points, so if your voice channel offers both balanced and unbalanced inputs, it may be best to use the unbalanced ones. Note that unbalanced connections are sometimes fixed at –10dBu sensitivity while the balanced connections are at +4dBu. The Input Gain control should enable you to optimise the input level, and most output stages have enough gain and headroom to bring the signal back up to the required level, but just occasionally you may find that the output limiter in your voice channel comes in at too low a level if you work this way. Should this be the case, or if you're getting distortion because of a level mismatch, make up balanced-to-unbalanced cables and used the voice channel's balanced connectors. Check your equipment handbook to find out how to wire up a cable for unbalanced use, as some require the 'cold' conductor to be grounded while others require it to be disconnected and left floating.

gain structure

When recording via a voice channel, you should always set the input gain trim so that the meters show a healthy reading – in a well designed unit, the level metering will come before the Output Level control. Signal peaks should push the meter close to the top of its scale, but not far enough to cause the peak or clip indicator to light up. After setting up the input gain correctly, use the Output Level control to set the record level, being aware that digital equipment often requires much higher signal levels than analogue. For example, a digital input with a nominal +4dBu sensitivity may require between 15dB and 18dB in order to hit the peak level. This means that many voice channels are running with their output sections almost flat-out to get enough level into the digital recorder, so if the recorder has a −10dBv sensitivity option, this may make life easier for the voice channel.

A final point concerning gain structure is to take care how you use the compressor make-up gain control. This is provided so that you can compensate for any gain loss caused by compression, and perhaps the best way to adjust it is to use the compressor's Bypass switch to compare the maximum-output meter readings (or your recorder's input meter, if your voice channel has no output metering) with compression switched in and out. The peak signal levels should be similar both with and without compression, although the average level will be higher with compression. Adjust the compressor make-up gain until this is the case.

recording instruments

If a voice channel has instrument inputs, does this mean that you can record guitar or bass directly?

Guitars and basses need to run into an input impedance of around 1Mohms in order to be recorded cleanly, and this is what the instrument input of a typical voice channel provides. Even so, don't expect the same sound as you'd get from a guitar amp – guitar amps have tailored frequency-response curves to give them their characteristic sound. Because of this, you may need to use some EQ to get the sound just the way you want it. You can also use compression to even out both guitar and bass sounds, but if you want an overdriven sound, it's best either to use a dedicated guitar recording preamp or, in the case of a computer system, to process the clean DI'd guitar signal using a software guitar-amp-modelling plug-in.

esoterics

Many voice channels boast tube circuitry, but that doesn't automatically ensure that you'll get a good sound. The vintage tube gear that's still so highly valued was designed to operate as cleanly as possible, so whatever the tube magic might be, it isn't audible distortion, at least not in the context of mic preamps. Traditional tube circuitry runs at a plate voltage of around 300 volts, so if you come across a design that uses an external power adaptor, it's likely that it uses so-called 'starved-tube circuitry', where the plate voltage is barely ten per cent of its normal value. Some of these models can sound good, but the tube behaviour isn't the same as a traditional high-voltage circuit and the worst examples sound muddy rather than warm. A good tube circuit should maintain clarity and transparency while also sounding warm and full.

You might also find a voice channel with a built-in de-esser. These are useful in dealing with singers who have a noticeably sibilant vocal character, but in order to work transparently the de-esser needs to be quite sophisticated, and in any event you might find a software plug-in that can do the job just as effectively after recording. The worst de-essers pull down the level of the entire audio signal when sibilance is detected, which can give the audio a noticeable lisping quality. A better option is to use a de-esser that turns down the level of only the upper part of the audio spectrum, but again heavy processing can cause audible side-effects. To date, the best option is the de-esser that pulls down the gain of a relatively narrow band of frequencies where sibilance is known to reside, leaving the low and the extreme high ends unaffected. When de-essing at source, listen very carefully to the sound (ideally via headphones) when setting up the control in order to ensure that there are no audible side-effects, as these will be almost impossible to rectify after recording. As with any other pre-processing, use as little as you can get away with while recording and add more later if necessary.

warmth and air

While compression and gentle low-end EQ can give a vocal a sense of warmth, the choice of microphone also has a big influence, as does exploiting the proximity effect produced by working fairly close to the mic. Tube mics and preamps are often said to sound 'warm', but the other end of the audio spectrum is also important, as many commercial records require a lively, transparent vocal sound. Conventional high-frequency EQ can leave vocals sounding harsh, but the secret to getting that airy high end is to apply a wide EQ boost at very high frequencies, typically between 14kHz and 16kHz. This needs to be only a couple of decibels, in most cases, with a bandwidth setting of around two octaves. The result is an airy transparency without harshness, although some equalisers sound sweeter than others in this respect. If your mixer EQ or plug-ins don't cut it, then you can add air at the recording stage using your voice-channel EQ.

glossary

AC

Alternating current.

active

A circuit containing transistors, ICs, tubes and other devices, that requires power to operate and is capable of amplification.

A/D converter

Circuit for converting analogue waveforms into a series of values represented by binary numbers. The more 'bits' a converter has, the greater the resolution of the sampling process. Current effects units are generally 16 bits or more with the better models being either 20- or 24-bit.

active sensing

A system used to verify that a MIDI connection is working, that involves the sending device sending frequent short messages to the receiving device to reassure it that all is well. If these active sensing messages stop for any reason, the receiving device will recognise a fault condition and switch off all notes. Not all MIDI devices support active sensing.

ADSR

Envelope generator with attack, sustain, decay and release parameters. This is a simple type of envelope generator and was first used on early analogue synthesizers, though similar envelopes may be found in some effects units to control filter sweeps and suchlike.

AFL

After fade listen; a system used within mixing consoles to allow specific signals to be monitored at the level set by their fader or level control knob.

Aux sends are generally monitored AFL rather than PFL (see PFL) so that the actual signal being fed to an effects unit can be monitored.

aftertouch

A means of generating a control signal based on how much pressure is applied to the keys of a MIDI keyboard. Most instruments that support this do not have independent pressure sensing for all keys, but rather detect the overall pressure by means of a sensing strip running beneath the keys. Aftertouch may be used to control musical functions such as vibrato depth, filter brightness, loudness and so on, though it may also be used to control some parameters of a MIDI effects unit, such as delay feedback or effect level.

alfa

Release version of software (but may still contain some bugs – see Beta).

algorithm

A computer program designed to perform a specific task. In the context of effects units, algorithms usually describe software building blocks designed to create specific effects or combination of effects. All digital effects are based on algorithms.

aliasing

When an analogue signal is sampled for conversion into a digital data stream, the sampling frequency must be at least twice that of the highest frequency component of the input signal. If this rule is disobeyed, the sampling process becomes ambiguous as there are insufficient points to define each cycle of the waveform, resulting in enharmonic sum and difference frequencies being added to the audible signal. See Nyquist.

ambience

The result of sound reflections in a confined space being added to the original sound. Ambience may also be created electronically by some digital reverb units. The main difference between ambience and reverberation is that ambience doesn't have the characteristic long delay time of reverberation – the reflections mainly give the sound a sense of space.

amp

Unit of electrical current. (Also abbreviation for 'amplifier'.)

amplifier

Device that increases the level of an electrical signal.

amplitude

Another word for level. Can refer to sound levels or electrical signal levels.

analogue

Circuitry that uses a continually changing voltage or current to represent a signal. The origin of the term is that the electrical signal can be thought of as being 'analogous' to the original signal.

anti-aliasing filter

Filter used to limit the frequency range of an analogue signal prior to A/D conversion so that the maximum frequency does not exceed half the sampling rate.

application

Alternative term for computer program.

ASCI

American Standard Code for Information interchange. A standard code for representing computer keyboard characters by binary data.

attack

The time taken for a sound to achieve maximum amplitude. Drums have a fast attack, whereas bowed strings have a slow attack. In compressors and gates, the attack time equates to how quickly the processor can change its gain.

attenuate

To make lower in level.

audio frequency

Signals in the human hearing range, nominally 20Hz to 20kHz.

aux

Control on a mixing console designed to route a proportion of the channel signal to the effects or cue mix outputs (aux send).

aux return

Mixer inputs used to add effects to the mix.

aux send

Physical output from a mixer aux send buss.

backup

A safety copy of software or other digital data.

balance

This word has a dual meaning in recording. It may refer to the relative levels of the left and right channels of a stereo recording, or it may be used to describe the relative levels of the various instruments and voices within a mix.

balanced wiring

Wiring system which uses two out-of-phase conductors and a common screen to reduce the effect of interference. For balancing to be effective, both the sending and receiving device must have balanced output and input stages respectively.

bandpass filter (BPF)

Filter that removes or attenuates frequencies above and below the frequency at which it is set. Frequencies within the band are emphasised. Bandpass filters are often used in synthesizers as tone shaping elements.

bandwidth

A means of specifying the range of frequencies passed by an electronic circuit such as an amplifier, mixer or filter. The frequency range is usually measured at the points where the level drops by 3dB relative to the maximum.

beta version

Software which is not fully tested and may include bugs.

binary

Counting system based on only two states – 1s and 0s.

bios

Part of a computer operating system held on ROM rather than on disk. This handles basic routines such as accessing the disk drive.

bit

Binary digit, which may either be 1 or 0.

boost/cut control

A single control which allows the range of frequencies passing through a filter to be either amplified or attenuated. The centre position is usually the 'flat' or 'no effect' position.

bouncing

The process of mixing two or more recorded tracks together and re-recording these onto another track.

BPM

Beats per minute.

breath controller

Device that converts breath pressure into MIDI controller data.

buffer

Circuit designed to isolate the output of a source device from loading effects due to the input impedance of the destination device.

buffer memory

Temporary RAM memory used in some computer operations, generally to prevent a break in the data stream when the computer is interrupted to perform another task.

bug

Slang term for software fault or equipment design problem.

buss

A common electrical signal path along which signals may travel. In a mixer, there are several busses carrying the stereo mix, the groups, the PFL signal, the aux sends and so on. Power supplies are also fed along busses.

byte

A piece of digital data comprising eight bits.

cardioid

Meaning heart-shaped, describes the polar response of a unidirectional microphone.

channel

A single strip of controls in a mixing console relating to either a single input or a pair of main/monitor inputs.

channel (MIDI)

In the context of MIDI, 'channel' refers to one of 16 possible data channels over which MIDI data may be sent. The organisation of data by channels means that up to 16 different MIDI instruments or parts may be addressed using a single cable.

chase

Term describing the process whereby a slave device attempts to synchronise itself with a master device. In the context of a MIDI sequence, chase may also involve chasing events – looking back to earlier positions in the song to see if there are any program changes or other events that need to be acted upon.

chip

Integrated circuit.

chord

Three or more different musical notes played at the same time.

chorus

Effect created by doubling a signal and adding delay and pitch modulation.

chromatic

A scale of pitches rising in semitone steps.

click track

Metronome pulse which assists musicians in playing in time.

clipping

Severe form of distortion which occurs when a signal attempts to exceed the maximum level which a piece of equipment can handle.

clone

Exact duplicate. Often refers to digital copies of digital tapes or discs.

common mode rejection

A measure of how well a balanced circuit rejects a signal that is common to both inputs.

compander

Encode/decode device that compresses a signal while encoding it, then expands it when decoding it.

compressor

Device designed to reduce the dynamic range of audio signals by reducing the level of high signals or by increasing the level of low signals.

computer

A device for the storing and processing of digital data.

conductor

Material that provides a low resistance path for electrical current.

console

Alternative term for mixer.

contact enhancer

Compound designed to increase the electrical conductivity of electrical contacts such as plugs, sockets and edge connectors.

continuous controller

Type of MIDI message used to translate continuous change, such as from a pedal, wheel or breath control device.

copy protection

Method used by software manufacturers to prevent unauthorised copying.

crash

Slang term relating to malfunction of computer program that necessitates restarting the program.

cut and paste editing

The ability to copy or move sections of a recording to new locations.

cutoff frequency

The frequency above or below which attenuation begins in a filter circuit.

CV

'Control voltage' used to control the pitch of an oscillator or filter frequency in an analogue synthesizer. Most analogue synthesizers follow a one-volt-per-octave convention, though there are exceptions. To use a pre-MIDI analogue synthesizer under MIDI control, a MIDI to CV converter is required.

cycle

One complete vibration of a sound source or its electrical equivalent. One cycle per second is expressed as 1Hertz (Hz).

daisy chain

Term used to describe serial electrical connection between devices or modules.

damping

In the context of reverberation, damping refers to the rate at which the reverberant energy is absorbed by the various surfaces in the environment.

DAT

Digital audio tape. The commonly used DAT machines are more correctly known as R-DAT because they use a rotating head similar to a video recorder. Digital recorders using fixed or stationary heads (such as DCC) are known as S-DAT machines.

data

Information stored and used by a computer.

data compression

A system for reducing the amount of data stored by a digital system. Most audio data compression systems are so-called lossy systems as some of the original signal is discarded based on psychoacoustic principles designed to ensure that only components which cannot be heard are lost.

dB

Decibel. Unit used to express the relative levels of two electrical voltages, powers or sounds.

dBm

Variation on dB referenced to 0dB = 1mW into 600 ohms.

dB/octave

A means of measuring the slope of a filter. The more dBs per octave, the sharper the filter slope.

dBv (dBu)

Variation on dB referenced to 0dB = 0.775 volts.

dBV

Variation on dB referenced to 0dB = 1 volt.

dbx

A commercial encode/decode tape noise reduction system that compresses the signal during recording and expands it by an identical amount on playback.

DC

Direct current.

DCC

Stationary head digital recorder format developed by Philips. Uses a data compression system to reduce the amount of data that needs to be stored.

DCO

Digitally controlled oscillator.

DDL

Digital delay line.

decay

The progressive reduction in amplitude of a sound or electrical signal over time. In the context of an ADSR envelope shaper, the decay phase starts as soon as the attack phase has reached its maximum level. In the decay phase, the signal level drops until it reaches the sustain level set by the user. The signal then remains at this level until the key is released, at which point the release phase is entered.

de-esser

Device for reducing the effect of sibilance in vocal signals.

defragment

The process of rearranging the files on a hard disk so that all the files are as contiguous as possible, and that the remaining free space is also contiguous.

deoxidising compound

Substance formulated to remove oxides from electrical contacts.

detent

Physical click stop in the centre of a control such as a pan or EQ cut/boost knob.

DI

Short for 'direct inject', where a signal is plugged directly into an audio chain without the aid of a microphone.

di box

Device for matching the signal level and impedance of a source to a tape machine or mixer input.

digital

Electronic system which represents data and signals in the form of codes comprising 1s and 0s.

digital delay

Digital processor for generating delay and echo effects – see DDL.

digital reverb

Digital processor for simulating reverberation.

DIN connector

Consumer multipin signal connection format, also used for MIDI cabling. Various pin configurations are available.

direct coupling

A means of connecting two electrical circuits so that both AC and DC signals may be passed between them.

disc

Used to describe vinyl discs, CDs, MiniDiscs and DVD.

disk

Abbreviation of 'diskette', but now used to describe computer floppy, hard and removable disks.

dither

A system of adding low level noise to a digitised audio signal in such a way as to extend the low level resolution at the expense of a slight deterioration in noise performance.

DMA

Direct memory access. Part of a computer operating system that allows peripheral devices to communicate directly with the computer memory without going via the central processor or CPU.

dolby

An encode/decode tape noise reduction system that amplifies low level, high frequency signals during recording, then reverses this process during playback. There are several different Dolby systems in use: types B, C and S for domestic and semi-professional machines, and types A and SR for professional machines. Recordings made using one of these systems must also be replayed via the same system.

DOS

Disk operating system. Part of the operating system of PC and PC compatible computers.

driver

Piece of software that handles communications between the main program and a hardware peripheral, such as a soundcard, printer or scanner.

drum pad

Synthetic playing surface which produces electronic trigger signals in response to being hit with drum sticks.

dry

A signal that has had no effects added.

DSP

Digital signal processor. A powerful microchip used to process digital signals.

dubbing

Adding further material to an existing recording. Also known as overdubbing.

ducking

A system for controlling the level of one audio signal with another. For example, background music can be made to 'duck' whenever there's a voiceover.

dump

To transfer digital data from one device to another. A Sysex dump is a means of transmitting information about a particular instrument or module over MIDI, and may be used to store sound patches, parameter settings and so on.

DVD

Digital versatile disc. High-capacity disc format capable of storing multi-format audio, video and computer data.

dynamic microphone

A type of microphone that works on the electric generator principle, where a diaphragm moves a coil of wire within a magnetic field.

dynamic range

The range in dB between the highest signal that can be handled by a piece of equipment and the level at which small signals disappear into the noise floor.

dynamics

Way of describing the relative levels within a piece of music.

early reflections

The first sound reflections from walls, floors and ceilings following a sound created in an acoustically reflective environment.

effect

Device for treating an audio signal in order to change it in some creative way. Effects often involve the use of delay circuits, and include such treatments as reverb and echo.

effects loop

Connection system that allows an external signal processor to be connected into the audio chain.

effects return

Additional mixer input designed to accommodate the output from an effects unit.

encode/decode

A system that requires a signal to be processed prior to recording, then that process reversed during playback.

enhancer

A device designed to brighten audio material using techniques such as dynamic equalisation, phase shifting and harmonic generation.

envelope

The way in which the level of a sound or signal varies over time.

envelope generator

A circuit capable of generating a control signal which represents the envelope of the sound you want to recreate. This may then be used to control the level of an oscillator or other sound source, though envelopes may also be used to control filter or modulation settings. The most common example is the ADSR generator.

equaliser

Device for selectively cutting or boosting selected parts of the audio spectrum.

erase

To remove recorded material from an analogue tape, or to remove digital data from any form of storage media.

event

In MIDI terms, an event is a single unit of MIDI data, such as a note being turned on or off, a piece of controller information, a program change, and so on.

exciter

An enhancer that works by synthesizing new high frequency harmonics.

expander

A devise designed to decrease the level of low level signals and increase the level of high level signals, thus increasing the dynamic range of the signal.

expander module

Synthesizer with no keyboard, often rack-mountable or in some other compact format.

fader

Sliding potentiometer control used in mixers and other processors.

FET

Field effect transistor.

figure-of-eight

Describes the polar response of a microphone that is equally sensitive both front and rear, yet rejects sounds coming from the sides.

file

A meaningful list of data stored in digital form. A 'standard MIDI file' is a specific type of file designed to allow sequence information to be interchanged between different types of sequencer.

filter

An electronic circuit designed to emphasise or attenuate a specific range of frequencies.

flanging

Modulated delay effect using feedback to create a dramatic, sweeping sound.

floppy disk

Computer disk that uses a flexible magnetic medium encased in a protective plastic sleeve. The maximum capacity of a standard High Density disk is 1.44Mbytes. Earlier Double Density disks hold only around half the amount of data.

flutter echo

Resonant echo that occurs when sound reflects back and forth between two parallel, reflective surfaces.

foldback

System for feeding one or more separate mixes to the performers for use while recording and overdubbing. Also known as a 'cue' mix.

formant

Frequency component or resonance of an instrument or voice sound that doesn't change with the pitch of the note being played or sung. For example, the body resonance of an acoustic guitar remains constant, regardless of the note being played.

format

Procedure required to ready a computer disk for use. Formatting organises the disk's surface into a series of electronic pigeon holes into which data can be stored. Different computers often use different formatting systems.

fragmentation

The process by which the available space on a disk drive gets split up into small sections due to the storing and erasing of files. See Defragment.

frequency

Indication of how many cycles of a repetitive waveform occur in one second. A waveform which has a repetition cycle of once per second has a frequency of 1Hz (pronounced Hertz).

frequency response

A measurement of the frequency range that can be handled by a specific piece of electrical equipment or loudspeaker.

FSK

Frequency shift keying. A method of recording a sync clock signal onto tape by representing it as two alternating tones.

fundamental

Any sound comprises a fundamental or basic frequency plus harmonics and partials at a higher frequency.

FX

Short for effects.

gain

The amount by which a circuit amplifies a signal.

gate

An electrical signal that is generated whenever a key is depressed on an electronic keyboard. This is used to trigger envelope generators and other events that need to be synchronised to key action.

gate (processor)

An electronic device designed to mute low level signals so as to improve noise performance during pauses in the wanted material.

general MIDI

An addition to the basic MIDI spec to assure a minimum level of compatibility when playing back GM format song files. The specification covers type and program number of sounds, minimum levels of polyphony and multitimbrality, response to controller information and so on.

glitch

Describes an unwanted short term corruption of a signal, or the unexplained, short term malfunction of a piece of equipment. For example, an inexplicable click on a DAT tape would be termed a glitch.

gm reset

A universal Sysex command which activates the General MIDI mode on a GM instrument. The same command also sets all controllers to their default values and switches off any notes still playing by means of an 'all notes off' message.

graphic equaliser

An equaliser whereby several narrow segments of the audio spectrum are controlled by individual cur/boost faders. The name comes about because the fader positions provide a graphic representation of the EQ curve.

ground

Electrical earth or 0 volts. In mains wiring, the ground cable is physically connected to the ground via a long conductive metal spike.

ground loop

A condition likely to lead to the circulation of currents in the ground wiring of an audio system. When these currents are induced by the alternating mains supply, hum results.

group

A collection of signals within a mixer that are mixed, then routed through a separate fader to provide overall control. In a multitrack mixer, several groups are provided to feed the various recorder track inputs.

GS

Roland's own extension to the General MIDI protocol.

hard disk

High capacity computer storage device based on a rotating rigid disk with a magnetic coating onto which data may be recorded.

harmonic

High frequency component of a complex waveform.

harmonic distortion

The addition of harmonics that were not present in the original signal.

head

The part of a tape machine or disk drive that reads and/or writes data to and from the storage media.

headroom

The safety margin in dBs between the highest peak signal being passed by a piece of equipment and the absolute maximum level the equipment can handle.

high-pass filter (HPF)

A filter which attenuates frequencies below its cutoff frequency.

hiss

Noise caused by random electrical fluctuations.

hum

Signal contamination caused by the addition of low frequencies, usually related to the mains power frequency.

Hz

Short for Hertz, the unit of frequency.

IC

Integrated circuit – see Chip.

impedance

Can be visualised as the 'AC resistance' of a circuit which contains both resistive and reactive components.

inductor

Reactive component that presents an increasing impedance with frequency.

initialise

To automatically restore a piece of equipment to its factory default settings.

insert point

A connector that allows an external processor to be patched into a signal path so that the signal now flows through the external processor.

insulator

Material that does not conduct electricity.

interface

A device that acts as an intermediary to two or more other pieces of equipment. For example, a MIDI interface enables a computer to communicate with MIDI instruments and keyboards.

intermittent

Usually describes a fault that only appears occasionally.

intermodulation distortion

A form of distortion that introduces frequencies not present in the original signal. These are invariably based on the sum and difference products of the original frequencies.

I/O

The part of a system that handles inputs and outputs, both digital and analogue.

IPS

Inches per second. Used to describe tape speed.

IRQ

Interrupt request. Part of the operating system of a computer that allows a connected device to request attention from the processor in order to transfer data to it or from it.

isopropyl alcohol

Type of alcohol commonly used for cleaning and de-greasing tape machine heads and guides.

jack

Commonly used audio connector. May be mono (TS) or stereo (TRS).

jargon

Specialised words associated with a specialist subject.

k

Abbreviation for 1000 (kilo). Used as a prefix to other values to indicate magnitude.

kHz

1000Hz

kOhm

1000 ohms

LED

Light emitting diode, type of solid state lamp.

LCD

Liquid crystal display.

LSB

Least significant byte. If a piece of data has to be conveyed as two bytes, one byte represents high value numbers and the other low value numbers, much in the same way as tens and units function in the decimal system. The high value, or most significant part of the message is called the 'most significant byte' or MSB.

limiter

Device that controls the gain of a signal so as to prevent it from ever exceeding a preset level. A limiter is essentially a fast acting compressor with an infinite compression ratio.

linear

A device where the output is a direct multiple of the input.

line level

A nominal signal level which is around -10dBV for semi-pro equipment and +4dBu for professional equipment.

load

Electrical circuit that draws power from another circuit or power supply. Also describes reading data into a computer.

local on/off

A function to allow the keyboard and sound generating section of a keyboard synthesizer to be used independently of each other.

logic

Type of electronic circuitry used for processing binary signals comprising two discrete voltage levels.

loop

Circuit where the output is connected back to the input.

low frequency oscillator (LFO)

An oscillator used as a modulation source, usually below 20Hz. The most common LFO waveshape is the sine wave, though there is often a choice of sine, square, triangular and sawtooth waveforms.

low-pass filter (LPF)

A filter which attenuates frequencies above its cutoff frequency.

mA

milliamp or one thousandth of an amp.

MDM

Modular digital multitrack; a digital recorder that can be used in multiples to provide a greater number of synchronised tracks than a single machine.

meg

Abbreviation for 1,000,000.

memory

A computer's RAM memory used to store programs and data. This data is lost when the computer is switched off and so must be stored to disk or other suitable media.

menu

List of choices presented by a computer program or a device with a display window.

mic level

The low level signal generated by a microphone. This must be amplified many times to increase it to line level.

microprocessor

Specialised microchip at the heart of a computer. It is here that instructions are read and acted upon.

MIDI

Musical instrument digital interface.

MIDI analyser

Device that gives a visual readout of MIDI activity when connected between two pieces of MIDI equipment.

MIDI bank change

A type of controller message used to select alternate banks of MIDI programs where access to more than 128 programs is required.

MIDI control change

Also knows as MIDI controllers or controller data, these messages convey positional information relating to performance controls such as wheels, pedals, switches and other devices. This information can be used to control functions such as vibrato depth, brightness, portamento, effects levels, and many other parameters.

MIDI controller

A term used to describe the physical interface by means of which the musician plays the MIDI synthesizer or other sound generator. Examples of controllers are keyboards, drum pads, wind synths and so on.

(standard) MIDI file

A standard file format for storing song data recorded on a MIDI sequencer in such as way as to allow it to be read by other makes or model of MIDI sequencer.

MIDI implementation chart

A chart, usually found in MIDI product manuals, which provides information as to which MIDI features are supported. Supported features are marked with a 0 while unsupported features are marked with an X. Additional information may be provided, such as the exact form of the bank change message.

MIDI in

The socket used to receive information from a master controller or from the MIDI Thru socket of a slave unit.

MIDI merge

A device or sequencer function that enables two or more streams of MIDI data to be combined.

MIDI mode

MIDI information can be interpreted by the receiving MIDI instrument in a number of ways, the most common being polyphonically on a single MIDI channel (poly-omni off mode). Omni mode enables a MIDI instrument to play all incoming data regardless of channel.

MIDI module

Sound generating device with no integral keyboard.

MIDI note number

Every key on a MIDI keyboard has its own note number ranging from 0 to 127, where 60 represents middle C. Some systems use C3 as middle C while others use C4.

MIDI note off

Message sent when key is released.

MIDI note on

MIDI message sent when note is played (key pressed).

MIDI out

The MIDI connector used to send data from a master device to the MIDI In of a connected slave device.

MIDI port

The MIDI connections of a MIDI-compatible device. A multiport, in the context of a MIDI interface, is a device with multiple MIDI output sockets, each capable of carrying data relating to a different set of 16 MIDI channels. Multiports are the only means of exceeding the limitations imposed by 16 MIDI channels.

MIDI program change

Type of MIDI message used to change sound patches on a remote module or the effects patch on a MIDI effects unit.

MIDI splitter

Alternative term for MIDI Thru box.

MIDI sync

A description of the synchronisation systems available to MIDI users – MIDI Clock and MIDI Time Code.

MIDI thru

The socket on a slave unit used to feed the MIDI In socket of the next unit in line.

MIDI thru box

Device which splits the MIDI Out signal of a master instrument or sequencer to avoid daisy chaining. Powered circuitry is used to 'buffer' the outputs so as to prevent problems when many pieces of equipment are driven from a single MIDI output.

minidisc

Consumer audio disc that uses data compression. Normally used for stereo recording but may also store multichannel audio and computer data.

mixer

Device for combining two or more audio signals.

monitor

A reference loudspeaker used for mixing. Or...

monitor

The action of listening to a mix or a specific audio signal. Or...

monitor

VDU display for a computer.

monophonic

One note at a time.

motherboard

The main circuit board within a computer into which all the other components plug or connect.

MTC

MIDI Time Code; a MIDI sync implementation based on SMPTE time code.

multi-sample

The creation of several samples, each covering a limited musical range, the idea being to produce a more natural range of sounds across the range of the instrument being sampled. For example, a piano may need to be sampled every two or three semitones in order to sound convincing.

multitimbral

A synthesizer, sampler or module that can play several parts at the same time, each under the control of a different MIDI channel.

multitimbral module

MIDI sound source capable of producing several different sounds at the same time and controlled on different MIDI channels.

multitrack

A recording device capable of recording several 'parallel' parts or tracks which may then be mixed or re-recorded independently.

near field

Some people prefer the term 'close field', to describe a loudspeaker system designed to be used close to the listener. The advantage is that the listener hears more of the direct sound from the speakers and less of the reflected sound from the room.

noise reduction

System for reducing analogue tape noise or for reducing the level of hiss present in a recording.

noise shaping

A system for creating digital dither such that any added noise is shifted into those parts of the audio spectrum where the human ear is least sensitive.

non-registered parameter number

An addition to the basic MIDI spec that allows Controllers 98 and 99 to be used to control non-standard parameters relating to particular models of synthesizer. This is an alternative to using System Exclusive data to achieve the same ends, though NRPNs tend to be used mainly by Yamaha and Roland instruments.

non-linear recording

Describes digital recording systems that allow any parts of the recording to be played back in any order with no gaps. Conventional tape is referred to as linear, because the material can only play back in the order in which it was recorded.

normalise

A socket is said to be normalised when it is wired such that the original signal path is maintained unless a plug is inserted into the socket. The most common examples of normalised connectors are the insert points on a mixing console.

nut

Slotted plastic or bone component at the headstock end of a guitar neck used to guide the strings over the fingerboard, and to space the strings above the frets.

nyquist theorem

The rule which states that a digital sampling system must have a sample rate at least twice as high as that of the highest frequency being sampled in order to avoid aliasing. Because anti-aliasing filters aren't perfect, the sampling frequency has usually to be made more than twice that of the maximum input frequency.

octave

When a frequency or pitch is transposed up by one octave, its frequency is doubled.

off-line

Process carried out while a recording is not playing. For example, some computer-based processes have to be carried out off-line as the computer isn't fast enough to carry out the process in real time.

ohm

Unit of electrical resistance.

omni

Meaning all, refers to a microphone that is equally sensitive in all directions, or to the MIDI mode where data on all channels is recognised.

open circuit

A break in an electrical circuit that prevents current from flowing.

open reel

A tape machine where the tape is wound on spools rather than sealed in a cassette.

operating system

The basic software that enables a computer to load and run other programs.

opto electronic device

A device where some electrical parameters change in response to a variation in light intensity. Variable photoresistors are sometimes used as gain control elements in compressors where the side-chain signal modulates the light intensity.

oscillator

Circuit designed to generate a periodic electrical waveform.

overdub

To add another part to a multitrack recording or to replace one of the existing parts.

overload

To exceed the operating capacity of an electronic or electrical circuit.

pad

Resistive circuit for reducing signal level.

pan pot

Control enabling the user of a mixer to move the signal to any point in the stereo soundstage by varying the relative levels fed to the left and right stereo outputs.

parallel

A means of connecting two or more circuits together so that their inputs are connected together, and their outputs are all connected together.

parameter

A variable value that affects some aspect of a device's performance.

parametric eq

An equaliser with separate controls for frequency, bandwidth and cut/boost.

passive

A circuit with no active elements.

patch

Alternative term for 'program', referring to a single programmed sound within a synthesizer that can be called up using program change commands. MIDI effects units and samplers also have patches.

patchbay

A system of panel-mounted connectors used to bring inputs and outputs to a central point from where they can be routed using plug-in patch cords.

patch cord

Short cable used with patch bays.

peak

Maximum instantaneous level of a signal.

PFL

Pre-fade listen; a system used within a mixing console to allow the operator to listen in on a selected signal, regardless of the position of the fader controlling that signal.

phantom power

48V DC supply for capacitor microphones, transmitted along the signal cores of a balanced mic cable.

phase

The timing difference between two electrical waveforms expressed in degrees where 360 degrees corresponds to a delay of exactly one cycle.

phaser

Effect which combines a signal with a phase-shifted version of itself to produce creative filtering effects. Most phasers are controlled by means of an LFO.

phono plug

Hi-fi connector developed by RCA and used extensively on semi-pro, unbalanced recording equipment.

pickup

The part of a guitar that converts the string vibrations to electrical signals.

pitch

Musical interpretation of an audio frequency.

pitch bend

A special control message specifically designed to produce a change in pitch in response to the movement of a pitch bend wheel or lever. Pitch bend data can be recorded and edited, just like any other MIDI controller data, even though it isn't part of the Controller message group.

pitch shifter

Device for changing the pitch of an audio signal without changing its duration.

poly mode

The most common MIDI mode that allows an instrument to respond to multiple simultaneous notes transmitted on a single MIDI channel.

polyphony

The ability of an instrument to play two or more notes simultaneously. An instrument which can only play one note at a time is described as monophonic.

port

Connection for the input or output of data.

portamento

A gliding effect that allows a sound to change pitch at a gradual rate, rather than abruptly, when a new key is pressed or MIDI note sent.

post-fade

Aux signal taken from after the channel fader so that the aux send level follows any channel fader changes. Normally used for feeding effects devices.

post production

Work done to a stereo recording after mixing is complete.

power supply

A unit designed to convert mains electricity to the voltages necessary to power an electronic circuit or device.

PPM

Peak programme meter; a meter designed to register signal peaks rather than the average level.

PPQN

Pulsed per quarter note. Used in the context of MIDI Clock derived sync signals.

PQ coding

Process for adding pause, cue and other subcode information to a digital master tape in preparation for CD manufacture.

pre-emphasis

A system for applying high frequency boost to a sound before processing so as to reduce the effect of noise. A corresponding de-emphasis process is required on playback so as to restore the original signal, and to attenuate any high frequency noise contributed by the recording process.

pre-fade

Aux signal taken from before the channel fader so that the channel fader has no effect on the aux send level. Normally used for creating foldback or cue mixes.

preset

Effects unit or synth patch that cannot be altered by the user.

pressure

Alternative term for aftertouch.

print through

The undesirable process that causes some magnetic information from a recorded analogue tape to become imprinted onto an adjacent layer. This can produce low level pre or post echoes.

processor

Device designed to treat an audio signal by changing its dynamics or frequency content. Examples of processors include compressors, gates and equalisers.

program change

MIDI message designed to change instrument or effects unit patches.

pulse wave

Similar to a square wave but non-symmetrical. Pulse waves sound brighter and thinner than square waves, making them useful in the synthesis of reed instruments. The timbre changes according to the mark/space ratio of the waveform.

pulse width modulation

A means of modulating the duty cycle (mark/space ratio) of a pulse wave. This changes the timbre of the basic tone; LFO modulation of pulse width can be used to produce a pseudo-chorus effect.

punch in

The action of placing an already recorded track into a record at the correct time during playback, so that the existing material may be extended or replaced.

punch out

The action of switching a tape machine (or other recording device) out of record after executing a punch-in. With most multitrack machines, both punching in and punching out can be accomplished without stopping the tape.

PZM

Pressure zone microphone. A type of boundary microphone. Designed to reject out-of-phase sounds reflected from surfaces within the recording environment.

Q

A measure of the resonant properties of a filter. The higher the Q, the more resonant the filter and the narrower the range of frequencies that are allowed to pass.

quantise

A means of moving notes recorded in a MIDI sequencer so that they line up with user defined subdivisions of a musical bar, for example, 16s. The facility may be used to correct timing errors, but over-quantization can remove the human feel from a performance.

RAM

Abbreviation for Random Access Memory. This is a type of memory used by computers for the temporary storage of programs and data, and all data is lost when the power is turned off. For that reason, work needs to be saved to disk if it is not to be lost.

R-DAT

Digital tape machine using a rotating head system.

real time

An audio process that can be carried out as the signal is being recorded or played back. The opposite is off-line, where the signal is processed in non-real time.

release

The time taken for a level or gain to return to normal. Often used to describe the rate at which a synthesized sound reduces in level after a key has been released.

resistance

Opposition to the flow of electrical current. Measured in ohms.

resolution

The accuracy with which an analogue signal is represented by a digitising system. The more bits are used, the more accurately the amplitude of each sample can be measured, but there are other elements of converter design that also affect accuracy. High conversion accuracy is known as high resolution.

resonance

The characteristic of a filter that allows it to selectively pass a narrow range of frequencies. See Q.

reverb

Acoustic ambience created by multiple reflections in a confined space.

RF

Radio frequency.

RF interference

Interference significantly above the range of human hearing.

ribbon microphone

A microphone where the sound capturing element is a thin metal ribbon suspended in a magnetic field. When sound causes the ribbon to vibrate, a small electrical current is generated within the ribbon.

ring modulator

A device that accepts and processes two input signals in a particular way. The output signal does not contain any of the original input signal but instead comprises new frequencies based on the sum and difference of the input signals' frequency components. The best known application of ring modulation is the creation of 'Dalek' robot voices but it may also be used to create dramatic instrumental textures. Depending on the relationships between the input signals, the results may either be musical or extremely dissonant – for example, ring modulation can be used to create bell-like tones. (The term 'ring' is used because the original circuit which produced the effect used a ring of diodes.)

RMS

Root mean square. A method of specifying the behaviour of a piece of electrical equipment under continuous sine wave testing conditions.

roll-off

The rate at which a filter attenuates a signal once it has passed the filter cut-off point.

ROM

Abbreviation for read only memory. This is a permanent or non-volatile type of memory containing data that can't be changed. Operating systems are often stored on ROM as the memory remains intact when the power is removed.

safety copy

Copy or clone of an original tape or disk for use in case of loss or damage to the original.

sample

The process carried out by an A/D converter where the instantaneous amplitude of a signal is measured many times per second (44.1kHz in the case of CD). Or...

sample

A digitised sound used as a musical sound source in a sampler or additive synthesizer.

sample and hold

Usually refers to a feature whereby random values are generated at regular intervals and then used to control another function such as pitch or filter frequency. Sample and hold circuits were also used in old analogue synthesizers to 'remember' the note being played after a key had been released.

sample rate

The number of times an A/D converter samples the incoming waveform each second.

sawtooth wave

So called because it resembles the teeth of a saw, this waveform contains only even harmonics.

SCSI

(Pronounced SKUZZI) small computer system interface. An interfacing system for using hard drives, scanners, CD-ROM drives and similar peripherals with a computer. Each SCSI device has its own ID number and no two SCSI devices in the same chain must be set to the same number. The last SCSI device in the chain should be terminated, either via an internal terminator, where provided or via a plug-in terminator fitted to a free SCSI socket.

sequencer

Device for recording and replaying MIDI data, usually in a multitrack format, allowing complex compositions to be built up a part at a time.

short circuit

A low resistance path that allows electrical current to flow. The term is usually used to describe a current path that exists through a fault condition.

sibilance

High frequency whistling or lisping sound that affects vocal recordings, due either to poor mic technique, excessive equalisation or exaggerated vocal characteristics.

side-chain

A part of the circuit that splits off a proportion of the main signal to be processed in some way. Compressors use the side-chain signal to derive their control signals.

signal

Electrical representation of input such as sound.

signal chain

Route taken by a signal from the input to a system to the output.

signal-to-noise ratio

The ratio of maximum signal level to the residual noise, expressed in dBs.

sine wave

The waveform of a pure tone with no harmonics.

single-ended noise reduction

A device for removing or attenuating the noise component of a signal, but that doesn't require previous coding, as in the case of Dolby or dbx.

slave

A device under the control of a master device.

SMPTE

Time code developed for the film industry but now extensively used in music and recording. SMPTE is a real-time code and is related to hours, minutes, seconds and film or video frames rather than to musical tempo.

SPL

Sound pressure level measured in dBs.

SPP

Song position pointer (MIDI).

square wave

A symmetrical rectangular waveform. Square waves contain a series of odd harmonics.

standard MIDI file

A standard file format that allows MIDI files to be transferred between different sequencers and MIDI file players.

step time

A system for programming a sequencer in non-real time.

stereo

Two-channel system feeding left and right loudspeakers.

stripe

To record Time Code onto one track of a multitrack tape machine.

sub bass

Frequencies below the range of typical monitor loudspeakers. Some define sub-bass as frequencies that can be felt rather than heard.

subcode

Hidden data within the CD and DAT format that includes such information as the absolute time location, number of tracks, total running time and so on.

subtractive synthesis

The process of creating a new sound by filtering and shaping a raw, harmonically complex waveform.

surge

Sudden increase in mains voltage.

sustain

Part of the ADSR envelope which determines the level to which the sound will settle if a key is held down. Once the key is released, the sound decays at a rate set by the release parameter. Also refers to a guitar's ability to hold notes which decay very slowly.

sweet spot

The optimum position for a microphone, or for a listener relative to monitor loudspeakers.

switching power supply

A type of power supply that uses a high frequency oscillator prior to the transformer so that a smaller, lighter transformer may be used. These power supplies are commonly used in computers and some synthesizer modules.

sync

A system for making two or more pieces of equipment run in synchronism with each other.

synthesizer

Electronic musical instrument designed to create a wide range of sounds, both imitative and abstract.

tape head

The part of a tape machine that transfers magnetic energy to the tape during recording, or reads it during playback.

tempo

The rate of the 'beat' of a piece of music measured in beats per minute.

test tone

A steady, fixed level tone recorded onto a multitrack or stereo recording to act as a reference when matching levels.

thd

Total harmonic distortion.

thru

MIDI connector which passes on the signal received at the MIDI In socket.

timbre

The tonal 'colour' of a sound.

track

The term dates back to multitrack tape where the tracks are physical stripes of recorded material, located side by side along the length of the tape.

tracking

The system whereby one device follows another. Tracking is often discussed in the context of MIDI guitar synthesizers or controllers where the MIDI output attempts to track the pitch of the guitar strings.

transducer

A device for converting one form of energy to another. A microphone is a good example of a transducer as it converts mechanical energy to electrical energy.

transparency

Subjective term used to describe audio quality where the high frequency detail is clear and individual sounds are easy to identify and separate.

transpose

To shift a musical signal by a fixed number of semitones.

tremolo

Modulation of the amplitude of a sound using an LFO.

triangle wave

Symmetrical triangular-shaped wave containing odd harmonics only, but with a lower harmonic content than the square wave.

trs jack

Stereo-type jack with Tip, Ring and Sleeve connections.

unbalanced

A two-wire electrical signal connection where the inner or hot or +ve conductor is usually surrounded by the cold or -ve conductor which forms a screen against interference.

unison

To play the same melody using two or more different instruments or voices.

valve

Vacuum tube amplification component, also known as a tube.

velocity

The rate at which a key is depressed. This may be used to control loudness (to simulate the response of instruments such as pianos) or other parameters on later synthesizers.

vibrato

Pitch modulation using an LFO to modulate a VCO.

vocoder

Signal processor that imposes a changing spectral filter on a sound based on the frequency characteristics of a second sound. By taking the spectral content of a human voice and imposing it on a musical instrument, talking instrument effects can be created.

voice

The capacity of a synthesizer to play a single musical note. An instrument capable of playing 16 simultaneous notes is said to be a 16-voice instrument.

vu meter

Meter designed to interpret signal levels in roughly the same way as the human ear, which responds more closely to the average levels of sounds rather than to the peak levels.

wah pedal

Guitar effects device where a bandpass filter is varied in frequency by means of a pedal control.

warmth

Subjective term used to describe sound where the bass and low mid frequencies have depth and where the high frequencies are smooth sounding rather than being aggressive or fatiguing. Warm sounding tube equipment may also exhibit some of the aspects of compression.

watt

Unit of electrical power.

waveform

A graphic representation of the way in which a sound wave or electrical wave varies with time.

white noise

A random signal with an energy distribution that produces the same amount of noise power per Hz.

write

To save data to a digital storage medium, such as a hard drive.

XG

Yamaha's alternative to Roland's GS system for enhancing the General

MIDI protocol so as to provide additional banks of patches and further editing facilities.

XLR

Type of connector commonly used to carry balanced audio signals including the feeds from microphones.

y-lead

Lead split so that one source can feed two destinations. Y leads may also be used in console insert points in which case a stereo jack plug at one end of the lead is split into two monos at the other.

zero crossing point

The point at which a signal waveform crosses from being positive to negative or vice versa.

zipper noise

Audible steps that occur when a parameter is being varied in a digital audio processor.